Hyperinflation in Germany

Perceptions of a Process

Hyperinflation in Germany

Perceptions of a Process

ERIC E. ROWLEY

© Eric E. Rowley, 1994

All rights reserved. No part of this publication may be reproduced, stored in a retrieval system, or transmitted in any form or by any means, electronic, mechanical, photocopying, recording, or otherwise without the prior permission of the publisher.

Published by
SCOLAR PRESS
Gower House
Croft Road
Aldershot
Hants GU11 3HR
England

Ashgate Publishing Company
Old Post Road
Brookfield
Vermont 05036
USA

British Library Cataloguing-in-Publication Data
Rowley, Eric E.
  Hyperinflation in Germany: Perceptions of
  a Process
  I. Title
  332.4

ISBN 1-85928-039-0

Library of Congress Cataloging-in-Publication Data
Hyperinflation in Germany : perceptions of a process / Eric E. Rowley.
    p.   cm.
  ISBN 1-85928-039-0 : $59.95 (approx.)
  1. Inflation (Finance)—Germany—History—20th century.
  2. Germany—Economic policy—1918-1933.
  HG999.H96 1994
  332.4'1'094309042—dc20   93-45454
                                                    CIP

ISBN 1 85928 039 0

Phototypeset by Intype, London
Printed and bound in Great Britain at the University Press, Cambridge

Emmy Zehden*
einem Opfer des Terrors
gewidmet

Dedicated to
Emmy Zehden
Victim of the Third Reich

---

*Emmy Zehden, 1900–44. Newspaper seller, Berlin. Jehovah's Witness. Accused before the Volksgericht of sheltering three men liable for military service. Executed in Plötzensee Prison, Berlin, 9 June 1944. *Beiträge zum Widerstand 1933–45 8. . . . Für Immer Ehrlos. Aus der Praxis des Volksgerichtshofes.* Gedenkstätte Deutscher Widerstand, Berlin, 1985.

Contents

Acknowledgements   xi

1. Introduction   1

    Sources – Summary of the major causes of hyperinflation in Germany in 1923 – Interpretation of the written record – Blaming the Treaty of Versailles – Bias in reporting – The context – The occupation of Germany after the Armistice – German fears of French territorial ambitions

2. The Agricultural Situation and Food Supplies   11

    General problem – Aggravated problems due to territorial losses – Illustration of territorial losses and their importance for the supply of agricultural products and raw materials – The political importance and reactions of the agricultural sector – Significance of the Kapp-Putsch for financial stability – Reports on the agricultural crisis in the press – Reports by H.J. Greenwall from Berlin – Poverty in Berlin and its consequences – Agriculture and budget deficits of the Reich

3. Attitudes, Hearts and Minds   24

    Reception of German troops in Berlin – Franco-German hatred – Nationalism and racialism as factors in inflation – Atrocity stories in the British press harden attitudes to post-war reconciliation – German experiences of hostility – Craven's part in the Great War – German responses to the occupation of the Ruhr – Atrocity stories in the German press

4. Living with Hyperinflation   44

    External value of the Mark 1921–23 – The Berlin foreign exchange market – Illicit trading in Marks – Arbitrage in currency markets – Movement of people and currency contrasted – Gustav Cassell and purchasing power parity theory – Measurement of inflation – Exchange rate movements or price indices? – The pressure for stabilization of the currency – Problems of a growing number of different types of money – Costs of using various types of money – Action against profiteers – Violence on the streets – Refusal of suppliers to trade – Hoarding and holding back supplies

5. The Average Citizen 72

The average citizen in Cuxhaven 1923 – Calculating the rent for November 1923 – Dealing with the bank – Buying the newspaper – Protecting the purchasing power of money – The 'value-protected' loan of 1923 – The Goldmark and associated calculations – The Festmarkbank – The Goldmark: an illustration – Shopping in Hildesheim, December 1923 – The plethora of forms of payment – Advertisements in Hildesheim, 1923 – The effects of inflation on an individual family: Emmy Zehden of Berlin – Letter appealing for mercy stresses the impact of inflation on the family – Inflation and public morality – Inflation, desperation and theft – The burial of the dead

6. Loans and Public Sector Finance 93

Finance of the Great War by Germany – The 1915 War Loan – Budgetary problems after the war – The Compulsory Loan of 1922 – Treaty of Versailles and budget problems – Compulsory Loan and 'Crowding-Out' – Too many employed in the public sector? – Guaranteed Real Value Loan of August 1923 – The role of the State Loans Office – City finance: the 1923 budget of Hildesheim

7. Emergency Money – Notgeld 115

A theoretical framework – Is the money supply cause or effect? – The size of Notgeld issues – Some examples of Notgeld – The origins of Notgeld – From a shortage of small change to large denomination notes – Increases in the velocity of circulation show up as an apparent 'shortage' of money – Financial burdens on local authorities exacerbate the sense of a shortage of money – Recognition that a note may have more direct use than its value in exchange – Notgeld as a means of acquiring interest-free loans and resources effectively cost free – Collector interest recognized and encouraged – The use of Notgeld by industrialists – Comparison with Britain – Political comment on Notgeld issues – Redemption of Notgeld

8. The Views of Hjalmar Schacht, President of the Reichsbank ... 139

The money supply as the cause of inflation – The problem of Notgeld – Lack of control over the note issue in Germany in 1923 – The establishment of an independent central bank – The Autonomy Law of 26 May 1922 – The assertion of independence by the Reichsbank – Reducing the size of the note issue

9. The Stabilization of the Currency ... 148

Schacht and stabilization – The Rentenmark as an interim solution – Recognition of the importance of controlling monetary expansion – Is money cause or consequence? – Hyperinflation: a shortage of money? – Money in short supply, reported by Friedrich Lange – Other reports of money in short supply – The optimum supply of money, a contribution of Von Seipio – View of President of the Reichsbank, Rudolf Havenstein – The opinions of Friedrich Pilot – Reports on currency reform in the *Cuxhavener Zeitung* – Success for the Rentenmark only on certain assumptions – Recognition of the need to balance the budget – Curbing the private sector's contribution to inflation – Attempts to establish local areas of currency stability

10. Relevance of the Events of 1923 for Economic Policy Today ... 174

The importance attached to balancing the budget today as a direct consequence in Germany of these events and experiences – The need for an independent central bank prepared to resist government demands for inflationary financing – Reflection of the events of 1923 in political campaigning in Germany

11. Postscript 180

Fundamental causes of economic problems seen as political in nature – Resentment of French imperialism expressed in cartoons and poetry – The desire for a saviour

Index 184

Acknowledgements

I am grateful to the following for their help and assistance with material used in the preparation of this text: the staffs of the IWWA, Hamburg; the city archives in Cuxhaven, Heilbronn and Hildesheim; and the archive of the Nordsee Zeitung, Bremerhaven.

I must also thank the relatives of the late Harry Greenwall, *Daily Express* correspondent in Paris before the Armistice in 1918 and subsequently in Berlin, for the loan of his personal collection of press cuttings of his reports.

I am particularly grateful to Herr Edgar Staiger in Heilbronn and Frau Hannelore Theuerkauf in Hildesheim for their assistance with locating material.

Thanks are also due to the German Historical Institute, London.

Words such as billion and trillion have different meanings in the various languages. The following units are used in this narrative and conform to German usage both in 1923 and at the present time:

10^6	million
10^9	milliard
10^{12}	billion
10^{15}	billiard
10^{18}	trillion
10^{21}	trilliard

CHAPTER ONE

Introduction

The great inflation in Germany, particularly in the second half of 1923, is arguably one of the most significant of modern times. Between 1 June and 20 November 1923, the United States dollar rose from 75,000 to 4,200,000,000,000 Marks.[1] Using the exchange rate as a proxy for changes in the internal purchasing power of the Mark, it is easy to see that this period saw the total destruction of the purchasing power of the currency. This destruction of the currency was accompanied by dramatic social, political and economic changes, some of the consequences of which are evident in our own time.

But what did those who lived through these years make of the events that touched their lives so dramatically? Much information is available to answer this question. The newspapers of the period reflected public concerns and popular ideas of cause and effect. The Emergency Money or Notgeld issues are yet another source of information, as are the diaries and letters written by those affected by the process.

Using principally the sources mentioned above, this narrative attempts to describe the perceptions of the process of hyperinflation of those who lived through these years, whose sources of information were their daily experiences, passed down to us in the form of contemporary newspaper articles, the currency of the period, diaries and letters.

The impressions of Friedrich Lange, Stadtsyndikus and Erster Bürgermeister of Berlin, contrast with the experiences of Emmy Zehden, newspaper seller in the same city but at the opposite end of the social structure of the capital city of the Reich. Their own words tell the stories of their lives and experiences during this period.

The perceptions of industrialists such as Hugo Stinnes are inferred from their actions on financial markets and from reports by others in their memoirs.

The views of Hjalmar Schacht, Currency Commissioner of the Reich responsible for carrying out the currency stabilization programme of 1923 and later President of the Reichsbank, are discussed at some length.

The reports from Paris and Berlin of Harry Greenwall, War Correspondent of the *Daily Express*, helped to form and inform opinion in Britain towards Germany. His reports from Berlin immediately after the Armistice in November 1918 provide graphic description of the background against which the inflation drama of 1923 would unfold.

For insights into the perceptions of the great majority of the population, reports in the press and inscriptions on the Emergency Money or Notgeld issues are at least an indication of the thoughts of their authors as both reflectors of and formers of opinion. It seems reasonable to assume that circulation considerations alone would have ensured that the views expressed would be broadly those that would be endorsed by at least a significant proportion of the readership.

Comments by Erich Maria Remarque, German infantryman in the Great War and author, express something of the hopelessness of the situation of those inextricably caught up in the destruction of the currency.

Looking back at that time, a German writer could say:

> *Im Jahre 1923 gerät die Republik an den Rand des Abgrunds. Äusserer Druck und innere Zerissenheit treffen zusammen. Die Ruhrbesetzung durch französische und belgische Truppen; der deutsche passive Widerstand und der damit einhergehende Wirtschafts- und Währungsverfall; die separatistischen Bestrebungen im Rheinland und in der Pfalz; die umstürzlerische Opposition der Kommunisten und Nationalsozialisten.*[2]

(In 1923 the Republic was approaching the edge of a precipice. External pressure coincided with internal dissension. The occupation of the Ruhr by French and Belgian troops; German passive resistance and the associated collapse of the economy and currency; the separatist aspirations in the Rhineland and Palatinate; the revolutionary opposition of the Communists and National Socialists.)

Summary of the major causes of hyperinflation in Germany in 1923

The main body of the text deals with the impact of the inflation on the lives of individuals and what they thought of the underlying causes of the phenomenon. It is useful before proceeding to consider these experiences to have a summary of the major causes of the destruction of the purchasing power of the Mark in the years after the First World War.

The disciplines of the Gold Standard were abandoned on the outbreak of war in August 1914. The transfer of resources to the war effort was largely achieved in Germany by the direct printing of notes to finance the budget deficits of the war years. Formally, the procedure for increasing the note issue still relied upon the discounting of government securities by the Reichsbank, but in effect notes were printed to meet the deficits. The virtually total dependence of the Reichsbank on the government meant that such securities (*Reichsschatzanweisungen*) were discounted at the behest of the state without the Central Bank being able to exercise any control on the amounts involved. As a result, the money supply increased four-fold during the war. Much of the immediate impact was suppressed by price controls and the dislocations of war that caused a fall in the velocity of circulation of money.

Budgets continued to be in deficit after 1918 and financed essentially as during the war. This was due to the costs of resettling displaced persons from territories lost under the terms of the Treaty of Versailles; the fact that post–1918 German governments did not have full control over the territory of the Reich, the ability to control and tax trade across its borders in the west being limited by the Allied Occupation; and the need to raise funds initially in Marks to meet the reparations demanded by the Treaty of Versailles. As inflation rose, people tried to shift from money into goods (*Flucht in die Sachwerte*). By June 1923, a 2000-fold rise in the money supply was associated with a 24,618-fold increase in the general level of prices. Prices rose faster than the associated increases in the money supply as a result of the attempt to shift from money into goods. People held smaller and smaller money balances for shorter and shorter periods of time. This was observed as an increase in the velocity of circulation of money. It led to yet more destabilizing consequences. Prices rising faster than the money supply created the impression of a shortage of money rather than pointing directly at excessive money printing as the cause of the inflation. The response to this perceived shortage of money was to print yet more varied monies. Vast quantities of Emergency Money or Notgeld were printed by companies, cities, towns and individuals. Such a positive feedback situation, of course, drove price levels ever higher. A temporary palliative for a difficult commercial situation very rapidly made the problem still worse.

On 11 January 1923, French and Belgian troops marched into the Ruhr. The immediate pretext was the failure of Germany to make a particular delivery of a reparations payment in kind – 100,000 telegraph poles! The response of the Germans in this area was one of passive and sometimes not-so-passive resistance. The supply side of the German economy in these areas collapsed as output stopped with the strikes called in opposition to the occupation taking effect. The tax base also fell as incomes were reduced, but the budgetary expenditure of the government in Berlin was increased to support the resistance in the Ruhr. Deficits increased, money supplies rose and inflation surged to new levels: the Mark finally became worthless.

The effects on prices of the above may be measured either by exchange rate movements or by a number of price indices available during the period. The price of the United States dollar had risen from 4.2 Marks in 1914 to 4.2×10^{12}, the value at which Hjalmar Schacht, Currency Commissioner of the Reich and later President of the Reichsbank, was to attempt to stabilize the currency in November 1923. The Mark had depreciated even further on foreign exchange markets outside Berlin. The inflation gave an impetus to the development of price indices. One Wholesale Price Index rose from 1 in 1913 to 1422 × 10^9 on 26 November 1923. An overall Cost of Living Index rose over the same period from 1 to 1535 × 10^9. With numbers such as these, the differences hardly matter. The Mark was worthless by November 1923.

Much is made in the German press at this time of the responsibility for Germany's financial plight of the Treaty or 'Diktat' of Versailles, as it was often called at this time. Certainly, many features of the Versailles Treaty made a return to 'normality' difficult. Territorial losses and resettlement costs added to budgetary expenditure whereas the Occupation meant that the German government was not master in its own territory. The demands for reparations payments made it imperative for the Reich to generate balance of payments surpluses, but political hatred and hostilities to a resumption of normal trading relationships made it impossible to do so.

Germany's problems were exacerbated by the population growth of the nineteenth century and the growth of cities due to migration from rural to urban areas. The concentration of population off the land in urban areas presented the major problem of feeding a nation faced with the consequences of low productivity in agriculture and the Allied blockade during the war.

This text looks at what those living through this period made of financial and economic events. It looks at reports that illustrate what they made of causes and consequences and what it was like to live through these events on a daily basis.

Interpretation of the written record

Written testimony passed down to us by those who directly experienced particular historical events is often incomplete in a number of ways. The writer records events that are a partial and incomplete record of what happened, he selects what to record and how it should be recorded. There is also another problem. Facts need ideally to be set within a theoretical framework to offer an explanation of the processes and interrelationships at work. This presents a problem of interpretation. At 70 years remove from the events, an interpretation that we may make of likely relationships between stated events may well not be the explanation accepted or even perceived as possible at the time they occurred. Often, for example, the reports in the *Hildesheimer Allgemeine Zeitung* are presented in isolation one from the other. It is often possible to fit a number of these reports into a theoretical framework but the idea that this would have found widespread understanding and acceptance at the time needs to be advanced with a great deal of caution. Consider the following example:

> *[Die Berliner] Verwaltung hat sich dazu entschliessen müssen, im Winter eine längere Pause im Unterricht eintreten zu lassen, weil die Heizung der Schulen zu einer unerschwinglichen Ausgabe geworden ist.*[3]

(Due to exorbitant heating costs, the [Berlin] Administration has been forced to extend the winter break for schools.)

Compare the above extract with another report in the same newspaper published in the same edition.

> *Die deutsche Regierung hat den Staatssekretär Schröter beauftragt, bei der Kriegslastenkommission in Paris die Herabsetzung der deutschen Kohlenlieferungen an die Entente um monatlich 500,000 Tonnen zu beantragen unter Hinweis auf die Unmöglichkeit der Innehaltung der bisher vorgeschriebenen Kohlentonnage und auf die deutsche Kohlennot.*[4]

(The German goverment has instructed Secretary of State Schröter to apply to the War Reparations Commission in Paris for a reduction in German coal deliveries to the Entente [Britain and France] of 500,000 metric tons per month, for two reasons: the impossibility of maintaining the tonnage so far stipulated and the German coal shortage.)

It is tempting for the reader today to put these two quotations together in a way that it seems obvious that the reader in Hildesheim would have done in 1923. Because interpretation does not always accompany reports and one is even less likely to find a report set into an overall theoretical context, such a temptation must be viewed with some caution.

Presumably some of the readership would have asserted that the schools could have been heated with the coal sent abroad in payment of war reparations! This fairly obvious linkage would not, however, have been a complete analysis of the coal price situation in Germany that led to the closure of the schools. Consider Figure 1.1. The lowest price, P, would have been established in the absence of the inflationary financing of budget deficits on the demand side and the absence of reparations deliveries of coal on the supply side. P1 would apply with reparations payments and a non-inflationary financing of the budget deficits. P2 would have arisen with the inflationary financing of deficits and no reparations. P3, the actual price prevailing, reflects

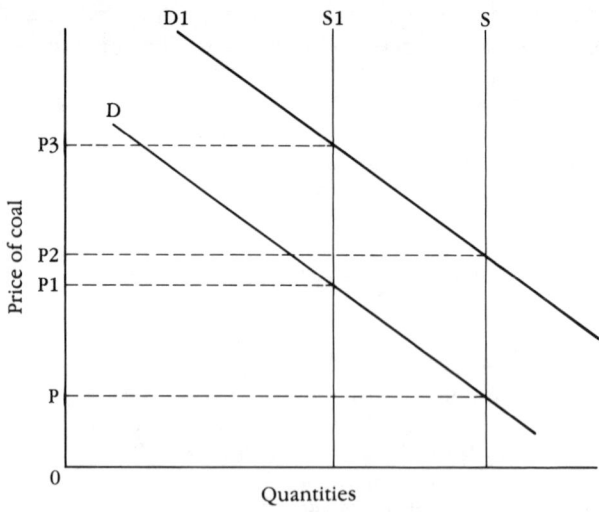

Key:

S = total production of coal

S1 = coal available to the home market

S−S1 = coal sent abroad to meet reparation payments

Figure 1.1 German coal market, 1923

contributions from both the supply and the demand sides, that is, from a demand inflated in nominal terms by the consequences of deficit financing, and from the supply side by the reductions in supply to the home market caused by the deliveries made under the terms of the Treaty of Versailles. The difference between P and P3 can therefore be split conceptually into the components caused by factors operating from both the demand and the supply sides. One would not have expected the broad mass of the readers of the *Hildesheimer Allgemeine Zeitung* in 1923 to have drawn these distinctions in quite this kind of way.

The general blaming of the Treaty of Versailles for just about every undesirable aspect of life in Germany in the 1920s was common. There was often no attempt to spell out the interrelationships and linkages between events that would establish the degree to which the Treaty provisions were to blame compared to other factors simply present at that time and unrelated to the Treaty itself. Rarely is the theoretical reasoning spelled out. An exception in the *Hildesheimer Allgemeine Zeitung* during these years was an account of the role of money in the inflationary process. As discussed elsewhere, there is explicit consideration given[5] as to whether the inflation observed is caused by an excessive growth in the money supply or whether the monetary growth itself is caused by price increases that arise from the operation of other factors.

Some of the press reports considered were written by H.J. Greenwall, *Daily Express* Special Correspondent in Paris during the 1914–18 war and subsequently in Berlin from shortly after the Armistice. His detailed reports of events illustrate another problem of interpreting the written commentary of those present at the time. As far as his period in Paris was concerned, Greenwall was often reporting secondhand on experiences and stories told to him by alleged eye-witnesses. In Berlin, he was much closer to the events he reported. For this reason, it seems likely that his reports from Berlin are much more to be trusted as a record of what actually happened than his reports from Paris. There is, of course, always the problem with such reports of realizing that the correspondent is writing with at least one eye on the tone and content expected by his editor and the general requirements of the 'folks back home'. Even reports that are factually incorrect may well be useful, however, in the sense that they are evocative of attitudes and views prevailing at the time.

The context

The Armistice of Réthondes that was signed at 5.00am on 11 November 1918 signalled the end of the fighting on the Western Front when it came into force at 11.00am on the same day. The Great War, or the First World War as it was later more commonly to be called, was at an end. Some ten million people had lost their lives. For millions that survived, the future held malnutrition, even outright starvation and the illnesses associated with an inadequate diet.

The German armies were not driven by military force from their trenches. They withdrew under the terms of the Armistice back towards Germany, followed at a distance by the Allied armies. By the time peace negotiations began at Versailles in January 1919, forces of the Allied Powers had occupied German territory up to the left bank of the Rhine with bridgeheads on the right bank. The Occupation was to last until 1930 when, at 9.30am on 30 June, the British, French and Belgian flags were taken down from the Wilhelm Hotel, Wiesbaden.[6]

For most of its length, the border between Occupied and Unoccupied Germany followed the River Rhine. With bridgeheads at Cologne and Mainz on the right bank of the Rhine, effective control over river traffic was achieved. A customs barrier was established between the two parts of Germany on 18 January 1923. This effectively meant that Germany did not have full control over foreign trade flows. From the 1914 western frontier of Germany to the Rhine, the Allies could exercise

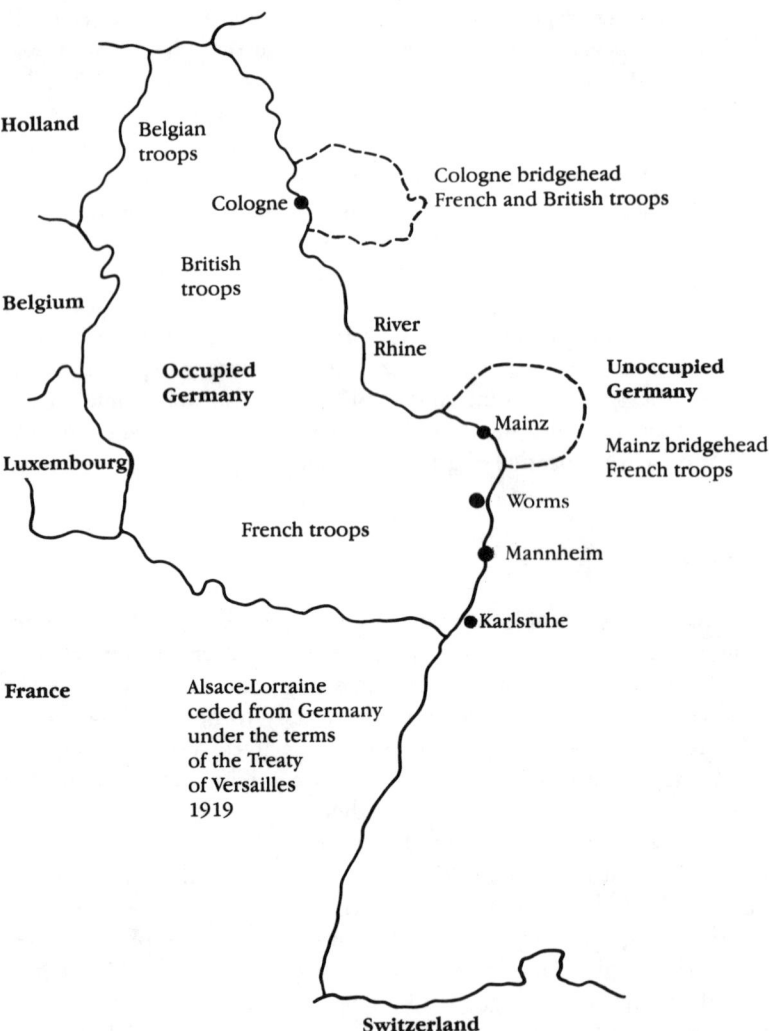

Source: Roosevelt N. 'The Ruhr Occupation'
Foreign Affairs, vol. 4, no. 1,
October 1925

Figure 1.2 The Occupation of Germany after the Armistice November 1918

effective control. The area of occupation contained most of the productive industrial areas of Germany, thus limiting a supply-side recovery after the end of hostilities. The Occupation thus hampered Germany's ability to achieve the balance of payments surpluses needed both for domestic recovery and to begin to pay off the reparations payments levied on it by the Treaty of Versailles. It also aroused German fears that the French push to the Rhine was intended to serve a French ambition to establish the Rhine as the Franco-German frontier. The author of the following extract makes this point explicitly to his Hildesheim readership:

> *Eine jede der in Frage stehenden Massnahmen wäre nur eine teilweise Befriedigung der völlig überhaupt nicht zu befriedigenden Rach- und Hasssucht Frankreichs, könnte aber an der Zahlungsfähigkeit Deutschlands nicht das Geringste ändern.*
>
> *Uebrigens ist dieser Gedanke der Pfänder nichts Neues, sondern ein Rückgreifen auf alte französische Praktiken in moderner Form. Es sei hier nur an die berüchtigten Reunionskammern Ludwigs XIV erinnert, deren Tätigkeit gleichfalls nur ein Vorwand zur Losreissung des linken Rheinufers vom Deutschen Reich war. Eine andere Form war der Rheinbund Napoleons. Heute wird solchen Bestrebungen nach Machterweiterung ein wirtschaftliches Mäntelchen umgehängt und man nennt Pfand, was man dauernd besitzen möchte.*[7]

(Any one of the measures in question would only partially satisfy the French obsession with vengeance and hatred, which will never be entirely satisfied, and could not have the slightest effect on the ability of Germany to pay.

Incidentally, the idea behind these forfeits is not new, rather a reversion to old French practices in a modern form. We need only refer here to the infamous 'Reunionskammern' of Louis XIV, the activities of which were also merely a pretext for seizing the left bank of the Rhine from the German Empire. Napoleon's Confederation of the Rhine was another form of the same thing. Today such attempts to extend French power are cloaked in economic terms, and the term forfeit is used to mean something one would like to own permanently.)

Notes

1. These figures dramatically illustrate the destruction of the currency in the second half of 1923. The rates are from the strictly controlled Berlin foreign exchange market. Data from other markets would even more dramatically illustrate the same point.
2. *Der Reichstag in der deutschen Geschichte*, 1988. Sonderdruck des Deutschen Bundestages, p. 1.

3. *Hildesheimer Allgemeine Zeitung*, 16 September 1922. *Die Not der Städte*: the crisis in the cities.
4. Ibid. *Deutschland fordert Herabsetzung der Kohlenlieferungen*: Germany demands reductions in coal deliveries.
5. *Hildesheimer Allgemeine Zeitung*, 28 August 1922. 'The Dollar near 2000!'
6. For a detailed survey of this period and the various phases of the allied occupation, see *The Occupation of the Rhineland 1918–1929*, Imperial War Museum. Facsimile edition with an introduction by G.M. Bayliss. London, HMSO, 1987.
7. *Hildesheimer Allgemeine Zeitung*, 25 August 1922. 'The Berlin Negotiations'.
   Reunionskammern: Special courts of Louis XIV set up to push his claims to territory on the eastern frontier of France.
   Rheinbund: Confederation of the Rhine established by Napoleon embracing territory that by 1914 was part of the German Reich.
   forfeit: The payment in kind by the delivery of goods instead of cash. Payment in timber would carry the concern that the French wanted the land on which the trees were growing and not just the timber.

The Occupation of the Ruhr in January 1923 would have come as no surprise to the author of this article written four months earlier!

CHAPTER TWO

The Agricultural Situation and Food Supplies

German agriculture

The agricultural situation in Germany both during the Great War and afterwards was critical. Not only had the British blockade reduced German ability to import foodstuffs during the war but also the territorial loses imposed on Germany by the Peace Settlement included some of the most fertile agricultural areas and sources of industrial raw materials. For example, the supply of food to Berlin became progressively more difficult. In 1915, Berlin, together with 44 neighbouring areas, issued a common ration card. After the 'Turnip Winter' of 1916–17, the weekly food allowance per person was reduced to an egg, 20g of butter and 70–80g of meat. Heating, lighting and clothing were also rationed. Hunger was one of the contributory factors that led to major strikes in April 1917 and January 1918.[1]

There was no chance for Germany to recover from this situation after the Armistice before the Treaty of Versailles compounded the difficulties by insisting on territory being seceded to other nations. The title and information of Figure 2.1 are taken from a map of the time showing German territorial losses under the terms of the Treaty of Versailles, as well as losses in terms of food supplies and raw materials.

One of the consequences of the losses of territory, especially in the east, was a feeling of outrage on the part of those landowners who had been dispossessed. Their political weight was in 1923 to be such that the detailed stabilization policy pursued by the government and carried out by Hjalmar Schacht would reflect their concerns as expressed by such right-wing politicians as Karl Helfferich. The landed interests had been of importance earlier in an attempt to overthrow the government in 1920. This was the Kapp-Putsch, named after one of the leading figures, Wolfgang Kapp.

The Kapp-Putsch and General Strike, Berlin, March 1920

At the beginning of 1920, it appeared that internal political conditions in Germany were returning to normal. The economy was improving

and the value of the Mark was rising. Foreign confidence in Germany seemed to be increasing. Conservative forces, however, believed the time to be right to overthrow the young Republic. As discussed above, the territorial losses imposed by the Versailles Treaty had alienated agricultural interests as well as increasing the difficulty of feeding the nation. The Treaty also provided for a reduction of the navy to 15,000 men. The Erhardt Naval Brigade stationed near Berlin objected to the likely enforced return to civilian life. There was thus an alliance of arch-conservative politicans, embittered members of the armed forces and large landowners. Because other troops refused to defend the government, it was forced to flee, first to Dresden and then to Stuttgart. The armed occupation of Berlin was opposed by the left with a general strike. The failure to destroy the government was partly due to the loyalty to the legal government shown by the civil service. It was one of the political events noted by Schacht that caused a sharp fall in the value of the Mark on foreign exchanges.[2]

Source: Landesarchiv Berlin

Figure 2.1 *Vom Reiche sollen in Ost und West 5.5 Millionen Deutsche getrennt werden* (5.5 million Germans will be cut off in the east and west from the Reich)

The Kapp-Putsch is a major example of provisions of the Versailles Treaty creating internal situations that led to reactions that in turn adversely affected the financial position of the Weimar Republic.[3]

The problems of agriculture shaped the form of the stabilization policy and were responsible for some of the post-stabilization problems faced by Germany.

Territorial losses in the Versailles Settlement caused a major problem of population resettlement, the expenditure for which added to the budgetary deficits of the Reich. These losses of territory reduced the land available for cultivation thus requiring a more intensive cultivation of what remained. A policy of 'internal colonization' was adopted, under which displaced families from the lost territories were provided with the infrastructure investment necessary to take up agricultural work within the new boundaries. Increasing the intensity of cultivation of the available land was largely restricted by a lack of capital. As reported in the *Hildesheimer Allgemeine Zeitung*, the agricultural situation could be summarized as follows:

Die Krise der deutschen Landwirtschaft wird vor allem charakterisiert durch drei Momente.

1. *Durch die überaus hohe Belastung der Landwirtschaft durch Steuern und andere öffentl. Abgaben (Rentenbankbelastung).*
2. *Durch einen der allgemeinen Entkapitalisierung der deutschen Wirtschaft herrührenden Mangel an Kreditkapital und die Auswirkung beider Momente.*
3. *Durch die sich für den Landwirt ergebende Notwendigkeit, seine Produkte zur Erfüllung seiner Verpflichtungen um jeden Preis und zu dem ungünstigsten Zeitpunkte zu veräussern, die naturgemäss einer Senkung des Preises für landwirtschaftliche Erzeugnisse und damit ein Missverhältnis zum Preise der landwirtschaftlichen Betriebsmittel herbeiführt.*

Der niedrige Preis der landwirtschaftlichen Produkte in Deutschland rührt also von dem Steuerdruck und der Kreditnot her; er ist eine Folge des in bestimmten Zeitpunkten zu starken Angebots. Ganz anders jedoch liegen die Dinge auf dem Weltmarkt. Auch hier zeigt sich die Krise in einer Senkung der Preise für die wichtigsten landwirtschaftlichen Produkte, die jedoch ganz andere Ursachen hat als in Deutschland.[4]

(The crisis in German agriculture is characterized mainly by three factors.

1. The extremely high burden placed on agriculture by taxes and other public levies such as the Rentenbank charges.

2. The lack of credit available, caused by the overall decapitalization of the German economy and the effects of both factors.
3. The need for the farmer to meet his commitments by selling his goods at any price and at the most unfavourable time, leading naturally to a drop in prices for farming products and thus to a disproportionate relationship to production costs.

The low prices for agricultural products in Germany are therefore caused by the pressure of taxation and the lack of credit; they are the consequences of excess supply at certain times. On the world market, however, things are quite different. Here too the crisis is characterized by falling prices for the most important agricultural products but the causes are quite different to those in Germany.)

This is an illustration of the general problem of never being able to satisfy everybody. The form of the stabilization policy of 1923 reflected the importance of the agricultural interest and their political representatives in the Reichstag. The idea of backing for the issue of Rentenmark notes or, as they were often called, Bodenmarks,[5] in the form of a land charge tax on the agricultural sector was partly to flatter the sensitivities of the politically powerful landed interests.

The need to modernize German agriculture to feed the increased population within Germany's post–1919 boundaries was a major threat to the stability of the currency. Attempting to control the money supply in a situation of a desperate need for bank advances to finance working capital requirements for the agricultural sector was to prove a major problem after 1919 and throughout the 1920s.

Taxation was therefore seen as a factor that both burdened agriculture with additional costs and depressed the demand for its products. In the large cities, the situation was much worse. People were dying from starvation.

> Nach einer Ausführung von Dr Goeb – Berlin, erhält etwa ein Sechstel der deutschen Bevölkerung öffentliche Unterstützung ... die Not, die selbst bis zu Hungertodesfällen (in Berlin 43 Hungertodesfälle während 10 Monate des Jarhes 1923) führt.[6]

(According to a comment by Dr Goeb in Berlin, about a sixth of the German population is in receipt of state benefits. The deprivation has even caused people to die of starvation (43 cases in Berlin during the first 10 months of 1923).)

No wonder that Hjalmar Schacht, President of the Reichsbank, felt inhibited from using normal discount rate methods of curbing the demand for credit in such a situation. The draconian credit squeeze that he adopted in 1924 resulted in an absolute fall in the level of credit advanced on discounted bills. Such a credit squeeze exceeds what would be expected today and is explicable in terms of the special circumstances of 1924 in Germany and in particular of the need to make companies use their own resources instead of relying on Reichsbank credits. At least one modern effect of a credit squeeze is noted: the contraction of the home market forces more attention on promoting exports! The political and economic conditions in the agricultural sector in Germany at this time do highlight the considerable risks attached to the stabilization policy pursued by Schacht.[7]

A graphic picture of hunger in Berlin is contained in the reports from that city by the *Daily Express* Correspondent, H.J. Greenwall. On 22 November 1918, he reported that,

> Although the food situation is very bad, the bread ration is now 2lbs. 6ozs. weekly as compared with 1lb. 14ozs. two months ago. The meat ration is now 9ozs. weekly, compared with the same quantity fortnightly two months ago. There is an allowance of 1oz. of butter weekly and about 2ozs. of horribly smelling margarine made from turnips. There are now plenty of potatoes and the ration is 12lbs. weekly. One egg is allowed every three weeks.

On 12 December 1918, Greenwall reported an interview with Walther Rathenau.[8] He is reported as saying that,

> Germany has been hungry for three years, but is not yet starving. Everybody who sees Germany will say that she is not starving now, and that is perfectly true; but if you talk of the provisions to be found in Germany you must truthfully say that they will be exhausted in two months, and if you wait until then to send food it will be too late, because seventy million people cannot be fed as easily as, say, seven million Belgians.

In an interview with Fritz Ebert, First Chancellor of the German Republic, the question of food supplies was raised by Greenwall. Ebert was keen to stress the consequences of the territorial losses of Germany for the supply of food.

> Supplies quoted in the statistics existed in many cases only on paper, and supplies were wasted in the hope that the War would end earlier. Then there came, as you know, the separation of rich agricultural districts in consequence of the Armistice conditions and of the political surrender in the East, the surrender of trucks and locomotives, the lack of coal, and, finally, difficulties of transport throughout the whole country.[9]

Food shortages dominate Greenwall's reports from Berlin. In a report of 2 December 1918, he wrote,

Rathenau Memorial, Koenigsallee, Berlin

> The Liberal-Democratic Party of Germany
> in Memory of
> **WALTHER RATHENAU**
> Foreign Minister of the German Reich
> He fell murdered on this spot
> on the 24th June 1922
> The Health of a People stems from its
> inner Life – from the life of its Soul
> and from its Spirit
>
> October 1946

Political killings reflected the violence of the times and hampered the pursuit of economic stabilization measures by the Reich government. Significant assassinations at the other end of the political spectrum included Karl Liebknecht and Rosa Luxemburg.

Figure 2.2 The murder of Walther Rathenau

THE AGRICULTURAL SITUATION AND FOOD SUPPLIES 17

> I have noticed that there is absolutely no nourishment in the food. One is always hungry ... one sees people munching apples to assuage their hunger. Poor people live on acorn coffee, sour bread – four slices a day – and vegetable soup. The meat ration is nominally 8³⁄₄ozs. a week but in reality, no more than half that is obtainable.... For breakfast, I have the choice of acorn coffee, Ersatz tea, or Ersatz cocoa. There is no sugar, butter, or milk but I can have Ersatz jam – made from turnips – or Ersatz honey. For lunch and dinner there is a variety of dishes, but nothing to eat.[10]

By 4 December 1918, Greenwall was complaining of having to pay 71/- (£3.55) for a meal at a restaurant in Berlin. He further reported that, 'One is always hungry. I have decreased four inches in girth in a fortnight.'[11] More seriously, he reported on breeding stocks being killed for immediate consumption thus jeopardizing future food supplies and encouraging the hoarding of supplies by peasants. The tone is sometimes jocular but never disguises the underlying seriousness of the report. On hoarding by the peasants of food supplies, Harry Greenwall wrote that,

> If you ask a peasant to sell you a goose he replies: 'I have none.' But if you go on: 'Well, I have a box of cigars and a couple of pairs of socks', the peasant says, 'Well, perhaps I can find a goose!'[12]

Thus, barter replaces money transactions, available food supplies are hoarded and the economic situation becomes progressively more difficult.

Greenwall's interview with Dr Wurm, the German Food Controller since the outbreak of the Revolution, is also interesting for a quantitative estimate of the food shortage.

> On December 1st 1914, there were 25,300,000 hogs in Germany. On December 1st 1916, on account of the food shortage, the number had been reduced to 17,000,000 ... by next March, it is expected that there will be only 3,000,000 hogs in Germany.... During this winter, we had to have four meatless weeks. Last September we had 18,500,000 cattle. The average weight of the beasts in 1914 was 440lbs. The average weight is now 290lbs. There are now 1,500,000 fewer cows than in 1914. The average amount of milk given by German cows in 1914 was seven to eight quarts daily. Now they give only three and a quarter daily. One reason for this is the shortage of horses, so that oxen and cows have to work in their place.[13]

On the same day, he could also report that,

> In Unter den Linden this afternoon I saw a cab-horse fall and break

its leg. The authorities forbid that horses should be shot. The one I saw removed to the slaughter-house was taken for food.[14]

Poverty

People died from hunger on the streets of Berlin in 1923. Many more were malnourished as a consequence of several factors converging simultaneously; these include the blockade of Germany during the 1914–18 war that prevented the import of the foodstuffs needed to feed the population, overpopulation in relationship to its own agricultural productivity and the failure to provide adequate public assistance or index-linked incomes to maintain purchasing power during the years of hyperinflation.

The suffering reported in Lange's diary can be seen as an extension and intensification of a process started by the conduct of the First World War. Consider the following extracts:

Der Antiquitätenhandel blüht. Das Kulturgut verarmter Familien wandert zum Händler, um dort von Ausländern und Neureichen gekauft zu werden.[15]

(The antiques trade is flourishing. The cultural possessions of impoverished families find their way into the hands of dealers, to be sold to foreigners and the nouveaux-riches.)

Die Zahl der durch die Inflation verarmten Kleinrentner schätzt man auf etwa 30,000. Davon haben nur 8,000 öffentliche Hilfe Anspruch genommen. Der Rest lebt von der Verschleuderung seiner letzten Sachwerte.[16]

(It is estimated that there are about 30,000 people on low pensions who have been impoverished by inflation. Of these, only 8,000 have claimed state benefits. The remainder live by selling off their last material assets.)

Reich deficits and agriculture

Among the factors contributing to the budget deficits of the Reich government in Berlin were the financial implications of the new boundaries, especially those arising from territorial losses in the east. Unsettled boundaries had been the cause of conflict for centuries and were not to be settled by the Treaty of Versailles! They were to be one of the sources of financial stress for the Weimar Republic.

THE AGRICULTURAL SITUATION AND FOOD SUPPLIES 19

That the question of the eastern boundaries of the German-speaking states before unification in the nineteenth century and for the German Reich after Bismarck was not new, and that the provisions of the Versailles Treaty were regarded as yet one more stage in a continuing saga, is illustrated by one example of Notgeld of the period (Figure 2.3).

Figure 2.3 An example of Notgeld[17]

The period costumes of the figures emphasize the continuity of the problem, the lack of settled boundaries. At the present time, there is uncertainty about Germany's eastern boundaries. At the end of the First World War, doubts also existed about boundaries in the west, although the Treaty of Versailles was to provide a lasting solution to these particular problems. For Germany, in the immediate aftermath of the war, to have to provide considerable infrastructure investment for the newly arrived settlers from the lost territories was a major problem.

> *Es sind 21,886 Ansiedlerfamilien angesetzt worden, deren Kopfzahl einschliesslich der von ihnen nachgezogenen deutschen Nichtansiedler in den Ansiedlergemeinden auf rund 153,000 geschätzt wurde. Rechnet man auf ein Ansiedlerdorf rund 500 Hektar Fläche und 30 Siedlerfamilien, so bedeutete das Siedlerergebnis etwa 700 Dörfer. Erbaut waren 479 Schulen, 57 Kirchen, 34 Bethäuser, 53 Pfarrgehöfte, rund 70 andere Bauten für öffentliche Zwecke. Etwa 3,500 Bauerngehöfte, 220 Arbeitermiethäuser, 300 Gasthöfe sind vom Staate errichtet worden. 235,000 Acker waren dräniert, 30,000 Morgen Moorkulture und Wiesenverbesserungen ausgeführt, 468*

Kilometer Wegestrecken gepflastert oder chaussiert, rund 650,000 Obst- und Nussbäume gepflanzt.[18]

(It has been calculated that there are 21,886 settler families. The number of persons has been estimated at around 153,000, which includes German non-settlers who followed them into the settlement communities. Assuming 500 hectares of land and 30 families per settlement village, the result of settlement would amount to something like 700 villages. 479 schools, 57 churches, 34 places of worship, 53 vicarages and some additional public buildings were built. Approximately 3,500 farmsteads, 220 workers' rented houses and 300 inns have been built by the state. 235,000 fields were drained, improvements to 30,000 acres of moorland and meadow were carried out, 468 kilometres of road were tarred or cobbled. Some 650,000 fruit and nut trees were planted.)

Quite a financial burden for a country to carry immediately after the Great War! It can either be claimed that financing the resulting deficits by increasing the money supply meant that the money supply was responsible for the subsequent inflation, or that the Treaty of Versailles was responsible in that the deficits were incurred as a response to the terms of that Treaty. Stress on the territorial losses caused by the Treaty of Versailles does not necessarily mean that contemporary opinion was unaware that the political factors could not have caused inflation without the monetary expansion. But for many, the mechanism was rather different: they saw the attempts to implement the terms of the Treaty as leading firstly to a depreciation of the Mark on the foreign exchange market in terms of other currencies. This led to a rise in import prices that raised the general level of prices internally. An increase in the money supply then took place to enable trade to continue at the higher price level. The common factor in both explanations is, of course, the political. The above discussion regarding the consequences for public sector expenditure of the need to resettle displaced Germans from the east adds another factor to the explanation of inflation. The quotation from the *Hildesheimer Allgemeine Zeitung* illustrates the scale of the infrastructure investment requirements of resettlement. This added to the total Reich budgetary financing requirements and hence to the deficits, the financing of which played a major part in the monetary expansion that caused the inflation.

For Schacht, the conditions in Germany after the Great War were akin to a return to the standards of the middle of the nineteenth century. But what did this mean?

THE AGRICULTURAL SITUATION AND FOOD SUPPLIES 21

Der Zug in die Städte

In den 50er und 60er Jahren strömen in die immer grösser werdenden Industriestädte vor allem Arbeitskräfte aus der jeweils unmittelbaren Umgebung. Wenig später setzt die grosse Wanderung aus Ostdeutschland in die west- und mitteldeutschen Industriereviere ein. Gleichzeitig steigt zwischen 1850 und 1870 die Bevölkerungszahl von 35 auf 41 Millionen. Unmenschliche Wohnverhältnisse, 18-Stunden-Tag, Löhne am Rande des Existenzminimums und Kinderarbeit bestimmen die Lage der damaligen Industriearbeiterschaft.[19]

(Migration into the Cities

During the fifties and sixties of the nineteenth century, workers flooded into the ever-expanding industrial cities from the surrounding areas. A little later there began the great migration from eastern Germany into the industrial areas of western and central Germany. At the same time, between 1850 and 1870, the population grew from 35 to 41 millions. Degrading living standards, the 18-hour day, wages close to a subsistence level and child labour defined the situation of the industrial working classes at that time.)

These conditions were to establish the basic situation that was to cause difficulty in Germany after the Armistice. An exportable surplus of food would have found a ready market in a hungry Europe but there was none to export. A major factor that might have helped to restore exchange rates nearer to their purchasing power parities was missing. It also strengthened the political power of agricultural interests. This was so strong by 1923 that the currency stabilization programme itself had to be framed in line with the expectations of these groupings.

For Schacht, Europe was stifled by overpopulation. While Germany had, therefore, to place great emphasis on increasing its agricultural production, the fertility of the land was limited; mass movement of its population to thinly settled land elsewhere in the world was seen as the only hope of a long-term solution to the problem of feeding the nation. The population growth of the nineteenth century was the root cause of the problem and thus the only solution was to increase the ratio of land to population by large-scale emigration. Thus, population pressure generates its own inexorable demand for living-space (*Lebensraum*)![20]

The power of the argricultural interests is illustrated by the following patriotic call that the government in Berlin felt obliged to make in 1923.

Aufruf an die deutschen Landwirte

Berlin, 1 August.

Der Reichsausschuss der Deutschen Landwirtschaft erlässt einen Aufruf an die deutschen Landwirte. Der Aufruf führt aus, dass die deutsche Landwirtschaft keine Schuld an der Lebensmittelnot in den Städten trägt und schliesst mit den Worten: An alle deutschen Landwirte ergeht unser Ruf und unsere Mahnung; Helft, dass alles, was Ihr an Erträgnissen des Landes zum Verkauf stellen könnt, unverzüglich geliefert wird und in die Hand der Verbraucher gelangt. Die in allernächster Zeit zu erwartende Herausgabe einer wertbeständigen Anleihe soll Euch in die Lage versetzen, den Erlös so anzulegen, dass er Euch zur Fortführung Eurer Wirtschaft erhalten bleibt. Helft dem Vaterlande, Ihr helft damit am besten auch der deutschen Landwirtschaft.[21]

(An Appeal to the Farmers of Germany

Berlin, 1 August.

The Reich Agriculture Committee issues an appeal to all German farmers. The appeal states that German agriculture cannot be held responsible for the lack of food supplies in the cities and ends with the words: our call and exhortation goes out to all German farmers; help in bringing all the saleable products of the land into the hands of the consumer without delay. The distribution of an inflation-protected loan in the near future is intended to put you in a position whereby you can invest the profit in such a way as to retain it for the maintenance of your business. By helping the Fatherland, you will also be helping German agriculture in the best possible way.)

Notes

1. '*Feld und Hof, Haus u. Garten*': 'Field and Farm, House and Garden'. An illustration in the *Hildesheimer Allgemeine Zeitung*, 19 May 1924. It stresses the worth of rural life and the importance of agriculture. Similar sentiments were to be illustrated on Rentenmark notes issued as part of the currency stabilization measures in November 1923.
2. H. Schacht, *The Stabilisation of the Mark* (Berlin: Westkreuz Verlag 1927) ch. 2, 'From the Armistice to the Invasion of the Ruhr'.
3. Landesarchiv Berlin. *Kapp-Putsch und Generalstreik März 1920 in Berlin. Tage der Torheit, Tage der Not. 1990* .
4. *Hildesheimer Allgemeine Zeitung*, 19 May 1924. *Landwirtschaftliches Allerlei*: agricultural miscellany.
5. *Bodenmarks*: the term stresses the idea of the land as a backing for the new notes.
6. *Hildesheimer Allgemeine Zeitung*, 19 May 1924. *Die deutsche Landwirt-*

schaft und die Volksnot: German agriculture and the deprivation of the people.
7. H. Schacht, *The Stabilisation of the Mark* (Berlin: Westkreuz Verlag 1927) especially ch. 5, 'From the Rentenbank to the Gold Discount Bank'.
8. Walther Rathenau, 1867–1922. Son of the founder of AEG, Emil Rathenau. Minister of Reconstruction 1921. Foreign Minister 1922. Engineer, banker, merchant and writer. Close relations with the Kaiser before 1914. One of the 'Kaiserjuden' a privileged élite for whom religion was no bar to holding the highest offices of state. Murdered in the Grunewald, Berlin 1922. See Annemarie Lange, *Berlin in der Weimarer Republik* (Berlin: Dietz Verlag 1987).
9. *Daily Express*, 3 December 1918.
10. *Daily Express*, 4 December 1918.
11. Ibid.
12. *Daily Express*, 1 December 1918.
13. Ibid.
14. Ibid.
15. Friedrich C.A. Lange, *Gross-Berliner Tagebuch 1920–1933* (Berlin: Westkreuz Verlag 1982). Diary entry for 20 September 1922. The use of the word '*Kulturgut*' here translated as 'cultural possessions' is particularly poignant. It means not just goods but those items of cultural signficance, '*Werk der Kultur*', implying paintings and all forms of works of art, the very things that give life dignity and sophistication. Civilized standards in their lives are sacrificed to ensure basic physical survival.
16. Ibid., diary entry for 2 May 1923.
17. Issued by the Council of Saalfeld a. Saale, 1 August 1921. The inscription reads, 'Reception of political refugees on the market square'.
18. *Hildesheimer Allgemeine Zeitung*, 19 May 1924. *Landwirtschaftliches Allerlei*: agricultural miscellany.
19. 'Fragen an die deutsche Geschichte', Ausstellung im Reichstag, 1990.
20. H. Schacht, *The Stabilisation of the Mark* (Berlin: Deutsche Verlags-Anstalt, 1927), especially ch. 10, 'International Cooperation'.
21. *Cuxhavener Zeitung*, 6 July 1923.

CHAPTER THREE

Attitudes, Hearts and Minds

The German withdrawal from France had taken place under the terms of the Armistice and not as a result of military defeat. Nor did they arrive home in any sense as a defeated army. Greenwall reported from Berlin on 10 December 1918 that,

> At noon there must have been half a million persons packed in Unter den Linden. Punctually, at one o'clock the first detachment, consisting of a Bavarian infantry unit, fought its way through the serried ranks of cheering, screaming, and 'hoch-ing' multitudes. Handkerchiefs were waved, women threw flowers in the soldiers' path, and the men themselves were covered in flowers.... The people went mad with excitement. Bands blared out marching songs, in which the onlookers joined in chorus. I looked down on the sea of waving handkerchiefs, hats, and multi-coloured students' caps, and thought that the victorious home-coming troops in Paris, London and New York could have no reception to excel this. 'Do these people realize they are beaten?', I asked myself. Women dashed into the marching ranks and embraced the men, cavalrymen seized women round the waist and swung them up beside them on horseback. Red Cross nurses rode on guns, gun-carriages and field-kitchens were smothered in flowers, and the crowds cheered themselves hoarse. It was an unforgettable scene.[1]

The attitudes of such a people meant that there would be stubborn resistance to the allied attempt to impose a settlement on Germany that was not accepted by them.

German unification had been imposed from above. The Reich government in Berlin would be weakened in its relationships with the provinces because separatist tendencies had not been entirely eliminated by Bismarck. It would be further weakened as it struggled to cope with hunger at home and to meet the terms of the Versailles Treaty, seen by Germans as having been dictated in a spirit of revenge by countries unable to defeat Germany on the battlefield.

Franco-German hatred is a common theme to be found in the newspapers in Germany during 1922 and 1923. The devastation of northern France during the Great War and the insistent French demands for Germany to make reparation payments both in cash and kind were the immediate factors involved. However, the antecedents of these feelings involved the events of earlier years, 1792–1813 in particular, that had not by 1914 resulted in a settled mutually accepted common frontier. Two questions arise: firstly, the nature of the antagonisms reported and secondly, the impact of these events on the ability of the government of the Reich, even given the will, to balance its budget by adjusting expenditure and income from taxation flows so as to preclude inflationary forms of finance through Reichsbank credits.

The nature of the hatred is illustrated to an extent by the 10,000 Mark Reichsbank note issued in 1922 in Berlin. This was known as the 'vampire note', the man on the note appearing to have a bite on his neck. This was an allusion to the effects of French reparations demands on Germany after the Great War. The heroic sturdy figure of a man represents Germany, the 'bite' the fatally weakening effect on him of the French demands. Such an attitude may appear highly theatrical to us now but it does illustrate something of the feelings of the time.

Figure 3.1 The 10,000 Mark note of 1922. The 'vampire note' showing heroic Germany fatally wounded by the French bite into the neck sucking out its very life blood.

Nationalism and racialism as factors in inflation

Franco-German hatred in the aftermath of the Great War played a significant role in causing the hyperinflation in Germany in 1923. The border in the west between France and Germany was in dispute. There were grave suspicions in German minds about French intentions. These were seen historically as securing the west bank of the Rhine as the common frontier and opportunistically to grab territory on the east bank if at all possible. Securing the Rhine border was advanced by the return of Alsace-Lorraine to France under the terms of the Treaty of Versailles, but was seen in many German minds as only part of a greater French design. The loss of life during the war on both sides and the devastation of northern France added to hates and hostilities. The occupation of the Ruhr district by French troops only added to German convictions that they were dealing with an expansionist power. It was the stubborn resistance of the Germans to French occupation, fuelled by the hatreds discussed above, that caused the collapse of production in the occupied areas. This collapse of production was accompanied by a rise in demand as transfers were made to the occupied areas to maintain the striking population. The slump in supply added yet another twist to the inflationary spiral. German press comment reserves particular venom for the French at this time, the British being seen as much less hostile. British support, however, for what the Germans regarded as an impossible reparations burden was a factor in maintaining conditions favourable for the development of hyperinflation. Apart from the family tragedies of war and personal losses, the reporting back to Britain of atrocity stories by sections of the British press played a part in generating a demand to make Germany pay. In so far as they fuelled a refusal to buy German goods, they helped to make German recovery impossible and the future receipt of reparations less likely.

Atrocity stories in the British press

The stories cited are all reports sent back to the *Daily Express* by its Paris correspondent, H.J. Greenwall. The reports from Paris are probably more suspect than those filed later from Berlin. The latter are eyewitness accounts and reports of interviews he conducted with German politicians. They are also markedly less jingoistic in tone. The former are reports at least secondhand and perhaps even further removed. Greenwall simply could not have been in all the places in which the atrocities were reported to have occurred. He relied on secondhand testimony at best. These dubious reports do, however, have an economic significance. They helped to strengthen the hands of those politicians determined to make Germany pay for the war. They helped to justify a level of reparation demands that Germany could not meet and to provoke a German reaction that helped to push the inflationary spiral still higher. Headlines like the ones below of 1918 were common at the time and were presented as factual statements of events.

WORSE THAN BEASTS

By H.J. Greenwall
'Express' Special Correspondent
Paris, Sept. 18

The news has reached me here of how the Germans behaved when they entered the town of Fschenstochowa, known as the Rome of Poland. Fschenstochowa is looked upon by the Poles as a sacred city, and is visited every year by a million pilgrims.

The sacrilege of the Convent of the Virgin has created an indelible impression among the Russian Poles, and this fresh German outrage is certainly going to increase the Slav hatred of the Teuton.

German troops, under the command of Colonel Zollern, entered the cells of the convent and forced the nuns to drink wine with them. Scenes of indescribable excess followed.

Other acts of violation took place in the town, and husbands, brothers and sweethearts who tried to interfere were ruthlessly shot down. In the night most of the population left the town.

The peasants of the neighbouring villages burnt their reserves of corn so as to annoy the Prussians. Then they armed themselves with old shotguns, pitchforks, and scythes, and set out to avenge their kindred. Needless to say, the whole band was massacred.

GERMANY'S ORGANIZED POLICY OF MURDER

French Official Report Reveals Appalling Systematized Atrocities

EVERY CRIME IN THE CALENDAR

By H.J. Greenwall 'Express' Correspondent
Paris, Thursday, Jan. 7
1918

The policy of wanton pillage and murder which is an integral part of the German system of making war is relentlessly exposed in the official report of the commission appointed by the French Government to investigate violations of international law by the enemy in the parts of France which they have occupied.

The report, which will be published tomorrow, contains twenty-seven columns of small type, and should be entitled 'Germany's Shame'. It contains a chapter-and-verse recital of every crime known in the Newgate calendar, from robbery with violence to rape. All the names, places, and dates where outrages were committed are given by the prosecution, and Germany stands indicted before the world's jury.

The commission has collected sufficient evidence to prove everything up to the hilt. During the fighting on the Marne, both before and after the defeat, the German soldiers, with the complicity of their high officers, embarked on systematic pillage. Detachments entered villages fully equipped to burn and destroy.

Reading of the attacks on unprotected women and the murders of little children causes the blood to boil. The document is the most damning ever compiled and shows clearly what France has endured, and what Great Britain would suffer if she were to come under the heel of the Huns.

HUNS IN MEUSE VALLEY

Pillaging houses to make the trenches comfortable

'Express' Correspondent. Paris, March 2nd
1918

Since they have occupied Saint Mihiel, the Germans have applied their methods of pillage in the most systematic manner.

They have seized everything they could lay their hands on, including doors and locks. Armchairs, beds, benches, tables have all been transported to the trenches.

The Germans, being in fear of the French shells, live in the cellars, and, as they love comfort, they have installed fires and stoves in them.

The pipes open into the street, by the ventilation holes and chimney places on the street level, and fill the village with smoke, giving Saint Mihiel a strange appearance.

Information has also come to hand about the German occupation of St. Maurice-sous-les-Côtes. When they arrived, the Germans first called on the mayor and the priest. The officer who visited the latter declared that he had hanged six priests in Belgium, and ordered the priest to celebrate Mass in honour of the Kaiser and of German victories.

OUR MEN BEHAVED LIKE VANDALS

EXTRACTS FROM THE DIARY OF A GERMAN OFFICER

PLUNDER AND MURDER

By H.J. Greenwall, 'Express' Correspondent
Paris, Friday, 9th October 1918

A striking admission by a German officer of the pillage and outrages committed by the Kaiser's troops in France is published in the 'Matin'.

The material was gathered from a pocket-diary belonging to an officer of the 12th Saxon Army Corps.

After describing numerous acts of incendiarism and wanton destruction, this writer states:

'On August 23rd we were marching on Lisogne. Our men declared that they were unable to proceed owing to the fire of franc-tireurs from the houses. Some of these alleged franc-tireurs were then seized. They were placed one behind the other in groups of three so that three might be killed by one rifle shot.

In the village of Bouvines our men behaved like vandals. The spectacle of the heaps of slain inhabitants defies description. Not one house was left standing.

From the debris all around we dragged forth the trembling people one after another and killed them.

A large number of men, women and children whom we found huddled together in a cellar were shot down in groups. The place was then set on fire.

On the 26th we crossed the frontier at Gui d'Ossus. This picturesque village was reduced to a cinder heap, although no charge whatever had been made against the inhabitants.

The rifle of a cyclist who fell from his machine accidentally went off. The man alleged that he had been fired on. Immediately, by order of our commanding officer, all the inhabitants were seized and flung into the flames of their own burning houses.

Such horrors as these, I hope, will not occur again.'

WOUNDED SOLDIERS BURNT ALIVE

HARROWING STORIES OF GERMAN ATROCITIES

'Express' Correspondent
Paris, May 23

Revolting stories of German brutality are told by refugees from the Longwy district who arrived in Paris yesterday after a long journey by way of Metz and Switzerland.

There were 380 of them in all, including many young girls and little children, whose terrified condition bore witness to the horrors through which they had passed.

At Mont Saint Martin seventeen civilians were shot on the pretext that they had fired on the Germans; forty-two houses were burnt, and more than three hundred people rendered homeless.

At Romain the Huns devastated the cemetery, took the wreaths from the graves, and with these and the wooden crosses that marked the resting-places of fallen French soldiers they made bonfires, round which they danced in drunken fury.

At Fresnoy, near Longuyon, a patrol of uhlans arrived, and began firing right and left on the inhabitants in the streets. They picked up the wounded and flung them into the houses to which they set fire.

Further on, at Barlieux, the same men burnt alive in a barn forty French wounded soldiers. At Long-la-Ville the Germans destroyed three-quarters of the houses; the inhabitants were only allowed to eat raw beetroots, to which the Huns applied the name, 'Joffre's stew'.

VON KLUCK'S CONFESSION

PROUD OF BEING CALLED A HUN AND A BARBARIAN

ORDERS TO DESTROY BELGIAN TOWNS

By H.J. Greenwall 'Express' Correspondent
Paris, Monday, Jan. 11

Von Kluck, the German general who commanded the right wing during the advance on Paris, is proud of being called a barbarian and a Hun.

A journalist who is a citizen of a neutral country has just returned to Paris from a visit to von Kluck's headquarters on the Aisne. He says the place is a veritable fortress, surrounded by trenches and defended by massed batteries of machine guns.

In a conversation with him von Kluck said: 'They call us Huns and barbarians. This honours us, because it proves our strength.'

Speaking of the destruction wrought by the German army during the advance through Belgium, von Kluck said: 'I do not deny I have personally given orders in Belgium to destroy and burn entire towns.'

Von Kluck recently received a visit from the Kaiser. He is now living in great comfort in a chateau belonging to a member of the Chamber of Deputies.

LIEGE JACKBOOTERY

'Express' Correspondent
Paris, Feb. 2

Mme. de Calwaert, wife of the Greek Consul in Liege, has been sentenced to three years' confinement in a German fortress under extraordinary circumstances.

According to a correspondent of the 'Journal', a man of poverty-stricken appearance presented himself at her house and begged for assistance.

She at first refused, but was so moved by his piteous appeal that she eventually gave him four marks (4s.).

The next day German soldiers arrested the lady on the pretext that she had been 'encouraging recruiting for the Belgian army.'

She was brought before a war council, and the president observed severely in passing sentence 'When one wants to help a poor man one gives sixpence not four shillings.'

HUN CONDEMNED TO DEATH

CALLOUS RECORD OF VICE AND MASSACRE

By H.J. Greenwall 'Express' Correspondent
Paris, April 15

A court-martial sitting at Rennes has condemned to death Karl Vogelgesang, aged twenty-four, belonging to the 26th Regiment of the Line.

He was charged with having committed pillage and incendiarism on August 5 in Belgium; with having killed the wounded on the battlefield on August 24; and with further acts of pillage committed in September.

A diary found on the prisoner was the evidence that convicted him. 'We found a big shop', he wrote; 'I took three fine shirts, ten pairs of socks, a packet of cigarettes, matches, cigars, vests, wine and beer; in brief, everything that a man wants. We had hardly got out of the place before it burst into flames.'

Vogelgesang notes that on August 16 he and some friends stole 115 bottles of wine, which 'prevented us from fasting for a few days.'

GERMAN BRUTALITY TO PRISONERS

BRITISH PARTY BEATEN WITH CLUBS

By H.J. Greenwall
'Express' Correspondent
Paris, April 3

Some of the inhabitants of the towns and villages invaded by the Germans have now returned to France by way of Switzerland, and many of them have interesting tales to tell of their experiences in Germany and on their way to prison.

A former town councillor of Roubaix has come back from Hameln-on-the-Weser (Hanover). He was taken prisoner on October 10, when the Germans fired on all the people who tried to get away.

From Roubaix the prisoners went to Douai, where they remained five days without receiving food, and but for the kindness of the miners' wives they would have starved. The women took food every night to the church, and the prisoners managed to bribe the guards to fetch it for them.

In Hanover the ex-councillor found many British, French, and Russian military prisoners. He says the French were fairly well treated, but the Russians and the British received most brutal handling from the guards.

On one occasion the British soldiers were singing, and for this offence the guards beat them with clubs so severely that many of them were seriously injured.

A French boy who tried to interfere was struck with a bayonet. He was wounded in the head, and died almost immediately.

GERMAN BOASTS

The prisoners were kept in tents, where they were employed in making fibre mats. Their food consisted of beetroot soup, boiled rice, and herring salad. They were told they would never be able to go back to France, because the country was already half conquered; and on the occasion of the fall of Antwerp the camp commandant gave an order to the Belgian prisoners to 'fall in,' and when they were lined up he triumphantly announced the news, but if he expected to derive any satisfaction out of it he was mistaken, for the Belgians never moved a muscle.

The Germans only released men unfit for military service, but they were so proud of their captures that they hung on every man's back a big placard marked 'Prisoner-of-war,' and they were wearing these when they arrived in Geneva.

Another of the returned men is a priest, who was accused of being an officer in disguise. They evidently thought he was a spy, because the Germans themselves have adopted the clerical dress for their own spies.

Another is a woman of Buzancy, who states that in Argonne three hundred soldiers mutinied, killed their officers, threw away their rifles, and surrendered to the French.

Three thousand Germans came through Buzancy at the time of the invasion, and one of the soldiers who slept at her house stated that three-quarters of those who went through had been killed.

The Germans behaved with their usual brutality at Buzancy. This woman was forced to act as a servant to the soldiers who slept in her house, and once, when she did not get them what they wanted quickly enough, three of them seized her and held her against the stove. She was very badly burned, but the men only laughed at her suffering.

MURDER BY INCHES

AWFUL TREATMENT OF FRENCH CIVIL PRISONERS

CONSUMPTION GERMS SPREAD BY THE GERMANS

By H.J. Greenwall, 'Express' Correspondent
Paris, Wednesday, March 10

The second official report of the Committee appointed to inquire into acts committed by the Germans in violation of international law, which will be published to-morrow, is even more horrible than the first.

About 1,000 civilian prisoners who have been interned in Germany recently returned to France. Of these, 300 have been examined on oath by the Committee.

Many men of military age were taken and underwent an operation rendering it impossible for them to bear arms.

A thousand old people and children, even women in an enceinte condition, were also taken, either on the false pretext that their neighbours had fired on the Germans, or that they were merely being taken to a place of safety in case of the imminent battle.

Families were separated and the children put in different camps from their mothers, who were vainly seeking their husbands.

During the railway journeys, generally no food or drink was given. Many of the prisoners from Northern France would have died of hunger, except for charity.

Women prisoners from Roubaix travelled eighty-five in a truck for seventy-two hours, and were unable to sit down.

They endured horrible suffering in the concentration camps, where the filth was indescribable. Only one person examined was found to have slept in a bed.

GERMANS KILLING THE WOUNDED

FRENCH SOLDIERS' TERRIBLE STORY

By H.J. Greenwall
'Express' Correspondent. Paris, Jan. 27

Another proof that Germans kill the French wounded is afforded by a statement given to M. Louis Vincent, late Prefect of the Nord, by a soldier named Felix Herbert, who is now in the hospital at Marseilles.

Herbert states that at the dawn of a day early in September, when the French trenches were being heavily bombarded by the enemy, he and three others were left there wounded.

The Germans captured the trench, and after robbing Herbert of his food and tobacco and his watch and chain, one of the Germans struck him on the head three times with the butt of his rifle.

A little later another German fired on the wounded men, and a bullet pierced Herbert's arm. He feigned death, but directly afterwards the Germans fired at him point blank.

Another of the wounded Frenchmen tried to crawl away, and a German officer shot him through the head with his revolver.

Herbert began to crawl away during the night and it took him twenty-four hours to reach a place of safety.

WOMEN AS SHIELDS

By H.J. Greenwall 'Express' Correspondent
Paris, Friday, Nov. 6

A dastardly act, in which the Germans made the mayor and mayoress and a row of inhabitants of Néry stand in front to protect the soldiers from the fire of the British, has just been described to me by one of the ambulance drivers.

One morning early, during a heavy mist, the encampment of the Queen's Bays was suddenly attacked by German troops, who got up within close range and opened fire with machine guns.

Our men were shaving and were taken at some temporary disadvantage. 'Boot-and-saddle' was sounded, and our men turned out quickly, the faces of many of them still covered with lather.

Swiftly forming and charging the Germans, the Queen's Bays drove the enemy back to Néry.

The Germans took up a position and got hold of the mayor and his wife and thirty-eight of the inhabitants and made them all stand up for three hours and a half to protect them from the British fire.

'Lie down!' cried the mayor to the others, but when they tried to do so in order to give the British a chance to fire at the enemy the German soldiers pricked them with their bayonets to make them stand up.

So terrible was the ordeal with the German soldiers using the standing line of civilians as a screen hour after hour, and threatening them with the bayonet, that the mayoress, distraught with terrror, became insane.

In the meantime the Queen's Bays were reinforced. They swept along at top speed and took the enemy in the rear. Every one of the Germans was accounted for. Those who were not killed were taken prisoner.

It is not difficult to understand that, after reading reports such as these, there would have been universal support for the harshest terms to be imposed in any peace settlement with Germany. The effects that such reports would have had are more important than the accuracy of the details they contain. There was certainly evidence of a reluctance to have anything to do with Germans even at the highest levels in the immediate aftermath of the war. Schacht himself relates an example of this involving himself.

Indessen herrschte im Ausland unmittelbar nach dem Kriege eine derart hasserfüllte Atmosphäre, die jahrelangen Lügen über das deutsche Hunnentum, die angeblichen deutschen Greuel und Verbrechen hatten sich so eingefressen, dass man nun nicht plötzlich den Weg zur Wahrheit und Vernunft zurückfinden konnte. Dabei gebärdeten sich oft gerade diejenigen am schlimmsten, die am wenigsten Veranlassung hatten. Im März 1919 kam ich als Vorsitzender einer Kommission über Warenablieferungen zu Verhandlungen mit einer gleichartigen alliierten Kommission nach Rotterdam und werde den lächerlichen Eindruck, den es auf mich machte, nie vergessen, als ich auf der amerikanischen Gesandschaft im Haag vorsprach, um die Adresse eines amerikanischen Mitgliedes dieser Kommission zu erfahren. Da erlebte ich es, dass ein Attaché zu mir herauskam und, meine Besuchskarte in der Hand haltend, mich fragte: 'Are you a German subject?' Als ich selbstverständlich bejahte, kamen die lapidaren Worte aus seinem Munde: 'Then I cannot speak to you.' Als ich darauf zu erklärenden Worten meinen Mund öffnen wollte, ertönte sofort wieder das: 'I cannot speak to you', worauf ich mich mit einem gut berlinischen ‹Na denn nich› umdrehte und dieses ‹diplomatische› Haus verliess. Das war die Mentalität noch drei Monate nach Waffenstillstandsabschluss, und es hat Jahre und Jahre gebraucht, um sie nur ein weinig zu bessern.[2]

(There was, however, an atmosphere abroad that was full of hatred towards Germany immediately after the War that was based for years on lies about the Hun and alleged German crimes and atrocities. This had been so deeply entrenched that the way back to truth and reason could not immediately be found. Those who behaved the worst in this respect often had the least cause to do so. In March 1919, I came to Rotterdam as Chairman of a Commission on the Supply of Goods for talks with a similar Allied Commission. I will never forget the comical impression I had on a visit to the American Legation in the Hague to enquire about the address of an American member of this Commission. An attaché came out to see me with my visiting card in his hand and asked, 'Are you a German subject?' As I naturally answered in the affirmative, the succinctly expressed words came out of his mouth, 'Then I cannot speak to you.' As I tried to open my mouth to offer words of explanation, the words were repeated, 'I cannot speak to you.' Whereupon, with a good Berlin expression, I said, 'Then don't' and turned around and left this 'diplomatic' establishment. That was the mentality three months after the Armistice and it took years and years for a small improvement to take place.)

It was the practice of many towns and villages in England to publish short biographies of those killed in the Great War. The communities were more closely knit at that time than in any period since and the sense of community losses was therefore all the greater. One of these volumes was published in Skipton, Yorkshire in October 1919. In his introductory note, the editor of the *Craven Herald* could write that,

> This volume of 'Craven's Part in the Great War' is a humble but sincere expression ... of the gallant, heroic and self-sacrificing spirit shown by the sons of Craven in resisting the unscrupulous, malignant and prearranged design of Germany and her dupes to crush the British Empire and the civilized countries associated with her.

The volume contains a photograph of every man in the area killed in action and lists the total British casualties killed, wounded or missing at 2,917,718. Material such as this would have contributed to a desire for revenge on Germany and no easy passage back to normal economic relations with other countries.[3]

The Armistice of 11 November 1918 was accepted by Germany for a number of reasons. Apart from war fatigue at home, losses of men and materials on the Eastern and Western Fronts and food shortages, there was reassurance in Woodrow Wilson's Fourteen Points of January 1918 that Germany would not be punished by the terms of the subsequent Peace Treaty. There was widespread anger and resentment in Germany at the terms of the Treaty of Versailles or 'Diktat' of Versailles as it was widely known. Yet the Fourteen Points alone implied substantial territorial concessions on the part of Germany. The 'wrong done to France by Prussia in 1871 in the matter of Alsace-Lorraine' was to be righted and 'An independent Polish State ... should be assured a free and secure access to the sea.'

The slaughter of war must be expected to cause hatred. The citizens of Craven, Yorkshire were informed that 'the Hun armies over-ran Belgium, destroying and plundering some of its greatest treasures and committing crimes which horrified the world.'[4]

French hatred of Germany was inevitable given the destruction of Northern France during the war and was a major factor complicating the restoration of normal economic relationships after 1918. The occupation of the Ruhr by the French and Belgians further deepened hostilities between these major nations of Continental Europe. Consider the reaction in reports of this event in the German press. In an article entitled, 'The Occupation of the Ruhr' published in the *Hildesheimer Allgemeine Zeitung*, we read as follows:

Der Feind ist da!

... Der Feind steht im Lande. Er hat sich in dem Herz der deutschen Wirtschaft eingenistet, um unser Herzblut zu trinken und unsere staatliche Existenz zu vernichten.... Der Truppeneinmarsch häuft auf das Ruhrgebiet neue Menschenmassen, die die Wohnungs- und Nahrungsnot ins Ungeheure steigern werden. Auch im unbesetzten Deutschland werden die Kohlen noch knapper und die Preise noch höher werden als bisher.... Deutschland ist nicht imstande, durch Aufbietung militärischer Macht die eingedrungenen Räuber der verdienten Strafe zu überliefern....

‹*Kein Zwingherr und kein Heer besiegt
Den Mann, der lieber bricht als biegt.*'[5]

(The Enemy is here!

... The enemy is in our land. He has built his nest in the heart of the German economy, drinking our life-blood and destroying our existence as a state.... The arrival of the troops piles new masses of people on the Ruhr district, who will increase the shortages in housing and food. In the unoccupied areas of Germany too coal will be in shorter supply and prices will be higher than before.... Germany is not in a position to call on military power to punish the robbers and intruders. They certainly deserve to be....

'No tyrant and no army defeats the man
who would rather break than bend.')

Apart from personal experience of the events, the major source of information would have been the newspapers of the day. The series of extracts from the *Hildesheimer Allgemeine Zeitung* during the early months of 1923 describe a vivid picture of hatred and resentment between the Germans and the French during the Occupation of the Ruhr. Supply problems made worse by the French occupation of vitally important industrial areas, transport difficulties caused by French occupation of railway stations making a difficult food situation even worse, German citizens being abused and shot by French troops on the streets of German cities, German citizens being sentenced to death by French courts-martial, and women and children being deliberately starved by French actions preventing food supplies getting through. This was the picture painted by news reports in one German city; it cannot have been much different in other cities. The economic effects of these events are fairly inevitable given human nature. The prolonged German will to resist meant even higher rates of inflation, which were produced in a number of ways. The collapse of the production of industrial goods decreased the goods available for sale. The government in Berlin lost a substantial part of its tax base, so revenue fell. As a consequence of this and a determination to assist the Occupied Area, the level of government expenditure rose and thus the deficit to be financed by accommodation at the Reichsbank; notes printed in exchange for Treasury securities also increased.

Der Terrorismus der Rheinlandkommission
Ueberfallene Ruhrbahnhöfe.

Honnef, 1. März. Der Bahnhof Honnef wurde heute vormittag von etwa 60 französischen Truppen besetzt. Die deutschen Eisenbahnbeamten wurden vom Bahnhof verwiesen. Der Zugverkehr liegt still.

Berlin, 1. März. Im Bezirk Köln sind heute vormittag die Bahnhöfe und zum Teil auch die Stellwerke an der Strecke Ehrenbreitstein – Troisdorf von französischem Militär besetzt und das meiste Personal vertrieben worden. Der Verkehr Köln-Frankfurt ist unterbrochen worden.

Berlin, 1. März. In den Bestimmungen über den Belagerungszustand in Bochum ist seit heute insofern eine neue Verschärfung eingetreten, als die Stunde des Geschäftsschlusses, des Inkrafttretens der Verkehrssperre usw. auf 4 Uhr nachmittags heraufgesetzt worden ist. Gestern abend sind zahlreiche Zivilpersonen, die angeblich die französische Verkehrsordnung hinsichtlich der Zeit überschritten hatten, inhaftiert und in der rohesten Weise unter den Augen französischer Offiziere misshandelt worden.[6]

(The Terrorism of the Rhineland Commission
Attacks in Railway Stations in the Ruhr.

Honnef, 1 March. The Railway Station at Honnef was occupied this morning by about 60 French soldiers. The German railway officials were required to leave the station. Railway traffic has stopped.

Berlin, 1 March. In the Cologne area the railway stations and also some of the signal boxes on the line between Ehrenbreitstein and Troisdorf were occupied this morning by French military units, and most of the staff were expelled. Traffic on the line from Cologne to Frankfurt has been interrupted.

Berlin, 1 March. There has been a further intensification of the provisions governing the state of siege conditions in Bochum. Shop closing times and the traffic curfew have been brought forward to 4pm. Yesterday evening numerous individuals who had allegedly infringed the French traffic order with regard to time were detained and mistreated in the crudest manner in the presence of French officers.)

Französische Hungerblockade gegen Frauen u. Kinder
Die Erdrosselung der Ruhrbevölkerung

Durch die immer neuen Verkehrsstörungen durch die Franzosen ist die Lebensmittelversorgung im Ruhrgebiet äusserst bedenklich geworden. In Gelsenkirchen, Bochum, Dortmund, Langendreer, Herne usw. ist fast gar nichts mehr zu haben. Die Milchzufuhr hat in den meisten Städten nicht mehr funktioniert. Kartoffeln sind, wenn überhaupt, nur für 20,000 Mk. zu haben. In Gelsenkirchen ist Fleisch so gut wie nicht mehr erhältlich. In Herne machen sich die Schwierigkeiten in der Lebensmittelversorgung immer fühlbarer, desgleichen in Bochum. In Gelsenkirchen ist der Kartoffelmangel sehr stark, auch Fleisch ist kaum noch zu haben. Die Lebensmittelversorgung von Wattenscheid ist nur noch über Gelsenkirchen möglich. In Kastrop musste die Milch mit Autos unter schwierigsten Verhältnissen herangebracht werden. Auf dem Bahnhof Lünen beschlagnahmten die Franzosen am 16. Juni für die Stadt bestimmte Lebensmittel der Ruhr- und Auslandshilfe.[7]

(French Hunger Blockade against Women and Children
The Strangulation of the Population of the Ruhr

The supply of foodstuffs in the Ruhr has become extremely critical because of the interruptions to traffic by the French. There is practically nothing to be had in Gelsenkirchen, Bochum, Dortmund, Langendreer, Herne and other places. Supplies of milk have ceased in most cities. Potatoes when available cost 20,000 marks. In Gelsenkirchen, meat is as good as unobtainable. Food supply difficulties in Herne are becoming increasingly apparent and severe. The same is true in Bochum. In Gelsenkirchen the potato shortage is severe and meat is virtually unavailable. The supply of foodstuffs to Wattenscheid is only possible via Gelsenkirchen. Milk had to be brought by car to Kastrop under the most difficult conditions. At the Railway Station in Lünen on the 16th of June the French confiscated foodstuffs from the Help for the Ruhr campaign and from foreign sources that were intended for the City.)

Französische Rache: 5 Deutsche in Dortmund erschossen

Die Meldung von der Erschiessung zweier Militärs in Dortmund hat sich leider bestätigt. Doch sind die Getöteten nicht Offiziere, sondern Unteroffiziere.... Dass die Franzosen sofort blutige Rache nehmen würden, war ebenfalls leider vorauszusehen. Wohin wird der französische Terrorismus im besetzten Gebiete noch führen! Die Verantwortung für die Folgen trägt die französische Politik vor dem Richterstuhl der Geschichte.

Dortmund, 11. Juni. Zu der Mordtat an den zwei französische Militärs wird von zuständiger Seite mitgeteilt, dass die Tat nicht von deutscher Seite verübt wurde.... Infolge des verschärften Belagerungszustandes kam es am gestrigen Abend zu Zwischenfällen. Die Räumung der Strassen um 9 Uhr wurde teilweise unter grossen Misshandlungen der Passanten durchgeführt, wobei die Franzosen Ohrfeigen und Fusstritte ausübten. Einer der Zivilisten erhielt im Laufe des Abends den tödlichen Schuss. Drei weitere Personen wurden in der Nacht erschossen und zwei verletzt. Durch Augenzeugen wurde festgestellt, dass die Franzosen ... ohne vorherigen Wortwechsel die Personen erschossen haben.[8]

(French Revenge: 5 Germans shot in Dortmund

The report of the shooting of two military personnel in Dortmund has unfortunately been confirmed. The dead are not officers but other ranks... That the French would immediately take bloody revenge was also unfortunately foreseeable. Whither French terrorism in the Occupied Area! French policy will carry the responsibility for the consequences before the court of history.

Dortmund, 11 June. Responsible sources have confirmed that the act of shooting the two French military personnel was not the responsibility of Germans. Incidents took place yesterday evening as a result of the intensification of the state of siege. The streets were cleared at 9.00pm with great violence on the part of the French with face slapping and kickings being meted out to passers-by. One of the civilians received a fatal shot during the evening. Three more were shot during the night and two injured. Eye-witnesses confirm that no exchange of words took place prior to the shots being fired.')

Sieben Deutsche zum Tode verurteilt
Ein Explosionsunglück bei Duisburg
Neues Urteil des Mainzer Kriegsgerichts

Paris, 30. Juni. In Mainz wurde gestern vor einem französischen Kriegsgericht gegen neun Leute im Alter von 18 bis 24 Jahren wegen versuchten oder beabsichtigten Attentats auf die Eisenbahnstrecke verhandelt. Sieben der Angeklagten stammen aus dem unbesetzten

Gebiet. Das Gericht verurteilte sieben zum Tode, zwei erhielten Freiheitsstrafen. Die Namen der Verurteilten sind nach der Pariser Meldung Sasse, Maurer, Grube, Hahne, Schneider, Freier, Fren, Lauth und Kögler.[9]

(Seven Germans Sentenced to Death
Explosion at Duisburg
Latest Sentences of the Court Martial
at Mainz

Paris, 30 June. In Mainz yesterday, a French court martial dealt with the cases of nine people between the ages of 18 and 24 years charged with attempted or planned attacks on the railway track. Seven of the accused come from the unoccupied area. The court sentenced seven to death and two received prison sentences. The names of the accused according to the report from Paris are Sasse, Maurer, Grube, Hahne, Schneider, Freier, Fren, Lauth and Kögler.)

The Germans had cause for resentment and anger directed against the allies in general and the French in particular. Consider the following report in the *Hildesheimer Allgemeine Zeitung* of 23 July 1923.

Die Kameradschaftliche Vereinigung ehem. 231er hielt gestern abend im Restaurant Wente eine gutbesuchte Monatsversammlung ab. Nach Aufnahme von 4 neuen Mitgliedern fand eine Durchberatung der Vereinsstatuten statt. Die Versammlung beschäftigte sich weiter mit der Ehrung der Gefallenen des Regiments durch Fertigstellung der Ehrentafel für das Ehrendenkmal auf dem Ehrenfriedhof. Eine Sammlung freiwilliger Beiträge hierzu ergab den Betrag von 145,000 Mk.

(The Old Comrades Association of the former 231st Regiment held a well-attended monthly meeting yesterday evening in the Wente Restaurant. The admission of four new members was followed by a detailed discussion of the Association's statutes. The meeting also considered the honouring of the fallen members of the Regiment by completion of the panel of names on the Memorial in the War Cemetery. A voluntary collection for this purpose raised 145,000 Marks.)

The Old Comrades Association had met and raised 145,000 Marks to honour those who did not return from the Great War. Presumably they had reached deeply into their pockets, so what had they raised in real terms? Elsewhere in the same newspaper, we read the following:

Mit Wirkung vom 23. Juli 1923 wird der Abgabepreis der Reichsgetreidestelle für das von ihr an die Kommunalverbände zur Markenbrotversorgung gelieferte Getreide von 800,000 Mark für die Tonne auf im Durchschnitt 2.4 Millionen Mark erhöht werden. Die Erhö-

hung soll erfolgen wegen der sich durch die Markentwertung immer mehr steigernden Verluste der Reichsgetreidestelle, die auch mit der neuen Massnahme noch bei weitem keine volle Deckung finden. Die Heraufsetzung des Abgabepreises wird auch eine Steigerung der Brotpreise naturgemäss zur Folge haben, die man etwa auf durchschnittlich das Doppelte der bisherigen annehmen kann. Dabei ist zu beaufsichtigen, dass wegen des Verfalls der Mark und weil im Brotpreis der Getreidepreis nur etwa drei Fünftel ausmacht, seit dem 4. Juni, dem Tage der letzten Erhöhung der Abgabepreise, Erhöhungen der Markenbrotpreise durch die Kommunalverbände fast wöchentlich, z.B. in Berlin viermal, erfolgten. Auch nach der am 23. Juli bevorstehenden Erhöhung wird das Markenbrot noch nicht den dritten Teil von dem kosten, was bereits heute für eine gleiche Menge von markenfreiem Brot aufzuwenden ist. In Hildesheim kostet ein markenfreies Brot zurzeit schon 18,000 Mark.

(With effect from 23 July 1923, the price of grain delivered by the Reich to the local organizations responsible for the supply of rationed bread will be increased on average from 800,000 Marks per tonne to 2.4 million Marks. The increase is intended to reflect the losses to the Reich that are constantly increasing due to the depreciation of the Mark. The present increase will by no means cover all the losses. Bread prices will automatically rise as a consequence of the increase in the price of grain. Bread prices will on average double. What is to be noticed is that bread prices since 4 June, the date of the last increase in Reich delivered grain prices, have been increased practically weekly by the local organizations, e.g. four times in Berlin. This is despite grain costs only amounting to some three-fifths of the bread price. After the planned increase on 23 July, rationed bread on coupons will not cost as much as one-third the price of unrationed bread at the present. Unrationed bread at the moment in Hildesheim costs 18,000 Marks.)

The Old Comrades Association had raised between them just about the price of eight loaves of unrationed bread! Thus 145,000 Marks would just about have raised that much given the price quoted in the extract of 18,000 Marks per loaf. They could not have been unaware of their extreme poverty as illustrated by these figures.

The winter in Heilbronn in 1923 was extremely cold. On 31 December 1923, 'Sehr kalt: −22°C' was recorded. Already in October, as the following extract illustrates, winter conditions had necessitated welfare distributions to the poorest of secondhand clothing from stocks held by the British Army:

Wegen der Notlage der minderbemittelten Einwohnerschaft im Winter genehmigt der Gemeinderat den Erwerb von 200 Mänteln, 300 Röcken, je 500 Hosen, Unterhosen, Hemden und Schnürschuhen aus gebrauchten Beständen der englischen Armee.[10]

(In view of the plight of the less well-off citizens in winter, the Municipal Council authorizes the supply of 200 coats, 300 jackets, 500 trousers, underpants, shirts and laced shoes from the second-hand stocks of the British Army.)

Long before 1914, the economies of Europe had become progressively more closely linked and inextricably interdependent in matters of trade. This became progressively more so as populations rose and trading volumes grew. The destruction of one country would severely damage the others. As Keynes wrote in 1919:

> If the European Civil War is to end with France and Italy abusing their momentary victorious power to destroy Germany and Austro-Hungary now prostrate, they invite their own destruction also, being so deeply and inextricably intertwined with their victims by hidden psychic and economic bonds.... Europe, if she is to survive her troubles, will need so much magnanimity from America, that she must herself practise it. It is useless for the Allies, hot from stripping Germany and one another, to turn for help to the United States to put the States of Europe, including Germany, on to their feet again.[11]

To meet the demand for reparations ideally required the simultaneous achievement of a budgetary surplus and a balance of payments surplus. The balance of payments surplus would produce the required net inflow of foreign exchange into the Reichsbank. From this fund, payments could be made to the foreign creditors of the Reich. Achievement of such a surplus was the *sine qua non* of the ability to fund reparation payments. Such an achievement would be reinforced by a budgetary surplus. Itself deflationary in nature, such a surplus would tend to reduce the demand for imports and increase the pressure on producers to export in so far as resistance to German goods abroad would permit. It would also have provided the government of the Reich with the means to purchase the required foreign exchange from the Reichsbank. This would be more likely to succeed than any attempts at outright confiscation of foreign exchange.

The reports of such alleged atrocities as those examples cited above, as well as the large casualties in the great land battles of the Great War, would harden public resolve in the UK to see Germany punished. This made it all the more difficult to restore the trading relationships on which the prosperity of both nations depended. The overwhelming majority view in the UK would not distinguish between those losses caused by the willingness of the British High Command to sacrifice wantonly thousands of lives for a few yards of ground and those losses inevitable in armed conflict. The opprobrium was totally visited on Germany.

The true extent of the contempt for the lives of its own soldiers by the British High Command is becoming more evident in the 1990s, as the Public Records Office makes available details of courts-martial during the Great War. Many soldiers who could take no more suffering, often after years of distinguished conduct and who refused orders or deserted their posts, were court-martialled and shot. These were secret executions. Their relatives at home were lied to and informed that their sons, fathers and husbands had 'died of wounds' or had been 'killed in action'. As John Crossland wrote,

> The victims had to go blindly to meet the great Moloch; any voting with the feet against the bloody lunges of the generals that passed for grand strategy must receive condign punishment.[12]

Notes

1. *Daily Express*, 11 December 1918.
2. Hjalmar Schacht, *The Stabilisation of the Mark* (Berlin: Deutsche Verlags-Anstalt, 1927), p. 29.
3. *Craven's Part in the Great War* edited by John T. Clayton. Editor of the *Craven Herald*, Skipton. From the volume presented to Driver James Woodhead.
4. Introduction to *Craven's Part in the Great War* compiled and edited by J.T. Clayton. A volume presented to each member of His Majesty's Forces who joined up from the Skipton Parliamentary Division.
5. *Hildesheimer Allgemeine Zeitung*, Friday, 12 January 1923.
6. *Hildesheimer Allgemeine Zeitung*, Friday, 2 March 1923.
7. *Hildesheimer Allgemeine Zeitung*, Tuesday, 19 June 1923.
8. *Hildesheimer Allgemeine Zeitung*, Tuesday, 12 June 1923.
9. *Hildesheimer Allgemeine Zeitung*, Monday, 2 July 1923.
10. *Chronik der Stadt Heilbronn 1922–1933*. Durr, F., Wulle, K., Schmolz, H. and Foll, W. Stadtarchiv Heilbronn 1986.
11. John Maynard Keynes, *The Economic Consequences of the Peace* (London: Macmillan 1920), pp. 3 and 135.
12. John Crossland, 'The Pity of War', *History Today*, vol. 41, July 1991, pp. 9–11.

CHAPTER FOUR

Living with Hyperinflation

The Berlin foreign exchange market

The data on exchange rates taken from the diary of Friedrich Lange were all from the official Berlin market. That the true market clearing rate in a free market might be radically different from these official rates was freely acknowledged. The reasons why such other rates might differ was the subject of press comment. Foreign currencies in 1923 were, of course, traded in a large number of centres. The values that Lange chose to record show selected values from the Berlin foreign exchange market. They show clearly enough the total destruction of the purchasing power of the Mark. For many commentators, however, the exchange rate was used not only to measure the external depreciation of the currency but also as a measure of the internal decline in the purchasing power of the Mark, raising the question of its adequacy for this purpose.

The Berlin market could be influenced to an extent by Reichsbank policy. Intervention did on occasions temporarily halt and even reverse the decline in the value of the Mark. In other markets, the Reichsbank could not directly influence the prices at which the Mark was traded. The market in Cologne, for instance, was in the Occupied Zone of Germany and was as removed from the influence of decisions in Berlin as markets in Paris and London. On these markets in particular, much larger falls in the value of the Mark took place than are recorded in Table 4.1.

The motivation of the Reichsbank not to allow the excess demand for dollars to be removed by a further increase in price is clear. It tried periodically to hold the dollar price to prevent further depreciation of the Mark. This was partly to reduce the rate of internal price inflation but was only ever successful for short periods of time. The Reichsbank could not, of course, control trade in the Mark beyond Germany's boundaries. Neither was it in control of foreign exchange markets elsewhere in Germany.

> Die Frage, wie der Dollar steht, ist zur Zeit in Deutschland schlechthin die Tagesfrage. Aber sie ist leichter gestellt als beantwortet. Freilich, die amtliche Notierung gibt eine klipp und klare Auskunft. So wurde beispielsweise urbi et orbi verkündet, dass der Dollar am

LIVING WITH HYPERINFLATION

Sonnabend ‹amtlich› 176,000 notierte, aber die Börsenauguren lachen einander zu, wenn sie sich begegnen. Die Nachfrage nach Devisen war an diesem Tage so stark, dass beispielsweise der Dollar, das Pfund, der Gulden, die Finnmark, die Lire, der französische Franken und die tschechoslovakische Krone nur mit je 5 Prozent zugeteilt wurden. Das heisst, die Nachfrage überstieg das Angebot so ungeheuer, dass unter diesen Umständen von einer wirklichen Kursnotierung kaum noch die Rede sein kann.... Es ist ein offenes Geheimnis, dass eben mit Rücksicht auf die Repartierungen die sogennanten ‹Konzertanmeldungen› Platz gegriffen haben. Das heisst, wenn der Devisenreflektant von vornherein damit rechnen muss, dass nur ein Teil seiner Anmeldung befriedigt wird, so wird er ‹vorsorglicher Weise› eben mehr verlangen, als er braucht. Ein Umstand, der wiederum in hohem Masse kurstreibend wirkt!

Man ersieht ... dass die zahlreichen Verordnungen, die seit zwei Monaten zur Stützung der Mark ergangen sind, immer wieder Lücken aufweisen, immer wieder neue Ergänzungen erforderlich machen, ohne dass es gelingt, die Lücken völlig zuzustopfen. Auf eine dieser Lücken, vielleicht die bedenklichste, hatten wir erst unlängst hingewiesen, nämlich auf das schwunghafte Wiederverkaufsgeschäft. Als Abgeber von Devisen tritt ja im wesentlichen nur die Reichsbank auf, und bei einer so scharfen Repartierung, wie sie jetzt bei der Zuteilung erfolgt, stellt das eine Art Lotteriespiel dar.

Mit dem Lotteriegewinn! Denn wem beispielsweise die von der Reichsbank bewilligten fünf Prozent Devisen in den Schoss fallen, der kann damit ein sehr einträgliches Arbitragegeschäft machen. Da er Devisen zu dem ‹amtlichen› Kurs bekommt, der eben nur amtlich ist, so kann er, wenn er sonst will, sie fünf Börsenminuten später mit erheblichem Agio verkaufen; sie werden ihm aus den Händen gerissen zu ‹Höchstpreisen›....

Jedenfalls bedeutet diese Massnahme das Zugeständnis, dass die amtliche Dollarnotierung nur noch eine Fiktion ist. In der Tat stellte sich zur Zeit, als die amtliche Notierung 176,000 lautete, die Newyorker Parität auf 228,571, und in Danzig, wo der Dollar frei und schwunghaft gehandelt wird, war der Kurs noch wesentlich höher.... Dem Markschwund nicht zu begegnen ist, wenn es nicht gelingt der Inflationswirtschaft, dem chronischen Defizit mit seiner alle Dämme fortspulenden Papiergeldflut ein Ziel zu setzen. Vorbedingung hierfür ist aber wiederum die Beendigung der französischen Ruhrsabotage, der von dort aus betriebenen Atomisierung der deutschen Wirtschaft.[1]

(In Germany today question number one is 'how's the dollar doing?'. It is however more easily asked than answered. Of course the official quotation gives a straight answer. On Saturday, for example, the whole world was told that the dollar 'officially' stood at 176,000, but stock exchange prophets laugh about it with each other when they meet. On that day the demand for foreign exchange was so strong that for instance only five per cent of the demand for the dollar, the pound sterling, the guilder, the Finnish mark, the lire, the French franc and the Czech crown could be met. In other words, demand exceeded supply so enormously that a true exchange rate is impossible under these circumstances.... It is no secret that, given the fractional allocation criterion, so-called 'concert bookings' become widespread. That is to say, when the prospective purchaser of foreign exchange expects from the outset to receive only a fraction of the amount requested, he will 'as a precaution' ask for more than he needs. This in its turn has a considerable impact on the rate of exchange!

It is evident ... that the numerous decrees introduced in the last two months as a means of supporting the Mark have a series of loopholes and again and again require supplementary decrees, which fail to close the gap entirely. We reported on one of these gaps recently, perhaps the most disquieting one, *viz.* the roaring trade in reselling currency. The Reichsbank is of course generally the sole

Table 4.1 The external value of the Mark in United States dollars

Date	Dollar price in Marks
1. 1. 1921	75
13.10	140
15.11	258
28.11	183
24. 3. 1922	326
26. 6	349
31. 7	670
15. 8	1,040
16. 9	1,460
24.10	4,000
16.11	7,500
18. 1. 1923	18,200
1. 2	48,000
1. 6	75,000
16. 6	107,000
30. 7	1,100,000
8. 8	4,700,000
1. 9	10,600,000
14. 9	106,000,000
4.10	440,000,000
23.10	56,000,000,000
1.11	142,000,000,000
8.11	630,000,000,000
17.11	2,500,000,000,000
20.11	4,200,000,000,000

Source: Dollar rates as quoted in Friedrich C.A. Lange, *Gross-Berliner Tagebuch 1920–1933*. No post-stabilization rates are quoted. The daily exchange rate had ceased to have the importance it held throughout 1922 and 1923. That Lange saw fit to include these rates in his diary suggest the importance of the prices of foreign currencies in the daily life of the citizen.

supplier of foreign exchange, and when the allocation is so tight as at present, obtaining foreign currency is a kind of lottery.

But a winning lottery! For those who, for example, receive the five per cent of currency authorized by the Reichsbank can do extremely lucrative arbitrage business. Having obtained foreign exchange at the 'official' rate, they can sell five minutes later, if they so wish, at a substantial premium; the foreign exchange will be grabbed at 'top' prices.

This measure implies the admission that the official dollar rate is pure fiction. As a matter of fact, at the time when the rate of the dollar was announced as 176,000 marks, in New York it was 228,571 and in Danzig, where the dollar is freely and briskly traded, it was significantly higher still. . . . The depreciation of the Mark can only be countered if we succeed in putting an end to the inflationary economy, to the chronic deficit with its floods of paper money washing away all dams. Again this can only be done when the French cease sabotaging the Ruhr and destroying the German economy.)

There was simply no free market in dollars in Berlin. The readers of the *Cuxhavener Zeitung* were made clearly aware of the interference by the Reichsbank in Berlin with the operation of the forces of supply and demand.

The demand for dollars far exceeded the supply of dollars from the Reichsbank resulting in rationing such that generally five per cent of the demand would actually be supplied. The demand for dollars was itself somewhat speculative. Why not put in an application for more than the amount really required in the hope that the percentage received

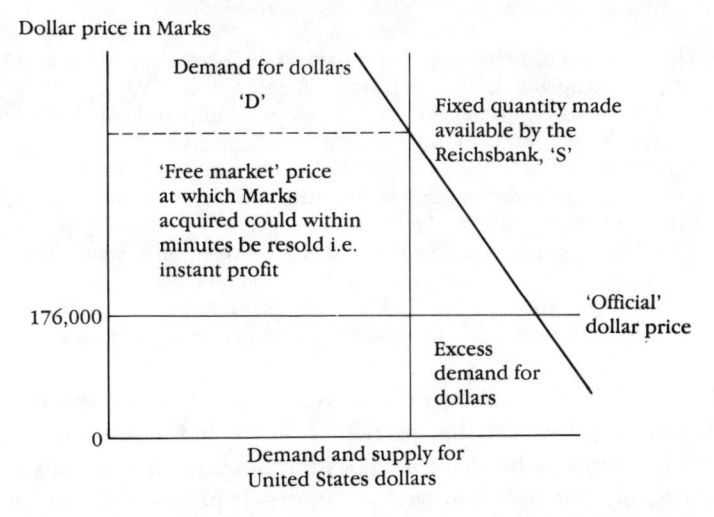

Figure 4.1 Berlin foreign exchange market, 7 July 1923

would actually be useful? The situation described in the *Cuxhavener Zeitung* is summarized in Figure 4.1.

The exchange rates quoted at the beginning of the chapter show clearly enough the depreciation of the German currency from 4.2 Marks to the dollar in 1914 to the 4.2×10^{12} at which the attempt was made to stabilize the rate in November 1923. As already discussed, these were the official Berlin rates and resulted from tightly controlled trading; it was by no means a free market. As illustrated above, on other markets, the Mark stood at a significant discount to these official rates. So how was this presented in the newspapers of the day? Consider the following extract:

Organisierte Markverschiebung?

Der Korrespondent des ‹Daily Express' in Hythe meldet, dass vor einigen Tagen auf dem Flugplatze von Hythe ein Fokkerapparat gelandet sei, aus dem ein deutschsprechender Passagier ausstieg, der zehn Pakete mit neuen 10-Millionenscheinen, im ganzen eine Summe von 500 Milliarden, bei sich führte. Während man den Pass des Deutschen untersuchte, sei ein englischer Flieger neben ihm gelandet, der den deutschen Fahrgast, sowie die Geldpakete bei sich aufnahm und in der Richtung nach Frankreich weiterflog. Das genannte Blatt versichert, dass dieses Ereignis sich seit 20 Tagen durchschnittlich dreimal in der Woche wiederhole.

Die Entwertung der Mark durch Frankreich ist bekannt, aber es ist wertvoll, dies immer wieder festzustellen.[2]

(Organized Illicit Trading in Marks?

The correspondent of the Daily Express in Hythe reports that a Fokker aeroplane landed at Hythe Airport a few days ago. A German speaking passenger got out carrying ten parcels of new 10 million Mark notes, in total a sum amounting to 500 thousand million Marks. While the German's passport was being checked, an English pilot landed alongside and then flew on again towards France together with the German passenger and the money packages. This newspaper confirms that this is repeated on average three times a week. It has been going on for some 20 days.

The depreciation of the Mark by sales in France is known but it is worthwhile to be able continually to confirm this fact.)

So the *Cuxhavener Zeitung* gave its readers in 1923 two examples of arbitrage: the pilot with his parcels of notes and those taking their chances on getting a Reichsbank allocation of currency and then selling it immediately at a premium within minutes. It points to the ineffective nature of controls on foreign exchange transactions when it is in the interests of buyers and sellers to arrange their transactions other than as expected by the regulatory authorities.

The newspaper presents its readers with a clear statement of cause and effect. The budgetary deficit arises from the consequences of the French occupation of the Ruhr district. It is financed by the printing of notes. This in turn causes the internal depreciation of the currency and leads people to seek protection from the resultant inflation by acquiring foreign exchange. This in turn is responsible for the decline in the value of the Mark in terms of foreign currencies. The cure for inflation is therefore seen as eliminating budget deficits by ending the French presence in the Ruhr district. Only in that way could tax revenues be expected to equal the expenditure of the Reich government and remove the need for recourse to the printing press.

It was not just the additional expenditure incurred by the Reich government in financing the occupied area that caused difficulties. The policy of passive resistance meant that a large part of German industry was closed down. The resultant unemployment meant a decline in the tax base, a fall therefore in tax yields and an increase in the deficit that was financed by printing notes. But this was not the only cause of inflation in 1923. The refusal to tax sufficiently during the Great War of 1914–18 and recourse to the printing press at that time was also a major factor not mentioned in the article.

Whereas foreign exchange markets outside Germany were not affected by decrees and notes could move across frontiers, the blockade by the French of the border between the occupied and unoccupied areas of the Ruhr effectively hindered the movement of people and goods.

Die brutale Absperrung des besetzten Gebiets

Essen 6. Juli.

Mit welcher Brutalität von den Franzosen die Absperrung des besetzten vom unbesetzten Gebiet ohne Rücksicht auf die hervorgerufene Lebensmittelkatastrophe gehandhabt wird, zeigt die Tatsache, dass Milchtransporte in das besetzte Gebiet nicht hereingelassen werden. Ferner wird den Geistlichen, die den Sterbenden die letzte Oelung bringen wollen, die Ein- und Ausreise verhindert. Ebenso sind die Krankentransporte zwischen dem besetzten und unbesetzten Gebiet verboten, was besonders die ländliche Bevölkerung bei dem Fehlen ausreichender ärztlicher Fürsorge sehr hart trifft.[3]

(The brutal blockage of the Occupied Zone

Essen, 6th July.

The brutality with which the French have cut off the occupied from the unoccupied zone regardless of the resulting food supply catastrophe is shown by the fact that the transport of milk into the occupied zone is being prevented. Priests bringing the last sacrament to the dying are impeded at the border. Inter-zonal transport of the sick has also been forbidden, which has very severe effects in particular on the rural population, who lack sufficient medical care.)

The rapid fall in the value of the Mark on the foreign exchanges was associated with two main factors, the depreciation of the purchasing power of the currency and the effects of speculation.

The first cause would be expected naturally enough and accords with the Purchasing Power Parity Theory of exchange rate movements. According to Gustav Cassell, this theory states that

> when two currencies have undergone inflation, the normal rate of exchange will be equal to the old rate multiplied by the quotient of the degree of inflation in one country and in the other.... The rate calculated by this method must be regarded as the new parity between the currencies, the point of balance towards which, in spite of all temporary fluctuations, the exchange rates will always tend. This parity I call purchasing power parity.[4]

There are a number of difficulties with this particular theory. Buyers are assumed to be indifferent as to the domestic or foreign origin of the assumed identical goods that are selected solely on the basis of price differences. Goods are also assumed to be freely available from both home and foreign sources. There is also the problem of determining the starting point at which it is assumed the exchange rates reflect purchasing power parities e.g. in the numerical example quoted in note 4, 4.2 Marks would buy exactly the same amount of traded goods as $1.

The account of Schacht illustrates clearly just how way out of line the Mark/dollar exchange rate was from that expected on a relative purchasing power basis. A rise in the rate in favour of the Mark over little more than two weeks from a dollar price of 50,000 to 20,000 marks shows the effect of speculation in the foreign exchange market.[5] Comments from other economists at the time supported Schacht's interpretation of exchange rate movements. It was argued that the German Mark was undervalued in purchasing power terms but stressed that 'Under normal circumstances an adverse balance of trade does not depress the exchange-value of a currency below its purchasing power parity.'[6]

Circumstances were thus clearly not normal! According to Cassell's estimate, the then current exchange rate of 15 Swedish Crowns = 100 Marks should have been 45 Swedish Crowns = 100 Marks if purchasing power parity criteria alone had determined the rate of exchange – a required increase of some 200 per cent in favour of the Mark. So, what were the abnormalities of the situation? As discussed elsewhere, Germany had been driven partly by hunger to agree to the Armistice. There was a situation of real starvation in parts of the land. To secure supplies, therefore, Germany was driven by circumstances to sell its currency at almost any price to get the goods it wanted so desperately. This was true of local bodies as well as of the central government. There could be no selection on the basis of price differences of equally available foreign and domestic alternatives. As the value of the Mark fell, a 'normal' response would have been for exports to rise but this was partly prevented by the existence of prohibitions on exports due to domestic shortages. Foreign currency holdings in Germany were often hoarded by speculators in anticipation of a further rise in its Mark value and thus were not made available to finance trade. The rate was further depressed by the export of capital from Germany caused by the taxation proposals of the Reich government. This mainly took the form of the export of bank notes. Germany did not control its western frontier. The Allies not only occupied the left bank of the Rhine but also bridgeheads on the right bank, making it difficult for the Germans to control outflows of capital. These exported notes were often sold on foreign markets, thus further depressing the value of the Mark. Cassell's estimate was of some ten thousand million (ten milliard) German bank notes held by France and Belgium. There would have been more if the Reichsbank had not ensured that Mark denominated bank note circulation in the German occupied areas had been kept to a minimum in favour of local issues of currency under Reich supervision during the war. The import of luxury goods continued. Thus, the 'normal' adjustments assumed by the purchasing power parity theory simply did not take place in Germany after 1918.

An important consequence for international trade follows if exchange rates are at or close to purchasing power parities. Relatively small price movements should then ensure, if the other conditions are also met, that a two-way flow of trade in goods and services takes place. That the German Mark was way below its puchasing power parity level was a threat to the re-establishment of international trade. Foreign goods would be less likely to find a market in Germany and so unemployment abroad would be higher than would otherwise be the case.

Hjalmar Schacht, President of the Reichsbank, was able to stress the limits to which reparations could be paid in foreign currencies. Germany's ability to pay reparations was limited to the extent of any balance of payments surplus. Any attempt to make Germany pay more than such a surplus would result in the value of the Mark being driven down on the exchanges. Any anticipation by speculators that foreign pressure, especially from France, would be successful in achieving such a level of payments would of itself encourage anticipatory selling of Marks and thus further depreciation in value and an increase in the internal cost of living.

> *Der Gedanke, der dieser vom Dawes-Komitee festgesetzten, und viel erörterten Regelung zugrunde liegt, ist der, dass Deutschland nur so viel an das Ausland abführen soll, als es an Wirtschaftsüberschüssen für seine ausländische Zahlungsbilanz herauswirtschaftet.[7]*

(The central idea of the Dawes Committee is that Germany should only deliver abroad an amount equal to the surplus on its balance of payments.)

The basic principal governing the maximum amount of reparations that Germany is able to pay is clearly stated by Schacht. The currency will be endangered if Germany is forced to pay an amount in excess of any balance of payments surplus. Any demands greater than this would trigger speculation and, in any case, would lead to depreciation of the Mark irrespective of the behaviour of the money supply within Germany. A close correlation would therefore be expected between political pressure on Germany to pay more, speculative selling of the Mark and therefore further depreciation of the currency.

The *Hildesheimer Allgemeine Zeitung* reported essentially the same point in rather more emotionally charged language.

Der Devisenschwindel

> *Wie lange ist es eigentlich her, dass man dem immer geduldigen deutschen Volke den Bären aufgebunden hat, das Sinken der deutschen Reichsmark wäre eine unmittelbare Folge der Reparationskrisis? ... Und je stärker der Druck der Entente sich geltend machte, je energischer besonders Frankreich forderte, dass Deutschland zahlen müsse, umso verzweifelter gestaltete sich Deutschlands finanzielle Lage.... Aber Deutschland ist nie in der Lage gewesen, die ihm auferlegten Reparationszahlungen zu leisten und deshalb ist der auf dem Wege über Belgien zeitweise gefundene Ausweg nicht als Lösung anzusprechen, sondern nur als Mittel der Verschleppung ... wir sind im Weltkriege selbst noch mit einem blauen Auge davongekommen dank dem deutschen Soldaten und seiner über alle Massen bewunderungswürdigen militärischen Leistungen, der Friede von Versailles ist für uns zu einer nationalen Katastrophe geworden, aber auf dem Valutaschlachtfelde verblutet das deutsche Volk. Wenn wir in diesen Tagen erleben, wie die Mark plötzlich auf ihrem Tiefstand weiter hinabgleitet und der Dollar wieder über 2000 steht ... so sollten wir doch endlich wissen, was die Glocke geschlagen hat. Wir gehen an der Devisenspekulation*

allmählich zugrunde, die Lebensfähigkeit des Staates genau so wie des Einzelmenschen scheitert an dem Börsentreiben, das unser aller Dasein nachgerade erdrosselt. Die Börse ist früher ein sehr selten trügendes Barometer für die politische Lage gewesen.[8]

(Foreign Currency Fraud

For how long now have the ever patient Germans been kidded that the depreciation of the Mark is a direct consequence of the reparations crisis? ... The more the pressure from the Entente made itself felt, the more France demanded that Germany must pay, the more desperate Germany's financial position became.... But Germany has never been in a position to meet the reparations payments imposed on her, and thus the temporary way out via Belgium cannot be regarded as a solution, but only as a means of postponement ... we came off lightly in the Great War thanks to the German soldier and his boundlessly admirable military performance. The Peace of Versailles has become a national catastrophe for us, and the German people are bleeding to death on the currency battlefield. When today we witness the Mark sliding down further from its low point and the dollar standing at more than 2000 Marks, then we should be aware of what's in store for us. Foreign exchange speculation is gradually destroying us, the viability of the state and the individual is foundering on Stock Exchange dealings which strangle our very existence. The Stock Exchange was previously nearly always reliable as a barometer of the political situation.)

The measurement of inflation

The inflation and its conseqences dominated daily life. The use of price indices, although known, was not as common as measuring inflation by reference to the decline in the external value of the currency, that is, by exchange rate changes. By late 1923, daily life was dominated by the latest exchange rate between the United States dollar and the Reichsmark. Wages and salaries were often indexed to this rate rather than to a price index. The importance of the exchange rate is reflected in some of the German literature that relates to this period. For example, writing of 1923 in his novel, *Der Schwarze Obelisk*, one of Remarque's characters says,

Gott sei Dank, dass morgen Sonntag ist.... Da gibt es keine Dollarkurse. Einen Tag in der Woche steht die Inflation still. Gott hat sicher nicht so gemeint, als er den Sonntag schuf.[9]

(Thank God that it's Sunday tomorrow.... There are no rates of exchange for the dollar. Inflation stops for one day in the week. That was surely not God's intention when he created Sunday.)

The idea in this quotation is an intriguing one. No publication of the inflation indicator implies no inflation! It is of course untrue but it does serve to highlight the importance for daily life of its publication.

How good a proxy?

Attention throughout Germany during this period focused on the daily publication of the Dollarkurs or exchange rate between the United States dollar and the German Papermark. This was normally published in the form of the number of Marks per dollar. Values of this rate noticed by the Mayor of Berlin, Friedrich Lange, are listed elsewhere in this text.

It assumed great importance as perhaps the most important single measure of the decline in the purchasing power of the Mark both externally and internally within Germany. But how good a proxy for the internal decline in the value of the currency was a measure of its changing external value in terms of the United States dollar? This was challenged in a short extract from an article in the newspaper, *Vorwärts*, published with endorsement of its main point by the *Hildesheimer Allgemeine Zeitung* on 25 August 1922.

> Es kann jetzt nicht scharf genug betont werden, dass zwischen der äusseren und der inneren Entwertung der Mark ein Unterschied besteht. Es ist nicht wahr, dass jeder Tagesbedarf des kleinen Mannes untrennbar mit dem Börsenkurs des Dollars verbunden sei. Das wäre nur richtig, wenn wir ausschliesslich von Einfuhrprodukten lebten. Wir haben aber auch einen innerwirtschaftlichen Markt, der in weitem Umfange die Bedürfnisse des Arbeiters und Angestellten befriedigt. Wir haben Warenvorräte im Lande, in denen kein Cents ausländischen Materials steckt.

> (It cannot now be stressed strongly enough that there is a difference between the internal and external devaluation of the Mark. To say that all the daily needs of the man in the street are indissolubly linked to the exchange rate of the dollar is not true. It would only be correct if we lived entirely on imported goods. We have however an internal economic market that satisfies the needs of workers and white-collar staff to a great exent. We have stocks of goods in the country that contain not a cent of imported materials.)

At the time, it was clear why the exchange rate was regarded as the most important statistic indicating the decline in value of the Mark. It was published daily in a number of centres throughout the country and was widely understood whereas the development of index numbers to measure changes in the purchasing power internally was relatively still in its infancy. Indices were produced relating to this period and so the claim in *Vorwärts* is in the form of a testable proposition.

Over the period under review in this text, it is immaterial whether the decline in the internal purchasing power of the Mark is measured by an index or by the exchange rate between the Mark and the dollar; both tell the same summary story, by the end of 1923, at the point at which the Rentenmark issues are introduced by Hjalmar Schacht – the Papermark is worthless!

But the article is dated August 1922. Using the exchange rate between the Mark and the dollar, a decline in the value of the Mark is noted, from 4.2 Marks = 1 US$ in 1914 to 1040 Marks = 1 US$ by August 1922. Over approximately the same period of time, wholesale prices rose from 1 to 287, the cost of living from 1 to 133, food from 1 to 154, heat and lighting from 1 to 161 and rent from 1 to 4. On the same basis of calculation, the value of the Mark fell from 1 to 248 (corresponding to the exchange rate change noted above).

Table 4.2 Index numbers in Germany, retail prices, 1913–14 = 1

Date 1922	Heating and lighting	Rent
March	30	3
June	48	3
September	161	4
December	1,038	17
1923		
March	5,529	113
June	10,378	301
July	36,904	714
August	890,539	4,932
September	23,300,000,000	300,000
October	5,175,000,000	54,000,000
November	834,000,000,000	22,000,000,000

Source: Fritz Sigler, 'The Adaptation of Wages to the Depreciation of the Currency in Germany', in *International Labour Review*, vol. IX, no. 5, May 1924. International Labour Office, Geneva.

On these figures, the writer of the extract from *Vorwärts* has a valid point. Over the period 1914 to August 1922, the cost of living generally, food prices, heat and lighting, and rent rose in price by significantly less than the amount 'predicted' from a knowledge of the exchange rate movement over the same period. Wholesale prices, however, rose by more than the amount suggested by the decline in the external value of

Table 4.3 Index numbers in Germany

Date 1922	Wholesale prices 1913 = 1	Cost of living	Retail prices 1913–14 = 1 Food	Clothing
March	54	26	36	48
June	70	41	51	65
September	287	133	154	260
December	1,475	1,120	807	1,161
1923				
March	4,888	2,854	3,315	4,328
June	19,385	7,650	9,347	11,995
July	74,727	37,651	46,510	66,488
August	944,041	584,045	670,485	1,089,571
September	23,900,000	15,000,000	17,300,000	26,500,000
October	7,100,000,000	3,657,000,000	4,301,000,000	6,160,000,000
November 5	129,000,000,000	98,500,000,000		
12	265,600,000,000	218,500,000,000		
19	1,413,600,000,000	831,000,000,000	862,000,000,000	816,000,000,000
26	1,422,900,000,000	1,535,000,000,000		
December 3	1,337,400,000,000	—		

Source: Fritz Sigler, 'The Adaptation of Wages to the Depreciation of the Currency in Germany', in *International Labour Review*, vol. IX, no. 5, May 1924. International Labour Office, Geneva.

the Mark. This was pointing the way towards a faster increase than hitherto in the level of retail prices during the following months.

The view that there might be islands of relatively greater price stability in the internal market has already been discussed. If so, then it is clear that the use of the depreciation of the Mark on foreign exchange markets as a measurement of the average decline in the internal purchasing power of the Mark would overestimate the latter. The empirical evidence considered at the time is not conclusive. Over a five-week period in October and November 1923, as illustrated on Figure 4.2 below, sometimes the price of the dollar in Marks rises more rapidly than the cost of living index and sometimes more slowly. The line of reasoning was, however, attractive to those who believed that the process of hyperinflation started in the foreign exchange market and was then followed by rising prices that had to be supported by monetary expansion to prevent unemployment rising. The quotation below, attributed to Hugo Stinnes, one of the leading German industrialists of the day, supports part of this line of reasoning. In effect, it is an argument that inflation is an inescapable concomitant of the monetary expansion necessary to maintain employment and output in a period of serious bottlenecks and supply inelasticities.

> First the reasons why Germany carried on the inflation policy which it did after the war were established. I pointed out that after the lost war it had been absolutely necessary for Germany to bring four million men then in the field, out of the habit of regular work, back into the regular routines of useful activity ... the weapon of inflation would have to be used in the future too ... because only that made it possible to give the population orderly and regular activity.[10]

As the rate of inflation rises, the discussion above shows how it becomes progressively more difficult to measure the process. Neither exchange rate data nor cost of living indices provide a single adequate basis of measurement. Although at the end of the process in November 1923, both measurements indicate the same conclusion – the complete destruction of the currency – there were significant differences over shorter periods between the two methods of measuring currency depreciation. The graph also illustrates the difficulty of producing a diagram for even this short period of time and the amusing solution found to accommodate the vertical axis!

The depreciation of the Mark on the foreign exchange market did, however, have a major advantage over the use of price indices in the measurement of inflation. The rapidly increasing Mark prices of foreign currencies such as the United States dollar and the British pound were

58   HYPERINFLATION IN GERMANY

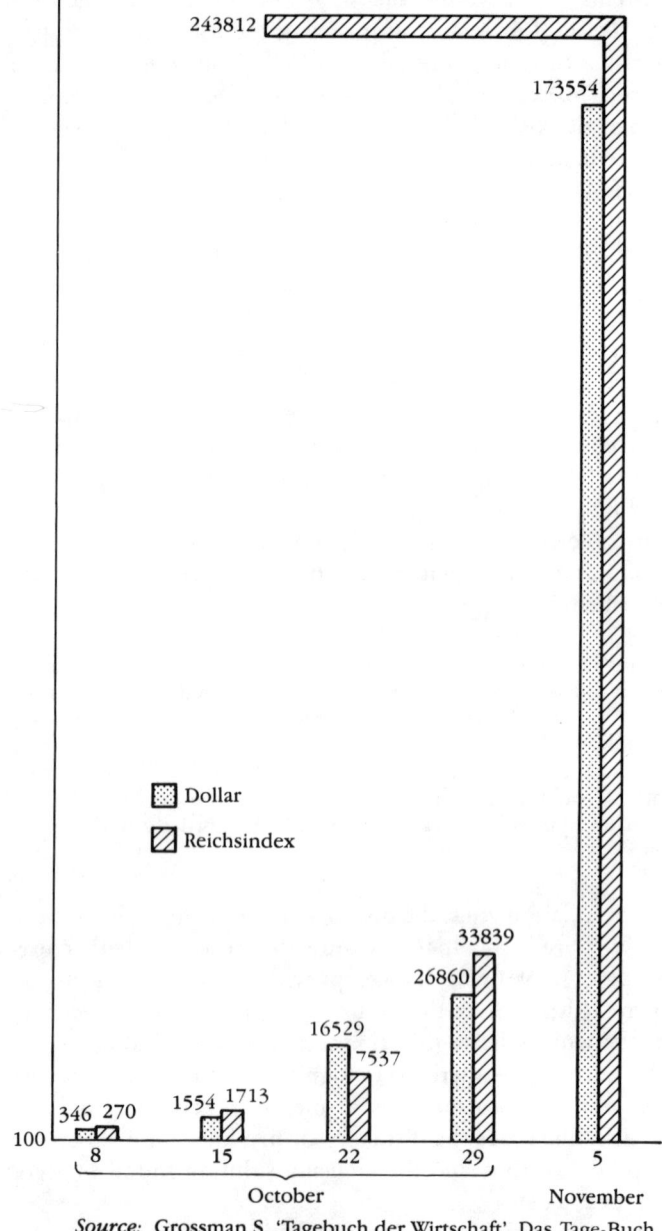

Source: Grossman S. 'Tagebuch der Wirtschaft', Das Tage-Buch, Heft 37. Jahrg. 4, S. 1605 Athenäum Verlag, Berlin 1923

Figure 4.2 The dollar and the cost of living index
(1 October 1923 = 100)

continuously available and the official Berlin rates were published and disseminated on a daily basis. The publication of price indices, however, inevitably lagged by a considerable amount of time the actual price increases measured. This can be a problem at any time but is particularly critical during a period of hyperinflation, when hours are important intervals of time for price rises and not days, weeks or months. Some of the deficiencies in the use of price indices were certainly understood at the time.

> *Am 5. Juni ist der Teuerungsindex des Statistischen Reichsamts pro Mai veröffentlicht worden. Spät kommen sie, diese Reichsindexe – so spät, dass sie für einen grossen Teil des Zweckes, dem sie dienen könnten und sollten, praktisch unverwendbar werden. Aber sogar das verspätete Erscheinen verzieche man leichter, wäre wenigstens die Ziffer selbst über jede Kritik erhaben. Das ist leider keineswegs der Fall. Der Mai-Index z.B. zeigt ein Erhöhen des Kostenniveaus um nur 29.2%, obwohl doch jedermann am eigenen Leibe erfahren hat, dass die Preise während des vergangenen Monats tatsächlich um 60–70%, wenn nicht um 100% gestiegen sind. Woher die Unstimmigkeit? Teilweise aus der Methode der Stichtage, deren letzter nicht einmal der Monatsultimo ist, teilweise wahrscheinlich aber auch aus der fortgesetzten Umgruppierung, will sagen Verschlechterung, der Warenklassen, die der Berechnung zugrunde gelegt werden. Wozu und in wessen Interesse diese Methode verwendet wird, bleibt unerörtert. Aber klar ist wozu sie führen muss. Der Lebenshaltungsindex des Statistischen Reichsamtes könnte, so lange uns ein fester Währungsmassstab fehlt, der Korrektivmassstab sein, der es dennoch gestattet, die soziale Lage im Gleichgewicht zu halten. Aber einem Index, der für den April eine Steigerung von 3% und im Mai eine Steigerung von 29% ausweis, kann diese justierende Funktion nicht mehr zugesprochen werden.*[11]

(The May cost of living index of the Reich Statistical Bureau was published on 5 June. These official indices arrive so late that they are practically useless for the majority of purposes for which they are intended. But even their late arrival would be excusable if at least the figures themselves were beyond criticism. Unfortunately this is certainly not the case. The May index, for example, shows an increase in the cost of living of only 29.2 per cent, although everyone knows from personal experience that during the last month prices in fact increased by 60–70 per cent, if not by 100 per cent. How does this discrepancy arise? Partly because of the method of taking sample dates, the last of which is not the end of the month, and partly due to the continual regrouping, or more correctly worsening of the commodities which form the basis of the calculation. No mention is made as to why and in whose interests this method is used. But where it leads is clear. In the absence of a stable currency yardstick the cost of living index of the Reich Statistical Bureau might act as a corrrective yardstick to keep the social situation in balance. But an index showing a 3 per cent increase for April and 29 per cent for May can no longer perform this levelling function.)

Should a cost of living index be judged by whether the rate of inflation calculated accords with common sense? The answer to this question would normally be in the negative. After all, an individual is only in a position to know something of the behaviour of prices that he deals with, itself a weak base from which to generalize about the economy as a whole. However, the official cost of living figures quoted for April and May 1923 in hyperinflationary Germany are at variance with price information available at the time from other sources.

A cost of living index produces a figure that is an average change of a large number of individual prices; it is a measurement of central tendency. There was, however, some contemporary recognition of the importance of the spread of prices around the average and the need to consider some measurement of dispersion. Dr Heichen[12] called attention to the significance of dispersion around the mean and presented his readers with an elementary lesson in statistical analysis in considering the interpretation of contemporary price data.

> *In Zeiten rapiden Falles des Aussenwertes der Mark wird die Streuung der Preise ausserordentlich gross; und umgekehrt verringert sie sich – wie das gegenwärtig der Fall ist – das Preisniveau stabilisiert.... Bei einer rapiden Markentwertung, die von der äusseren Valuta (der Zahlungsbilanz des Landes) ausgeht, rücken die Einfuhrwaren ... in weitem Abstand von dem Zentrum der mittleren Preislage ... während Erzeugnisse der Binnenwirtschaft verbleiben.... Erst späterhin, im Verlauf einiger Wochen, erfolgt ein ... Abstandsausgleich.*[12]

(At times when the external value of the Mark is falling rapidly the variation in prices is extraordinarily great; and conversely it is reduced, as is the case now, when the price level stabilizes. When a rapid depreciation of the Mark is caused by the balance of payments deficit, import prices deviate hugely from the mean price range ... while prices of the home economy remain constant.... Only after a few weeks is the imbalance corrected.)

Thus, the relative position of those who derive their incomes from the internal economy worsens relative to those whose business is associated with imported goods. The increased dispersion of prices around the mean thus involves distribution effects that increase inequality in the distribution of incomes. The effect is more pronounced because the prices of certain products such as potatoes are controlled by the authorities (*Preisprüfungsstellen*). The prices of imported goods such as cotton and items from the colonies (*Kolonialwaren*), on the other hand, rise immediately by the full amount of the decline in the value of the Mark. Two problems are noted: firstly, the general trade problem arising from paying for goods by the use of trade bills and secondly, the unsuitability of index-linking as a means of ensuring equitable treatment between debtors and creditors and between different sections of society. The commercial bill normally offered three months' credit to the debtor. By 1923, the rate of depreciation of the Mark was so high that such a period of credit could wipe out the real value of the debt. The creditor could protect his position by discounting the bill so that rarely was another trader to bear the loss but rather the loser would ultimately be the Reichsbank.

> *Der Verlierende, auf Kosten dessen Substanz der Wechselschuldner sein ‹Schlechtgeldgeschäft' macht, ist wohl nur selten ein anderer Warenkaufmann oder eine Privatbank (beide sind zu solchen Verlustgeschäften denn doch zu schlau geworden), sondern das Zentralnoteninstitut. Der Reichsbank sucht man alle Wechsel möglichst schnell und mit einem Minimum von Giros zuzuschieben.*[13]

> (Doubtless the loser, at whose expense the creditor makes his 'bad money' profit, is only rarely some other merchant or a private bank (for both have become wise enough not to incur such losses), but the central note issuing agency. People try to push their bills on to the Reichsbank as quickly as possible and with a minimum of endorsements.)

Although protection for the individual lay in rapidly discounting any bill that came into his possession, could the problem be solved by index-linking trade debts? Which index from the imperfect alternatives should be chosen?

> *Soll der offizielle – aber schlechte – Grosshandelsindex des Statistischen Reichsamts, oder sollen die besseren aber inoffiziellen Indexziffern privater Stellen als Basis dienen?*[14]

> (What should the calculations be based on? The official – but inferior – Wholesale Index as published by the Reich Statistical Bureau, or the superior but unofficial indices of private bodies.)

If this problem could be solved, then the Reichsbank would present the indexed bill back to its issuer for settlement. Indexing all bills in this way would not, however, be satisfactory because of the spread of individual price increases around the mean change that would be applied as the indexed adjustment to bills received by the Reichsbank. From the discussion above, such indexing would be a heavy burden for potato dealers and a relatively light burden for dealers in *Kolonialwaren*. It would not eliminate the inflation profits of the latter but might cause severely depleted profits or even losses for dealers in the products of the purely internal economy.

> Macht nun ein Indexwechsel ... solche Schlechtgeldgeschäfte der Warenkaufleute unmöglich? Nein! Der Indexwechsel verengert nur den Rahmen und das Feld.... Es wäre beispielsweise für Metall- oder Getreidehändler durchaus rentabel, denn deren Preise springen in Zeiten starken Markverfalls über den Index weit hinaus.... Für den Kartoffelhändler wäre ... der Indexwechsel ein gefährliches Instrument. Er kann ihm unter Umständen Kopf und Kragen kosten.... Der Indexwechsel ist zu milde.[15]

(Do indexed bills ... serve to prevent such profiting from bad money by merchants? No! Indexed bills merely reduce the extent and scope of their activities.... Metal and grain dealers for example would find it wholly worthwhile as their prices soar far above the index level at times when the Mark is falling heavily.... Indexed bills would be dangerous for potato dealers and could under certain circumstances cost them their livelihood.... The indexed bill is too lenient.)

So what does the author regard as the only satisfactory solution? The only all-round solution is seen in the introduction of gold-based bills, that is, effectively a return to the stable relative values of the gold standard as it operated prior to 1914.

> Der Goldwechsel ist ... vor allem das einzige wirksame Instrument demgegenüber alle Schlechtgeldkünste.... Wer einen Geldwechsel akzeptiert, muss eine Goldverpflichtung auch tragen können, wie das im Frieden normaler Weise üblich war. Im übrigen: keine Halbheiten. Nicht Indexwechsel, Goldwechsel brauchen wir.[16]

(The goldbill is ... above all the only effective way to stop these rackets in bad money.... Those accepting money bills must also accept a gold obligation, as was the practice in peacetime. In general: no half measures. We need goldbills, not indexed bills.)

The stabilization of the Mark

As the exchange rates quoted indicate, the need for stabilization of the currency became ever more urgent through 1923. The fall in the value of the Mark led throughout Germany to political unrest, violence and the breakdown of normal market relations between customers and sup-

LIVING WITH HYPERINFLATION 63

pliers. Some of the diary entries of Friedrich Lange chronicle the deteriorating situation:

21. September 1923
Die Not der Bevölkerung infolge der Markentwertung führt zur Plünderung der Kartoffeläcker und zur Selbstversorgung mit Brennholz in den städtischen Forsten, während die Reichsregierung endlich das Problem der Markstabilisierung berät.

14. Oktober 1923
Die Brotkarte ist verschwunden. Dollarkurs 3.8 Milliarden. Vor dem Rathaus Erwerbslosentumulte, in der Stadt Lebensmittelunruhen. Die Prominenz der Berliner Bühnen weilt nur noch vorübergehend hier, sonst auf Devisenjagd im Auslande.

5. November 1923
Bei den Arbeitsämtern sind 210,000 Erwerbslose eingetragen. In den Strassen Hungerkrawalle. Bäckereien und Lebensmittelgeschäfte werden gestürmt. Die Brotkarte muss vorübergehend wieder in Kraft gesetzt wrden.[17]

(21 September 1923
The deprivation arising from the depreciation of the mark is causing people to raid the potato fields and to help themselves to firewood from the municipal forests, while the Reich Government is at long last discussing the stabilization of the currency.

14 October 1923
The bread ration card has disappeared. Exchange rate 3.8 thousand million marks to the dollar. Demonstrations by the unemployed in front of the Town Hall. In the city, food supply unrest. Leading figures of the Berlin stage are only temporarily here, otherwise abroad looking for foreign currency.

5 November 1923
At the unemployment offices 210,000 unemployed are registered. On the streets, hunger riots. Bakeries and food shops are pillaged. The bread ration card must temporarily be reintroduced.)

The plethora of means of payment would in itself have been confusing for many shoppers but such a large number of different forms of payment would have caused a number of practical problems. The indexing mechanism was simple enough in theory; consult the exchange rate between the United States dollar and the Papermark and this would tell us the conversion rate between Goldmarks and Papermarks. But life was not as simple as this for the shopper in Germany in 1923!

Die Hauptrolle im Zahlungsverkehr wird die Goldanleihe übernehmen. Da die Goldanleihe kein gesetzliches Zahlungsmittel ist, sond-

ern die Rolle des gesetzlichen Zahlungsmittels nach wie vor für die Papiermark reserviert bleibt, so ist kein Händler verpflichtet, noch kann er dazu gezwungen werden, sie in Zahlung zu nehmen. Aber über diese juristische Möglichkeit wird die Praxis wohl zur Tagesordnung übergehen, und viel eher besteht die andere Möglichkeit, dass die Papiermark, das gesetzliche Zahlungsmittel, aus dem Verkehr völlig verschwindet. Es fragt sich nun, zu welchem Kurse die Goldanleihe in Zahlung genommen wird. Die grossen Berliner Geschäfte scheinen die Goldanleihe übereinstimmend mit der Börsennotierung zum Dollarkurs anzunehmen und gewähren noch dazu für Zahlungen in diesen Zahlungsmitteln einen fünfprozentigen Rabatt. Das können sie deshalb tun, weil sie für Papiermarkzahlungen vermutlich einen Geldentwertungszuschlag in die Papiermarkpreise einkalkuliert hatten, der nunmehr in Fortfall kommen kann. In kleinen Geschäften dagegen wird die Goldanleihe zunächst nicht so glatt in Zahlung genommen. Der Grund dürfte darin liegen, dass die Banken die Goldanleihe nicht zum Börsenkurs einlösen, sondern zu einem Kurse, der unter der Berliner Notierung liegt und durchaus nicht einheitlich ist. Sie führen zur Begründung an, dass sie nicht wüssten, wie die Goldanleihe am nächsten Tage notiert würde.[18]

(The Goldloan will become the main form of payment. Since the Goldloan is not a legal method of payment (this role is still reserved for the Papermark), no dealer is obliged to accept it in payment, nor can he be compelled to do so. But actual practice will doubtless override this legal objection and become the norm, and the much more likely possibility is that the Papermark, the legal method of payment, will fall into complete disuse. The question now is: at what rate of exchange will the Goldloan be accepted in payment? Big businesses in Berlin appear to accept the Goldloan at the dollar rate of exchange, at the same rate as that listed on the Currency Market, and in addition are giving a five per cent discount for payments in this form. They are able to do this because for Papermark payments they have presumably included a supplement for money depreciation in their Papermark prices, and this supplement can now lapse. In smaller businesses the Goldloan is not so readily accepted. The most likely reason is that the banks will not cash the Goldloan at the rate quoted on the Currency Exchange, preferring to use a rate below that quoted in Berlin and which is far from uniform. They justify this action by claiming that they do not know what the rate for the Goldloan will be on the following day.)

This extract illustrates one of the major problems facing shoppers with two payments media existing side by side, the exchange rate between them.

These problems would make shopping inconvenient to say the least. Good gains on the exchange rate were to be made if one were to frequent the large shops, extending to a small discount if paying with Goldloan notes even if it was a discount off an inflated Papermark price – inflated, that is, to take into account future expected depreciation.

Not such good deals were to be had in the small shops with the only exchange certainty being that the rate would be less to the customer's advantage than that indicated by the then current rate on the Berlin Exchange. Not knowing what they would get from the banks the following day, the small shops would pass on their uncertainty to their customers in the form of a less favourable rate than the current official Berlin rate of exchange for the dollar indicated.

So, what are the alternatives? Why not go to the bank, change the Gold-loan notes into Papermarks and then go shopping in the small shops? What sort of a deal could the individual shopper obtain from his bank?

> *Wenn für Goldanleihe an den Schaltern der Bank Papiermark gefordert wird, so kommt der Mangel an diesem Zahlungsmittel hinzu und es scheint, als ob einige Bankfilialen auch aus diesem Grunde einen Abzug vom Börsenkurse vornehmen.*[19]

(When people ask at bank counters for Papermarks in exchange for Goldloan, then the shortage of this form of payment also comes into play, and it seems as if some bank branches make a deduction from the official rate for this reason too.)

So both the banks and the small shops had their own somewhat different reasons for doing the same thing, paying out less to those who wished to pay in or change Goldloan notes into Papermarks than the current official rate of exchange. A source of confusion and no doubt some anger for the customer. Certainly, as the *Hildesheimer Allgemeine Zeitung* noted, it created a situation of confusion that sorely needed to be rectified.

> *Auf alle Fälle ist es nötig, dass sich hier in kürzester Zeit eine gleichförmige Praxis herausbildet um gerade in dieser Zeit der Einführung des neuen Zahlungsmittels Unklarheiten und Unruhe zu vermeiden.*[20]

(Whatever happens, in order to avoid confusion and anxiety while the new form of payment is being introduced, it is essential that a standard practice merges as quickly as possible.)

Failing this happening immediately, the newspaper could only advise its readers to devote some time and attention to making sure that they were not unwitting victims of this confusion and plethora of exchange rates in different shops and banks.

> *aber es wird doch für jeder einzelnen von Wichtigkeit sein, der weiteren Entwicklung viel Interesse und einiges Nachdenken zu widmen.*[21]

(but it is important for every individual to devote a lot of interest and some thought to further developments.)

This identifies one of the costs of this hyperinflation that was well identified and understood; negotiating one's way around the plethora of forms of payment with uncertain conversion rates between the various possibilities. But suppose our shopper had now solved his conversion rate problems between the various means of payment and was now ready to buy. What would he find in some of the markets? According to contemporary newspaper reports, a not infrequent problem encountered by the shopper was the lack of clearly indicated prices at which the trader was prepared to deal along with a lack of stated quantities for any given price. This appears to have given particular cause for concern in the case of bread, cakes and pastries in the discussions taking place in Berlin. There was talk of reintroducing the lapsed war-time regulations requiring, with compulsion if necessary, the posting of precise prices and quantities. There was a general feeling that profiteering by traders and the artificial forcing up of prices were taking place. As in other hyperinflations in other places at different times in history, those who marked up prices were attracting perhaps a little too much of the assumed responsibility for the inflation itself. There was even mention of establishing consumer circles to create, presumably, a countervailing force against the traders.

> *Das preussische Staatsministerium befasste sich am Freitag mit den Massnahmen gegen Wucher und Preistreiberei auf dem Lebensmittelmarkte. Als hauptsächlichste Mittel zur Sicherung der Volksernährung wurde unter anderem angesehen, die Wiedereinführung des vieleorts nicht mehr bestehenden Zwanges zur Preisauszeichnung sämtlicher Waren, insbesondere zur genauen Gewichts- und Preisbezeichnung der Backwaren in den Bäckereien. Massnahmen zur Heranziehung der Konsumentenkreise für auf den öffentlichen Lebensmittelverkaufsmärkten wurden gleichfalls besprochen.*[22]

(On Friday the Prussian State Ministry dealt with measures to combat profiteering and forcing up prices on the food market. The main means of ensuring that the people are fed properly was considered to be, among other things, the reintroduction of the requirement to display the prices of all goods, and in particular to indicate the weights and prices of goods in bakeries. In many places this requirement no longer exists. Measures to involve consumer groups in checking prices in shops and public food markets were also discussed.)

Shopping in Germany in 1922 and 1923 presented the consumer with a number of hurdles. Firstly, he had to overcome the problem of the varying degrees of acceptability of different forms of payment in different shops and markets and the value of one form in terms of another. Secondly, he could not be sure that prices and weights at which he could buy would be clearly displayed. He also probably felt exploited by traders he would see as substantially responsible for his immediate problems even if he endorsed the general blame attributed by the media to the terms of the Treaty of Versailles. In addition, he faced the possibility of street violence as he went about his everyday shopping.

> Zu schweren Zusammenstössen zwischen Plünderern und Beamten der Schutzpolizei ist es am Donnerstag in Eberswalde gekommen. Es kam zu einem förmlichen Strassenkampf, in dessen Verlauf etwa 20 Personen verletzt wurden, darunter acht schwer. Ein Verletzter, ein Russe namens Romanowski, ist im Krankenhaus gestorben. Auf dem Eberswalder Wochenmarkte herrschte schon seit Tagen Gärung. Bei dem gestrigen Markt wurde plötzlich das Gerücht verbreitet, dass die Kaufleute 120 Mk. für ein Pfund Zucker verlangten. Darauf kam es zu Zusammenrottungen. Die Menge drang in ein Manufakturwarengeschäft ein, zertrümmerte die Schaufenster und räumte fast den ganzen Laden aus. Weiter wurde eine Konditorei geplündert und die Schaufenster eines Delikatessengeschäftes ausgeraubt. Die Polizei wurde, als sie einschritt, mit Glasscherben und Steinen beworfen. Der Führer der Schutzpolizei sah sich schliesslich genötigt, den Befehl zum Gebrauch der Waffe zu geben. Es wurde eine Anzahl Schüsse abgefeuert, die zu den Verletzungen führten.[23]

(On Thursday police and looters clashed in Eberswalde. A real street battle developed, during which some twenty people were injured, eight of them seriously. One of them, a Russian called Romanovsky, died in hospital. There had been turmoil for days beforehand at the Eberswalde weekly market. Yesterday the rumour was suddenly spread that traders were asking 120 Marks for one pound of sugar, whereupon mobs formed. They forced their way into a draper's, smashed the windows and emptied almost the whole shop. A confectioner's shop was also ransacked and the shop windows of a delicatessen were robbed. the police intervened and were pelted with stones and broken glass. The police officer in charge was finally forced to give the order to use weapons. A number of shots were fired, leading to the injuries.)

Elsewhere in Germany, shopping was made difficult by the failure of shopkeepers to display prices at which they were currently prepared to deal. Their own attempt to delay sales in the hope of higher prices later made the already real threats of hunger in the population more likely. Often, prices were only displayed on the express orders of the police.

> Die Polizeidirektion ordnet an, dass Gegenstände des täglichen

> *Bedarfs in den Schaufenstern, Läden, und auf dem Wochenmarkt mit Preisschildern versehen werden müssen.*[24]

(Police headquarters order that prices must be displayed on all basic commodities in display windows, shops and on the weekly market.)

Orders of this nature would only be likely to result in yet higher prices being posted as traders sought to reflect future expected inflation in their current prices.

With at best inconvenience for shoppers together with growing threats to civil order, the pressures for an effective stabilization of the currency grew throughout 1923 and became ever more urgent.

On the morning of 12 November 1923, the Minister of Finance, Dr Luther, called in Hjalmar Schacht and offered him the job of Currency Commissioner of the Reich charged with carrying through the currency stabilization plans of the government.[25]

The dollar rates noted by Lange and quoted above were all the official dollar rates quoted on the Berlin Exchange. When Schacht took up office on 12 November, the official dollar rate in Berlin stood at 630×10^9 Marks whereas on the Cologne Exchange under the shield of the Occupation and out of reach of German foreign exchange law, the prevailing rate was around 4×10^{12} Marks. Although Schacht was convinced that only a contraction of the quantity of the legal tender could lead to price stabilization, the question as to which exchange rate should guide the policy deliberations was a difficult one.

Some factors responsible for price increases

Prices are determined by the forces of supply and demand. The standing textbook representation of price determination by these forces is illustrated in Figure 4.3. Consumers' attempts to hoard in the expectation of future price increases will be reflected in a shift to the right by the demand curve, whereas hoarding by suppliers for the same reason will cause the supply curve to shift to the left. Both will reinforce each other and cause the quantities traded to fall and the price level to rise.

That both these activities were at work in Germany in 1922 and 1923 is confirmed both by diary entries and press comment. Both actions create additional excess demand for the items being traded and this is the force that causes the price level to rise.

> *Die schärfste Kontrolle des deutschen Devisenverkehrs kann nicht verhindern, dass das Ausland in Markwerten spekuliert und sie in*

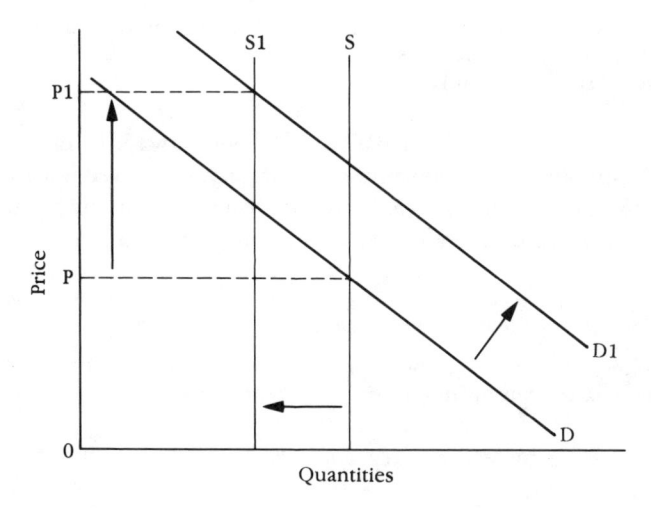

Key:

D–D1 hoarding by consumer

S–S1 hoarding by supplier

Figure 4.3 Price determination

Zeiten aussenpolitischer, für Deutschland ungünstiger Vorgänge und Massnahmen abstösst, wodurch eben automatisch die Devisen verteuert werden, auch wenn kein Deutscher Devisen hamstert oder in Devisen spekuliert.[26]

(The strictest supervision of German foreign exchange transactions cannot prevent foreigners speculating with the value of the Mark and selling it off cheaply at times of events or measures in foreign policy unfavourable to Germany, thus automatically raising currency prices, even if Germans are not hoarding currency or speculating in it.)

Die weitere Markentwertung führt zu Angstkäufen des Publikums in Textil- und Schuhwaren.[27]

(The further devaluation of the Mark is leading to panic buying by the public of textiles and shoes.)

Wegen der angespannten Versorgungslage – einerseits Hamsterkäufe, andererseits halten die Händler ihre Waren zurück, bis die Preise wieder gestiegen sind – kommt es im Gemeinderat zu einer heftigen Debatte.[28]

(Because of the tense supply situation caused on the one hand by hoarding and on the other side by dealers holding back their supplies until prices have risen further, a fierce debate took place in the District Council.)

Hyperinflation shifts the balance of power away from consumers towards suppliers. The consumer is certainly not sovereign in periods of hyperinflation. He can very rapidly come into his own again once the currency has been stabilized as the following entry shows:

Seit der Papierschein Dauerwert hat, ist aus dem gedemütigten Konsumenten wieder eine umworbene Persoñlichkeit geworden.[29]

(Now that new paper notes have long-term stability of value, the humiliated consumers are again persons to be courted.)

It is interesting to read a diary entry written barely a month after the introduction of the Rentenmark that asserts that the new currency has a long-term value in terms of its purchasing power, long before time would have proved this to be the case. After the catastrophic experiences of the previous two years and in particular the second half of 1923, the yearning for price stability must have been very great.

Notes

1. *Cuxhavener Zeitung*, 10 July 1923. *Wie steht der Dollar?*: What's the Position of the Dollar?
2. *Cuxhavener Zeitung*, 12 September 1923.
3. *Cuxhavener Zeitung*, 6 July 1923.
4. As a numerical example, consider an initial exchange rate of 4.2 Marks = $1. The price level in Germany rises by 200 per cent i.e. from an index level of 100 to 300. Over the same period of time, the price level in the United States remains constant at 100. On purchasing power parity reasoning, the new exchange rate should be 4.2 × 300/100 = 12.6 Marks = $1. Quoted in R.I. McKinnon, *Money in International Exchange* (Oxford University Press 1979), p. 118.
5. Hjalmar Schacht, *The Stabilisation of the Mark*, ch. 3. 'From the Invasion of the Ruhr to the Stabilisation of the Mark'.
6. G. Cassell, 'The Depreciation of the German Mark', *Economic Journal*, vol. 29, 1919, p. 493.
7. Hjalmar Schacht, *The Stabilisation of the Mark*, ch. 9. 'Foreign Credits'.
8. *Hildesheimer Allgemeine Zeitung*, Thursday, 5 October 1922.
9. Erich Maria Remarque, *Der Schwarze Obelisk* (Ullstein books 1978), p. 12.
10. F.K. Ringer (ed.), *The German Inflation of 1923* (Oxford University Press 1969), p. 91.
11. S. Grossman, 'Tagebuch der Wirtschaft', *Das Tage-Buch*. Heft 37. Jahrg. 4. S. 820. (Berlin: Athenäum Verlag 1923).

12. A. Heichen, 'Goldmarkweschsel kontra Schlechtgeldpolitik', *Das Tage-Buch*. Heft 37. Jahrg. 4. 569–571. (Berlin: Athenäum Verlag 1923).
13. Ibid.
14. Ibid.
15. Ibid.
16. Ibid.
17. Friedrich C.A. Lange, *Gross-Berliner Tagebuch 1920–1933* (Berlin/Bonn: Westkreuz Verlag, 2. Auflage 1982).
18. *Hildesheimer Allgemeine Zeitung*, 2 November 1923. *Unser tägliches Geld*: Our daily money.
19. Ibid.
20. Ibid.
21. Ibid.
22. *Hildesheimer Allgemeine Zeitung*, 2 September 1923. *Im Kampfe gegen die Teuerung*: The battle against price rises.
23. Ibid. *Blutige Schiesserei auf dem Eberswalder Wochenmarkt*: Bloody shoot-out at the Eberswalde weekly market.
24. *Chronik der Stadt Heilbronn 1922–1933*. Entry for 28 August 1923, p. 90.
25. Hjalmer Schacht, 1877–1970. One of the founders of the German Democratic Party DDP 1918. Harzburger Front 1931. President of the Reichsbank 1924–29 and 1933–39. Economics Minister 1934–37. Reichsminister 1937–44. Concentration Camp 1944–45. For a detailed account of his appointment as Currency Commissioner and the problems presented by the stabilization policy, see Ch. 4 'Die Stabilisierung der Mark', in *The Stabilisation of the Mark* (Westkreuz Verlag 1927).
26. *Hildesheimer Allgemeine Zeitung*, 25 August 1922. *Der Dollar an 2300!*: The dollar near 2300! The last sentence is an interesting reflection of the patriotism of the reporter for the *Hildesheimer Allgemeine Zeitung*. The foreign exchange price rose partly because of the very large speculative buying by some very big German names. See for example the description of the activities of the industrialist Hugo Stinnes elsewhere in this text.
27. Ibid.
28. *Chronik der Stadt Heilbronn 1922–1923*. Entry for 8 November 1923.
29. Friedrich C.A. Lange, *Gross-Berliner Tagebuch*. Diary entry for 16 December 1923.

CHAPTER FIVE

The Average Citizen

The average citizen in Cuxhaven

As well as being informed by his newspaper on economic and political explanations of the hyperinflation, the citizen would have had daily preoccupations that affected him more directly and obviously. One consequence of the flight from money was the appearance of barter. Advertisements for commodity swops are to be found in the press of the time. One advertisement in the *Cuxhavener Zeitung* advertised two iron ovens in exchange for potatoes while another wanted to swop a pig for corn.[1]

The average citizen in Cuxhaven needed to pay his rent. By November 1923, he needed to refer to the calculation method given in the newspaper in order to determine the amount to be paid. He was advised to cut out the formula and keep it for future reference!

As a small town on the coast where the Elbe meets the North Sea, barter advertisements might well have been more successful than in the larger cities inland. No town dweller in Cuxhaven was far from either the fishing industry or farms. It would have been much easier to find a mutual coincidence of wants than in larger cities such as Hamburg.

Ausschneiden! *Aufbewahren!*
Die November-Miete

Vom Mieteinigungsamt wird uns geschrieben:

Die im Voraus zu zahlende Novembermiete wird errechnet, indem man den 3. Teil der Monatlichen Grundmiete vervielfältigt an dem am 1. November 1923 gültigen Lebenshaltungsindex (einschl. Bekleidung) der Stadt Hamburg. Wird die Miete an einem Tage nach dem 1. November gezahlt, so ist immer der letzte vor dem Zahlungstage bekanntgegebene Index massgebend.

Der Index wird in den Tageszeitungen und durch Aushang im Rathaus und in der Zweigstelle der Sparkasse in Döse bekanntgemacht.

Die Indexzahl ist auf volle Milliarden abzurunden. Enthält die Indexzahl neben Milliarden Zahlen bis 500 Millionen einschliesslich, so wird nach unten, sonst nach oben abgerundet.

Die heute bekannte Indexzahl ist rund 13 Milliarden (genau 12 790 000 000).

Die so errechnete Miete setzt sich zusammen zur Hälfte aus Zus-

chlägen für laufende Instandsetzung und zur anderen Hälfte aus Zuschlägen für grosse Instandsetzung. Die übrigen unverändert gebliebenen Zuschläge zur Grundmiete sind so gering, dass sie nicht in Betracht kommen:

Beispiel:
  Friedensjahresmiete ... ... 600Mk.
  Friedensmonatsmiete ... ... 50Mk.
  Monatsgrundmiete
  (60% d. Friedensmonatsmiete) ... 30Mk.
1. *Grundmiete 100 % 30Mk.*
2. *Zuschlag f. Zinserhöh. 100 % ... 30Mk.*
3. *Zuschlag f. Verwaltungskosten 800 % ... 240Mk.*
4. *Zuschlag f. laufd. Instandsetzung*
   30Mk.: 6 = 5 × 13 (Index) 65 000 000 000Mk.
5. *Zuschlag f. grosse Instandsetz.*
   30Mk.: 6 = 5 × 13 (Index) 65 000 000 000Mk.
   _____
   130 000 000 000

rund 130 Milliarden Mark in November bei Zahlung am 1. November.

Die Zuschläge Abvermietung und gewerbliche Räume sind nicht geändert worden und so gering, dass sie gleichfalls nicht in Betracht kommen. Wesentlich neu ist, dass ebenso wie das Wassergeld und die Treppenbeleuchtungskosten die Strassenreinigungskosten anteilig auf die Mieter umgelegt werden können.[2]

(Cut it out!) Save it!
The November Rent
The Rents Conciliation Board has written to us as follows:

The November rent payable in advance is calculated by multiplying one-third of the monthly base rent by the cost of living index (including clothing items) of Hamburg valid on the 1st of November. Should the rent be paid after the 1st of November, then the index applicable will be the latest issued before the date of payment.

The index is published in the daily newspapers, displayed in the Town Hall and in the Döse branch of the Savings Bank.

The index figure should be rounded off to the nearest thousand million marks. Up to 500 million marks, it is rounded down, otherwise it is rounded up.

The index number given today is 13 thousand million (exactly 12,790,000,000).

The rent is comprised equally of additions for current maintenance and additions for larger items of maintenance expenditure. The other additions to the basic rent are unchanged and so insignificant.

Example:
  Annual peace time rent ... ... 600Mk.
  Monthly peace time rent ... ... 50Mk.

	Monthly base rent (60% of the monthly peace time rent)	...	30Mk.
1.	Base rent 100%		30Mk.
2.	Supplement for increased interest rates	...	30Mk.
3.	Supp. for administrative costs 800%	...	240Mk.
4.	Supp. for current maintenance 30Mk.: 6 = 5 × 13 (Index)		65,000,000,000Mk.
5.	Supp. for larger long-term maintenance 30Mk.: 6 = 5 × 13 (Index)		65,000,000,000Mk.
			130,000,000,000

The amount to be paid rounds off to 130 thousand million marks if paid on 1 November.

The supplements for sub-letting and commercial premises have not been altered and are so small that they may equally be disregarded. Significant new changes include street cleaning costs to be charged to tenants proportionately in the same way as payments for water and staircase lighting.)

The somewhat involved calculation, involving time and trouble, illustrates one of the costs of hyperinflation, indexing requires resources to implement! Parts of the formula are purely arbitrary. Why, for example, use 60 per cent of the monthly rent from 1914 as the basis for indexing? The addition for increased interest rates suggests a doubling of these rates from the base period. Should the property owner expect to double the rent because interest rates have doubled? This suggests the idea that a rent should reflect what the supplier of accommodation could have obtained from returns available on other investments. The addition for administration costs is presumably informed from data other than the price index to be used. The final two additions are for repairs and maintenance, addition number four for minor works and five for larger structural requirements. The multiplier of 13 is actually 13×10^9 or 13 milliard derived directly from the prices index used. Taking the last two items together, one-third of the total base rent of 30 Marks is then multiplied by the factor of 13 milliard derived from the index. This is presumably the proportion of the basic rent estimated to meet the maintenance requirements listed.

This is not necessarily an easy calculation for the ordinary citizen to make. Neither could he afford to wait too long! The example was published on 30 October 1923 to apply to rent payments to be made on 1 November. The 300 Marks of the first three items of the calculation are ignored in the final summation; they were worthless! Ignoring hundreds and even thousands of Marks in calculations was to be found in other financial transactions that would have affected the citizen in his everyday life. As the following notice in the *Cuxhavener Zeitung* shows, rounding off sums to multiples of one hundred thousand Marks was becoming increasingly common.

Wegen dringend erforderlicher Vereinfachung des Rechnungswesens ist ab 1. Oktober 1923

die MILLIONEN-MARK als EINHEIT

eingeführt und zwar mit einer Dezimalstelle, sodass auf Hunderttausende abzurunden ist.

Beispiel:

Die .... Bank in Cuxhaven wird ersucht, an

die .... Bank .... zu überweisen für ....

	Millionen	Mark
Mark Siebenmillionendreihunderttausend	7,	3

Cuxhaven, den .... 19..

....
Unterschrift.

Wir bitten demnach, bei Ausstellung von Schecks und sonstigen Zahlungsanweisungen auf uns künftig die Beträge

AUF VOLLE HUNDERTTAUSEND MARK ABZURUNDEN.

Wir werden in Zukunft bei allen von uns ausgehenden Berechnungen und bei Auszahlungen ebenso verfahren. Ausschliesslich bei Staatskonten sind bis auf weiteres 3 Dezimalstellen zulässig, d. h. also Abrundung auf Tausende.

Cuxhaven, den 2. Oktober 1923.

E. Calman.

Commerz- und Privatbank A. G. Filiale Cuxhaven.

Darmstädter und Nationalbank K. a. A.
  Zweigniederlassung Cuxhaven

Sparkasse des Amtes Ritzebüttel.

Vereinsbank in Hamburg Filiale Cuxhaven.[3]

(Because of the urgent need to simplify accounting procedures, from the 1st of October 1923, the

Million-Mark unit of account

will be introduced with one decimal place so that rounding off will be to units of one hundred thousand marks.

Example:

The.............. Bank in Cuxhaven is requested to transfer

an amount of seven million three hundred thousand marks

to the..................... Bank.......................

	Millions of marks	
Cuxhaven, the.................. 19..	7,	3

....
Signature.

We request therefore that in future amounts are rounded off to units of ONE HUNDRED THOUSAND MARKS when making out cheques and other forms of payment instruction.

All invoicing and payments made by us in the future will also be so calculated. Only in the case of Government accounts will rounding off to three decimal places be authorised until further notice i.e. rounding off to thousands of marks.

Cuxhaven, 2 October 1923.

E. Calman.

Commerz- und Privatbank A.G. Cuxhaven Branch.

Darmstädter und Nationalbank K.a.A.
            Branch Office, Cuxhaven.

Sparkasse [Savings Bank] Ritzebüttel

Vereinsbank in Hamburg, Cuxhaven Branch.)

The responses to hyperinflation were certainly causing confusion for the ordinary citizen. His rent rounded off to the nearest thousand million Marks, his transactions at the bank rounded off to the nearest hundred thousand Marks unless the transaction involved a government account, in which case rounding off to thousands of Marks was allowed. He needed knowledge of the latest prices index from Hamburg to calculate his rent with only the guidance as to the nature of the calculation that could be gleaned from the example published in the local newspaper.

A subscription to the *Cuxhavener Zeitung* had risen from 15,000 Marks for one month in July 1923 to 60×10^9 Marks for one week in November. Not only was it difficult for the individual to relate to the ever more rapidly increasing general level of prices, it was also difficult for him to know precisely what constituted money itself. The citizen needed guidance as to what forms of payment were in circulation and in particular what sources of inflation protection were possible. By October, the *Cuxhavener Zeitung* was looking forward to the forthcoming issue of Rentenmarks but reported to its readers the official list of inflation-protected monies. These were of course indexed to the exchange rate with the dollar and were protected in the sense that the necessary quantity of Papermarks would be paid out in the future to maintain the purchasing power as indicated by changes in the Mark price of the dollar.[4]

The confusion that these events caused for ordinary people can only be guessed at but was commented on at the time. Clearly, many Germans had difficulty in handling the new calculations with an ever increasing number of zeros in the actual amounts. 'Zero stroke' or 'cipher stroke' were names given by doctors in Germany to a nervous condition caused by the ever-increasing number of noughts on the notes and in the calculations. Dozens of cases of the 'stroke' were noticed in people struggling to calculate amounts expressed in thousands of billions.[5]

Wertbeständige Zahlungsmittel

Amtlich wird gemeldet: Die Ausgaben grosser Mengen wertbeständiger Zahlungsmittel beginnen in den nächsten Tagen. Folgende Massnahmen sind ergriffen:

1. *Stücke der Goldanleihe sind ununterbrochen gedruckt worden. Stücke über 1, 2 und 5 Dollar werden noch in dieser Woche in grosser Zahl zur Verfügung stehen. Am Ende dieser Woche werden täglich etwa für 8 Millionen Goldmark Goldanleihestücke hergestellt.*
2. *Um schon in wenigen Tagen Zahlungsmittel auch über kleinere Beträge in den Verkehr zu bringen, ist sofort die Herstellung von Zwischenscheinen der Goldanleihe beschlossen worden, die*

über ein Zehntel, ein Viertel und ein halb Dollar lauten werden. Der Druck hat bereits begonnen.
3. *Industriewerke, die eine für wertbeständiges Geld geeignete Sicherheit bieten können, wird auf Antrag die Genehmigung zur Ausgabe wertbeständigen Notgeldes erteilt, damit recht bald ein Teil der Löhne wertbeständig gezahlt werden kann.*
4. *Die Arbeiten zu dem Druck der Rentenmarkscheine erleiden durch die geschilderten Massnahmen keine Unterbrechung und werden mit der gleichen äussersten Beschleunigung wie bisher fortgeführt.*

Berlin, den 23. Oktober 1923.
Der Reichskanzler Dr. Stresemann.
Reichsminister der Finanzen Dr. Luther.
Wirtschaftsminister Koeth.[6]

(Inflation Protected Forms of Payment

The following has been officially announced: The issue of a large amount of inflation protected forms of payment will begin in next few days. The following measures have been adopted:

1. Units of the Gold Loan have been continuously minted. The 1, 2 and 5 dollar units will be available this week in large quantities. At the end of this week, Goldloan units to the value of around 8 million Goldmarks per day will be produced.
2. Smaller units will be brought into circulation in a few days. To this end, the decision has already been made to produce smaller units of the Gold Loan. These will have values of one-tenth, one-quarter and one-half of a dollar. Printing has started.
3. Industrial concerns which can offer suitable security for inflation-protected money will on application be given permission to issue such money. This will quickly allow a part of the wages to be paid in inflation-protected form.
4. The work involved in printing the Rentenmark notes has not been interrupted in any way by these measures and will be continued with the same exceptional rapidity as before.

Berlin, 23 October 1923.
Chancellor Dr. Stresemann
Minister of Finance Dr. Luther.
Economics Minister Koeth.)

The macroeconomic consequences of these policies are interesting! Inflation is responded to by making available yet more monies. The inflation protection is not to be produced by curbing the rate of growth of the various monies but rather by linking the value of the new monies to the exchange rate. In adding to the supplies of the various monies in existence, the effect will be to drive the price level yet higher. In the short term, they would be expected to slow the flight from money and provide a form of payment that need not immediately be spent.

The Goldmark

The higher the rate of inflation, the less adequately does money perform the functions normally required of it. The first functions to disappear are those of a standard of deferred payment and a store of value. Debtors therefore benefit at the expense of creditors. With very high rates of inflation, even the value of money as a form of payment for everyday transactions may break down. The search is then on for some form of transactions medium that is inflation-proof or, at least, one that offers a substantial degree of protection against its erosion in real value due to inflation. The need is for a *'wertbeständiger Zahlungsmittel'*. One of these in use in Germany during the hyperinflation was the Goldmark.

At the outbreak of war in 1914, the exchange rate had been 4.2 Marks to 1US$, reflecting the fixed parties of the Gold Standard. Both were thus equal to the same physical quantity of gold. As the Mark lost value during the period of inflation after the Great War, a distinction was drawn between the actual exchange rate against the dollar of the moment, the 'Dollarkurs', and the pre-war Gold Standard exchange rate of 4.2 Marks to the US dollar. The Gold Standard rate of exchange against the dollar became known as 4.2 Goldmarks.

This device could be used to price goods in a way more convenient for shops than constantly altering their prices to keep up with the depreciation of the Mark. Suppose that an item is priced at 4.2 Goldmarks or US$ 1 but the exchange rate is for the moment 7,500 Marks to the dollar. The pricing is in effect in dollars. There are two reasons why Goldmark pricing was used and not dollar pricing. Firstly, most shoppers would not have dollars and secondly, patriotic motives would have insisted on retaining a reference to the Mark in the pricing of goods for the domestic market in Germany.

The Goldmark prices could remain unaltered for relative lengthy periods of time thus saving the shopkeeper the problem of frequently adjusting his marked prices. The problem of coping with this situation was shifted to the consumer. He could pay 7,500 Papermarks or directly 4.2 Goldmarks with the increasingly available, Goldmark-denominated notes. As soon as the exchange rate altered with further depreciation of the Mark, the consumer would have to agree with the shopkeeper on the new Papermark equivalent of the Goldmark price.

The difficulty that this caused for the ordinary shopper can be imagined. The illustration has deliberately used simple amounts, that is, a Goldmark equivalent of a price of one US dollar. In a world without pocket calculators, the computational difficulties must have been immense and beyond the capabilities of many people when 'awkward' amounts of money were involved.

Goldnotes offered security of a kind. One could pay one's debts to public sector institutions with the bill either priced in the same units or multiplied up to its value of the moment in Papermarks, as discussed above.[7]

Another method of protecting holders of money against loss of real value due to inflation consisted of note issues by the Festmarkbank in Bremen. As the example illustrated below shows, these issues were linked directly to the United States dollar. There were risks involved in accepting such notes as a consideration of the 'small print' reveals.

Figure 5.1 One-dollar note of the Festmark Bank, Bremen

The conditions of issue were as follows:

1. *Für den Betrag der von uns herausgegabten Gutscheine haften wir mit unserem Gesamtvermögen, ausserdem sind dieselben in voller Höhe gedeckt durch kurzfristige wertbeständige Forderungen an Industrie und Landwirtschaft.*
2. *Die Gutscheine werden in Einzelbeträgen bis zu 10 Festmark jederzeit an unserer Kasse eingelöst. Grössere Beträge müssen unter Einreichung der Gutscheine zwei Börsentage vor der Auszahlung gekündigt werden. Der Auszahlungsberechnung*

wird der Durchschnitt der beiden amtlichen Berliner ‹Geld› – Notierungen für Auszahlung New-York zugrunde gelegt, die üblichen Bankspesen werden abgesetzt.
3. *Dieser Gutschein verliert am 31. Dezember 1926 seine Gültigkeit.*
4. *Für abhanden gekommene Gutscheine leisten wir keinen Ersatz.*

Bremen, im Oktober 1923
DEUTSCHE FESTBANK
Aktiengesellschaft

(1. We guarantee the amount of the notes issued by us with our total assets. These notes are completely covered by short-term inflation-protected demands on industry and agriculture.
2. The notes can be redeemed at our tills at any time in single amounts up to 10 Festmarks. For larger amounts notice must be given and the notes handed in two Stock Exchange working days before the withdrawal. The withdrawal will be calculated on the basis of the average of the two official money rates quoted in Berlin for New York payment. The usual bank charges will be deducted.
3. This note will be invalid after 31 December 1926.
4. No substitutes for lost notes will be issued.

Berlin, October 1923
Deutsche Festbank)

Here is an example of an interesting private enterprise initiative to redress the balance of interest between debtors and creditors. Debtors are issued with short-term loans presumably indexed to the exchange rate or 'Dollarkurs'. The creditors, the bank's customers, receive, on presentation of the Festmark note, the appropriate number of Papermarks equal to one dollar as indicated by the average of the two Berlin rates for notes, that is, the average of the buying and selling prices. The main area of risk for such a venture is obvious. If the borrowers cannot repay their exchange rate indexed loans, then the bank's customers would find their Festmark notes of diminished value.

Although the Festmarkbank of Bremen's activities are interesting, quantitatively the Goldmark pricing is much more significant and widespread at this time.

Shopping in Hildesheim in 1923 would have necessitated conversions of Goldmark prices into the corresponding Papermark prices. The example below is typical of the Goldmark-priced advertisements appearing in the *Hildesheimer Allgemeine Zeitung* in 1923 (see pp. 83–86). The alternative would be to advertise a product or service and leave off the price. It would then amount to turning up at the shop or theatre to find out! Occasionally, even as late as December 1923, a price would be stated in Papermarks.

The Goldmark – an illustration

Goldmark pricing did not need to be accompanied by the existence of Goldmark notes. It was tantamount to pricing in dollars while preserving an acceptable cover that the pricing was still in units of the German national currency. However, towards the end of 1923 in particular, the price level was spiralling upwards at such a rate that the issue of Goldmark notes was thought necessary in some areas to ensure acceptance. Figure 5.2 illustrates a ten-Goldpfennig note issued in November 1923 by the Dresden Chamber of Commerce.

Figure 5.2 A ten-Goldpfennig note[8]

The shopper would need to know how to convert from 'gold prices' into 'paper prices'. This was done with the aid of a published 'multiplier' or '*Schlüsselzahl*'. As discussed above, for a constant 'gold price', a corresponding 'paper price' would have to be calculated every time a new exchange rate was published.

The Goldmark did not, of course, contain any gold and neither did it give any conversion rights into gold. As a means of pricing goods, it was a harking back to the pre-war stability of the gold standard. It meant that advertisements for goods could have prices attached to them that would not change with the exchange value of the Papermark. As such, advertising copy could be accepted by newspapers and the prices would still be valid in Goldmark terms a few days later when the actual edition appeared on the newsstands. It was an accounting price and for most customers would have only been part of the price information they would require. Equipped with the relevant 'Dollarkurs', they could go shopping and bargain with the shopkeepers.

The device could just as accurately have been called 'Dollarmark' pricing. Clearly, in the aftermath of the Great War, patriotic reasons would have excluded this possibility!

Shopping in Hildesheim – December 1923

The cheapest available winter season coat advertised by J. Meyerhof in the Friday, 7 December 1923 edition of the *Hildesheimer Allgemeine Zeitung* was priced at 14.75 Goldmarks. Payment must have presented a puzzle for some shoppers!

The Rentenmark had been introduced the previous month at 1 RM = 10^{12} PM or 4.2 RM = 1 US$ as already discussed above. As 4.2 GM also equally 1 US$, 1 RM = 1 GM. The 14.75 GM priced coat would also have been sold at a price of 14.75 RM.

The price of the coat would also be fixed by this date in Papermarks. The November 1923 reforms had fixed the conversion rate of 1 RM = 10^{12} PM. The price of the coat in the devalued Papermarks would therefore be 14.75×10^{12}, that is, 14.75 billion Papermarks. The existence of a fixed conversion ratio for the old devalued paper currency in terms of the new issue effectively stabilized prices in Papermarks as well as in Rentenmarks and Goldmarks.

Consider the small advertisement for women's hair! For 100g of hair, 300 Milliarden, that is, 300×10^9 Papermarks were offered. Yet, apply the conversion ratio introduced the previous month and this reduces to $(300 \times 10^9)/10^{12} = 0.30$ Rentenmark = 0.30 Goldmarks.

A woman prepared to sell a substantial proportion of her hair for 30 Rentenpfennig = 30 Goldpfennig certainly would not have been able to shop for a coat at J. Meyerhof am Platze on the proceeds!

Was this advertisement aimed at the poorer members of society? That significant poverty existed at this time in Hildesheim is also suggested by the advertisement of the Rhineland Society (*Verein der Rheinländer*) for their meeting of 23 December in the Tivoli Room; Christmas presents were to be distributed to poor children.

For the local press, this diversity of means of payment was to be deplored; it had destroyed the monetary integrity of the German Reich one of the very cornerstones of unity. Consider the following extract from the *Hildesheimer Allgemeine Zeitung*.

Unser tägliches Geld

Wir befinden uns augenblicklich in einer Uebergangszeit von der Papiermarkzahlung zur Zahlung in wertbeständigem Gelde. Diese Neuordnung stellt sich äusserlich dar als eine gewisse Unordnung. Wir haben jetzt die Papiermark, die Goldanleihe in verschiedenen Stückelungen, die Dollarschatzanweisungen, die Rentenmark soll alsbald folgen; daneben erhalten wir eine Fülle sogenannten wertbeständigen Geldes, das die einzelnen Staaten und Kommunen herausgegeben haben bzw. ausgeben werden. Die Deckungsmodalitäten sind verschiedene, grösstenteils aber auf die Goldanleihe abgestellt. Sodann aber tritt noch eine neue Goldnote der Reichsbank hinzu, die, wie der Vizepräsident v. Glasenapp angekündigt hat, demnächst gegen volle Deckung durch Gold, Golddevisen und Goldhandelswechsel zur Ausgabe gelangen wird. Man glaubt sich in das erste Drittel des vorigen Jahrunderts zurückversetzt, als die deutsche Zerissenheit auf dem Hohepunkte war und Deutschland vor Begründung des Zollvereins ein wirtschaftliches Chaos bildete.[9, 10]

Our daily money

We are at present in a transitional phase from Papermark payment to payment in inflation-protected money. Externally this new order is manifested as a certain disorder. We now have the Papermark, the Goldloan in various denominations, dollar credits, with the Rentenmark soon to follow; in addition we receive a variety of so-called inflation-protected money that the individual states and local authorities have issued or will be issuing. The support arrangements vary, but for the most part are based on the Goldloan. But then we must add a new Reichsbank note, which according to an announcement by Vice-President von Glasenapp will be issued in the immediate future and will be fully covered by gold, gold foreign exchange and gold trade exchange. It feels as if we are back in the first half of the last century, when German disunity was at its height and Germany was in economic chaos before the foundation of the Customs Union.)

The content of the monetary reform programme to follow the immediate question of stabilizing the real value of the Mark is obvious from the discussion above: it is to establish a monetary system that serves the needs of the nation state. This includes only one central point at which notes are issued and a central bank to ensure that the monetary needs of the nation are met consistent with preserving the real value of the currency. It is, of course, the events of these years that led to the

Figure 5.3 Advertisements in the *Hildesheimer Allgemeine Zeitung*, Friday 7 December 1923

Damenmäntel als Weihnachtsgabe

Mein Angebot von ungewöhnlicher *Preiswürdigkeit bietet eine grosse Auswahl flotter Formen in nur guten Stoffen und sauberer Verarbeitung*

MANTEL 14.75 G.-Mk.	MANTEL 35.00 G.-Mk.	MANTEL 42.00 G.-Mk.
Stoffe englischer Art, hell und dunkel	*Astrachan, schwarz ganz gefüttert*	*Velour de laine in vielen Farben*
MANTEL 21.50 G.-Mk.	MANTEL 36.00 G.-Mk.	MANTEL 48.00 G.-Mk.
aus gutem Wollstoff, weite Gürtelform	*aus gemustert. Stoffen beste Qualität*	*gerippter Velourstoff, moderne Wickelform*
MANTEL 29.50 G.-Mk.	MANTEL 39.00 G.-Mk.	MANTEL 65.00 G.-Mk.
einfarbige und gemusterte Stoffe	*in bester Verarbeitung lange Form*	*aus erstklassig. Tuch marine und schwarz*

Elegante Modelle in Mänteln und Kostümen

Kinder- u. Mädchenmäntel in allen Grössen

J. Meyerhof am Platze

Frauenhaar

100 Gramm

300 Milliarden kauft

Ad. Raschke

Lutherstr. 19

Verein der

Rheinländer

Sonntag, den 9. Dez.

7 Uhr abends

im Tivoli- Saal

STIFTUNGSFEST.

Sonntag, den 23. Dez.

nachmittags 5 Uhr

Bescherung

armer Kinder

Figure 5.4 Advertisements in the *Hildesheimer Allgemeine Zeitung*, Friday 7 December 1923, translation

Ladies' Coats as Christmas Presents

My offer of *unusually* good value for money presents a large selection of stylish fashions all in good material and of excellent workmanship.

COAT	COAT	COAT
14.75 Goldmarks	35.00 Goldmarks	42.00 Goldmarks
English-style material, light and dark colours	astrakhan, black, fully lined	velour de laine in many colours
COAT	COAT	COAT
21.50 Goldmarks	36.00 Goldmarks	48.00 Goldmarks
good woollen cloth, broad belt style	patterned material, best quality	corded velvet material, modern wrapround style
COAT	COAT	COAT
29.50 Goldmarks	39.00 Goldmarks	65.00 Goldmarks
plain and patterned materials	best workmanship, long style	first-class cloth, navy and black

Elegant styles in coats and dresses

Children's and young ladies' coats in all sizes

J. Meyerhof am Platze

Women's Hair
purchased by
Ad. Raschke
19, Lutherstr.
100 grammes for
300 thousand million Marks

The Rhineland Society

Sunday, 9th December at 7.00pm

in the Tivoli Room

Founder's Day Celebration

Sunday, 23rd December at 5.00pm

distribution of Christmas presents to poor children

creation of the independent Reichsbank and its successor, the Bundesbank.

One source of information about the effects of the hyperinflation of these years on families would be, of course, the written testimony of those affected. For the lower social classes, there is a paucity of such material. One available example concerns the case of Emmy Zehden of Berlin, a newspaper seller and Jehovah's Witness, sentenced to death in 1943 for sheltering three co-religionists who refused to do military service. She was executed in Plötzensee Prison on 9 June 1944. In a letter pleading for the sentence to be commuted, she refers to the effects of the great inflation of 1923 on her parents and the whole family and of her contributions to maintaining the family at the cost of great deprivation to herself.

> *Meine Eltern, welche durch die Inflation alles verloren hatten, insbesondere meine Mutter als sie mit Horst-Günther ohne Ernährer da stand, habe ich unter Entbehrungen unterstützt.*[11]

> (At great cost to myself, I supported my parents who had lost everything because of the inflation, especially my mother who was on her own with Horst-Günther without a provider.)

Figure 5.5 is an example of a family ruined and the financial burden falling on the responsibility of one of the poorest-paid individuals, a newspaper seller. This is a testimony to the effects of the inflation at its most poignant.

Inflation and public morality

By July 1923, the *Hildesheimer Allgemeine Zeitung* editorial was well aware of the effects of inflation on the relationships between long-term loan debtors and their creditors and was reporting sympathetically on the attempts to introduce a law into the Reichstag to prevent borrowers repaying their lenders with inflation devalued Papermarks, the so-called 'Sperrgesetz' or 'Blocking Law'. The practice of repaying loans in devalued currency and the government not legally putting a stop to it, were regarded as indicative of a low moral tone in economic relationships:

> *Schön ist die Schädigung der Hypothekengläubiger und Obligationäre wahrlich nicht, und man kann es ihnen nicht verdenken, dass sie sich schmählich betrogen fühlen.... Dass der Staat zum Schutz dieser Gläubiger bisher nichts unternommen hat ... gehört auch zu den niederleidenden Begleiterscheinungen unserer wirtschaftlichen Lage ... dieser Fall ist ausserordentlich bezeichend für den heutigen*

Tiefstand der wirtschaftlichen Moral ... es sei direkt ‹unsittlich›, wenn eine Gesellschaft ... die Obligationäre nunmehr mit Papiermark schnöde abspeiss. Sie warten auf Hilfe vom Parlament und von der Regierung. Allerdings augenblicklich sind ja noch Ferien.[12]

(The damage done to mortgagees and other creditors is truly not nice, and one cannot blame them for feeling shamefully deceived. That the state has so far done nothing to protect these creditors is one of the depressing circumstances accompanying our economic situation.... This case is particularly indicative of the depths to which economic morality has sunk today.... It is said to be simply 'immoral' when a company now ... cynically fobs its creditors off with Papermarks. They are waiting for help from parliament and from the government. But of course it's still holiday time.)

The preservation of morality in society is undermined by inflation in a number of ways. In the example above, debtors take advantage of contracts with their creditors which do not provide for the index-linking of long-term debt repayments; the monetary system ceases to be neutral as between borrowers and lenders and the debtors take full advantage of what for them is a fortuitous turn of events.

As the rate of devaluation of the Papermark increased, so increasingly people turned to crime in order to survive. Entries in Friedrich Lange's diary illustrate the escalating nature of theft as 1922 is followed by a still faster depreciation of the Mark in 1923.

Auf den Kirchhöfen mehren sich die Bronze– und Metalldiebstähle. Der Strassenbahn stiehlt man die zentnerschweren Weichendeckel.[13]

(Thefts of bronze and other metal items from churchyards are increasing. Heavy points covers weighing a hundredweight are being stolen from the tramways.)

Die Not der Bevölkerung infolge der Markentwertung führt zur Plünderung der Kartoffeläcker und zur Selbstversorgung mit Brennholz in den städtischen Forsten.[14]

(The deprivation arising from the depreciation of the Mark is causing people to raid the potato fields and to help themselves to firewood from the municipal forests.)

Beim Überwachungsamt sind in diesem Jahre bereits über 3,000 Anzeigen der einzelnen Verwaltungen eingegangen. Gestohlen wurde besonders Altmaterial wie Bleirohre, Regentraufen, Gullydeckel, Leitungsdraht usw.[15]

(Over 3,000 prosecutions by individual authorities already this year

> Frauenstrafgefängnis Berlin NO 18, den 22. 11. 1943
>
> 1 J, 5643
>
> Gnadengesuch
>
> Herrn Oberreichsanwalt
> beim Volksgericht.
>
> Sehr geehrter Herr Präsident!
>
> Unterzeichnete wurde am 19. Nov. zu Tode verurteilt. Ich möchte auf diesem Wege um Gnade bitten. Meine Reue ist gross und bin ich mir meiner Tat doch nie so bewusst gewesen. Mein Leben lang war ich ein fleissiger und ordentlicher Mensch, immer nur Gutes getan.
>
> Meine Eltern, welche durch die Inflation alles verloren hatten, insbesondere meine Mutter als sie mit Horst-Günther ohne Ernährer da stand, habe ich unter Entbehrungen unterstützt. Die leiblichen Eltern haben sich tatsächlich bis zum 9. Lebensjahr nicht um den Jungen bemüht. So habe ich meine Jugendjahre geopfert, um ihm eine liebevolle Mutter zu geben. Es ist mir leider keine Gelegenheit gegeben für all meine Güte Beweis anzutreten. Auf der anderen durfte ich nicht beweisen wie rücksichtslos die leiblichen Eltern an dem Jungen gehandelt haben. Ich bitte höflichst um Herrn Präsidenten die Todesstrafe in eine Zuchthausstrafe umzuwandeln. Noch einmal möchte ich beweisen, wie sehr ich meine Tat bereue. So geben Sie mir bitte Gelegenheit im öffentlichen Leben wieder alles gut zu machen.
>
> Mit freundlichem
> Dank Frau
> Emmy Zehden
> Berlin NO 18
> Barnimstr. 10

Source: This letter and a facsimile of the original handwritten form is displayed at the Plötzensee Prison Memorial, Berlin.

Figure 5.5 Full text of the Clemency Appeal of Emmy Zehden

have been recorded. Thefts were particularly noted of old materials such as lead pipes, guttering, drain covers, wire, etc.)

One of the hallmarks of economic progress and rising living standards noted in the economic history of the United Kingdom was the dignity with which the dead were buried. Progress often took the form of incurring more expense to ensure burial in a family grave rather than what for many was a disgrace, burial in the cheaper public grave.

If the attention to the standard with which the dead are buried is

> Women's Prison   Berlin NO 18, 22.11.1943
>
> 1 J, 5643
>
> *Plea for Clemency*
>
> Chief State Lawyer of the People's Court.
>
> Dear Mr President,
>
> The undersigned was sentenced to death on the 19th November. I would like to request clemency. My contrition is great and I have never been so conscious of my action. I have been for my entire life an industrious and respectable person always only doing good things.
>   At great cost to myself, I supported my parents who had lost everything because of the inflation, especially my mother who was on her own with Horst-Günther without a provider. The natural parents showed no concern for the boy until his ninth year. So I sacrificed the years of my youth to give him a loving mother. I have been given no opportunity to tender proof of all my good deeds. On the other hand I was not allowed to prove how negligent the natural parents were in dealing with the boy. I request most politely Mr President for the death penalty to be converted into a period of imprisonment. Once again, may I prove how much I regret my deed. So please give me the opportunity in public life to make everything good again.
>
>   With friendly thanks,
>   Frau Emmy Zehden
>   Berlin NO 18
>   Barnimstr. 10

Figure 5.6 Full text of the Clemency Appeal of Emmy Zehden, translation

indicative of the level of human dignity in society, then, as the entries in Lange's diary show, this fell sharply in 1922 and 1923 in Berlin, coffin quality fell, 'mass' transport of bodies was introduced and cremation fees were linked to the price of the fuel used. Consider the following entries.

> *Da der Kokspreis zur Einäscherungsgebühr im Verhältnis 1 : 6 steht, erfolgt jetzt die Feuerbestattung nach der Koksklausel. Preisgrundlage: 1 Zentner Lichtenberger Schmelzkoks frei Krematorium, eine pietätlose Berechnung.*[16]

(Since the price of coke and cremation fees are in a ratio of 1 to 6, cremations are now carried out according to the coke clause. The basis of the price is: one hundredweight of Lichtenberg smelting coke at the crematorium, an impious calculation.)

Zur Verbilligung der ungeheuer gestiegenen Beerdigungskosten soll jetzt ein Massentransport bis zu vier Särgen erfolgen. Die Toten werden sich nicht daran stossen, für ihre Angehörigen weniger erfreulich.[17]

(To reduce the enormously high costs of a funeral, a form of mass transport for up to four coffins is being introduced. The dead will not object to this arrangement but it will be less pleasant for their relatives.)

Im Sitzungssaal der Stadtverordneten war der 50cm hohe Normalsarg, der sogenannte Nasenquetscher, ausgestellt, für den die einfache Gebühr zu zahlen ist. Wer höher hinaus will, hat das Zwei- und Dreifache zu entrichten.[18]

(In the conference (meeting) room of the councillors, the 50cm high 'normal coffin', the so-called nose-squasher, was put on display. It is for those who pay the standard fee. Those who want higher things must pay two or three times as much.)

Friedrich Lange was obviously not a man lacking a (grim) sense of humour! For further indications of Lange's humour in grim circumstances, see the diary entry for 3 October 1922 and the noting of the scene in the Council Chamber as the dog tax is discussed.

Notes

1. *Cuxhavener Zeitung*, Friday, 16 November 1923.
2. *Cuxhavener Zeitung*, 31 October 1923.
3. *Cuxhavener Zeitung*, 2 October 1923. Million Marks as the Unit of Account.
4. This form of inflation protection raises all the questions discussed elsewhere in the text. Are exchange rate changes good enough proxies for changes in the internal purchasing power of the currency? During a period of hyperinflation, can the payout ever be fast enough to fully compensate for inflation? If prices are posted in Papermarks and inflation protected units, are the two prices in line with exchange rate movements? How would the individual consumer check on this?
5. *New York Times*, 7 December 1923, quoted in J.K. Galbraith, *Money: Whence It Came, Where It Went* (London: Pelican Books 1976), p. 167.
6. *Cuxhavener Zeitung*, 24 October 1923.
7. Such Goldnotes were particularly useful for paying bills to public sector institutions as these bodies went over to Goldmark pricing in an attempt to place public sector revenues on a real rather than on a purely nominal basis.
8. The numbers shown on this example clearly link to the relationships discussed above. Ten Goldpfennig = 1/42 dollar. Therefore, one Goldmark = 10/42 dollar and it follows that 4.2 Goldmarks = one dollar, the

pre–1914 gold standard parity rate of exchange between the Mark and the United States dollar.
9. *Hildesheimer Allgemeine Zeitung*, 2 November 1923.
10. For the majority of the holders of these gold-linked issues, the reality was illusion in the sense that they were never likely to be able to get their hands on the gold equivalent of the paper they held. It meant that, in the majority of cases, the linkage to gold was through the United States dollar that had a gold value because America was still effectively on the gold standard. The key to the long-term preservation of real values lay not in stating a gold backing as such but in restricting the future growth of the amount of paper itself.
11. Letter, 22 November 1943. Published as a copy of the original handwritten form in *Beiträge zum Widerstand 1933–1945. 8 ... Für Immer Ehrlos. Aus der Praxis der Volksgerichtshofes* . Gedenkstätte Deutscher Widerstand Berlin. 'Ersatz-Vollstreckungsband der Strafsache Emmy Zehden', pp. 22–32. Published by the Landeszentrale für politische Bildungsarbeit, Berlin.
12. *Hildesheimer Allgemeine Zeitung*, 21 July 1913. *Wie man sein Geld verliert* : How to lose your money!
13. Diary entry 7 February 1923.
14. Diary entry 21 September 1923.
15. Diary entry 19 November 1923.
16. Diary entry 18 November 1922.
17. Diary entry 19 May 1923.
18. Diary entry 4 June 1923.

CHAPTER SIX

Loans and Public Sector Finance

Finance of the Great War by Germany

In Germany, for the most part, the war was financed by the Reich obtaining funds from the Reichsbank on the security of Treasury bonds and bills supplied by the former and discounted by the latter. The whole method of war finance was thus inflationary. Rapid increases in the money supply brought about in this way had little immediate impact on prices. As a not-insignificant part of the money supply was in the hands of troops in the field, price stability was helped by the reduced velocity of circulation. By the end of the war, a four-fold increase in the money supply per head had taken place. It was only rather late on in the war that it was decided to follow the example of England, where it was understood that the war should be financed contemporaneously to a significant extent by raising taxes. A quick victory would enable purchasing power to be withdrawn by a Victory Tax, or so thought the Reich government at the time.

There were, however, war loans. Figure 6.1 shows the 1915 five per cent war loan. The holder of this certificate for 10,000 Marks was doubly hit. As interest rates rose sharply after 1918, the value of his patriotic investment fell and so did the real value of the interest coupons. It is significant that it appears that the last coupon cashed was the one for 2 January 1922. The later ones were simply not worth presenting for payment. As the coupons are bearer securities, they were often directly used without being cashed as notes, adding yet again to the money supply. The exchange rate or 'Dollarkurs' had reached 670 Marks by July 1922 from around 5 at the time of issue of this loan, a fall in the value of the interest payment of 250 Papermarks from around 50 US dollars to 37 cents! No provision to remedy the plight of debt holders was to be included in the stabilization measures introduced in 1923.

From time to time during the period, press comment is preoccupied with considering the budgetary problems of the Reich. One of these occasions was in January 1922 when press coverage was given to the attempt by the government of the Reich to cover its deficit by raising a compulsory loan of 40 thousand million Marks (*Zwangsanleihe von*

Figure 6.1 Who loses from inflation! German War Loan issued in 1915 repayable in 1924. An example of a security rendered worthless by hyperinflation

LOANS AND PUBLIC SECTOR FINANCE 95

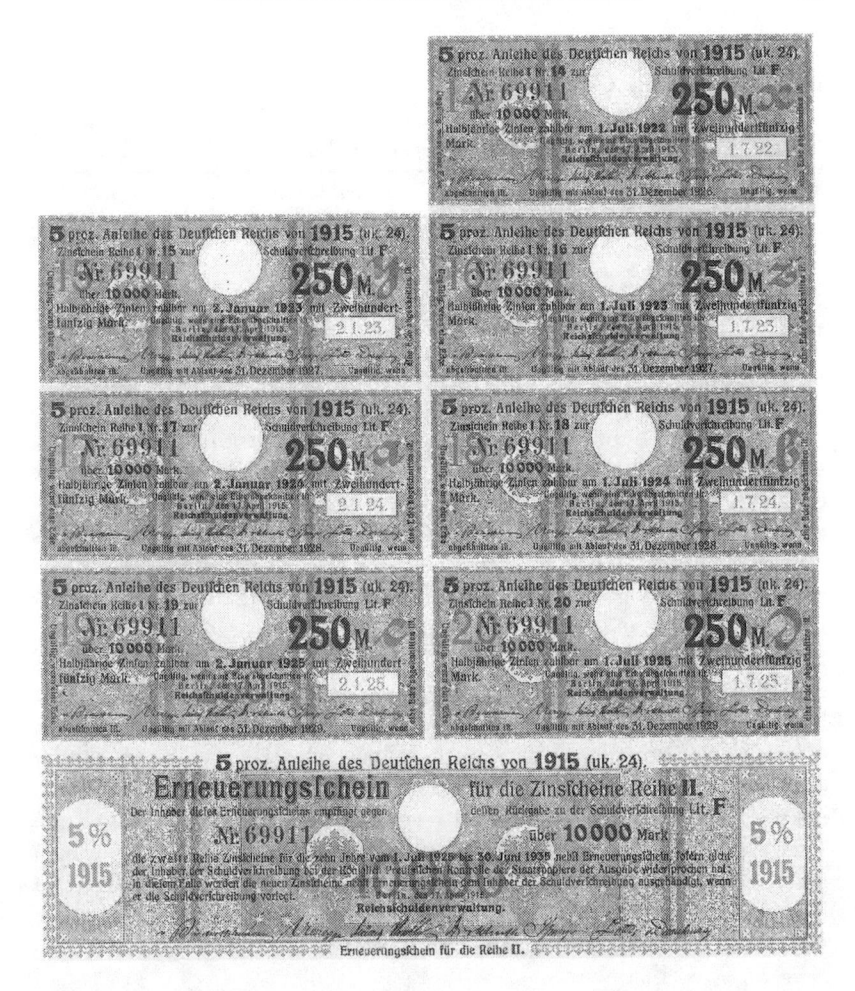

Figure 6.2 Interest coupons of the War Loan. The initial 250 Mark coupon would have been worth approximately $50. From July 1922 onwards, the interest was not worth collecting, such had been the depreciation of the currency

40 Milliarden). The severity of the budget deficit financing problem is indicated in Table 6.1.

Table 6.1 German Reich

Year	Revenue	Expenditure	Deficit
1919	2560	8560	−6000
1920	3178	9329	−6054
1921	2927	6651	−3676
1922	1488	3951	−2422
1923	519	5278	−4691

Source: Bresciani-Turroni, *The Economics of Inflation* (London 1937) pp. 437–8.

The units of account are Goldmarks. To convert them into Papermarks, the data in Table 6.1 would need to be multiplied by an appropriate exchange rate (Dollarkurs). It would be difficult to choose an appropriate rate in which to express the budget figures for any one year as this rate changed daily. The data are thus real values expressed in terms of the values of the gold standard that existed up to the outbreak of war in August 1914. A glance at the table can be misleading! The sharp fall in the real value of expenditure from 1921 to 1922 in particular does not arise from planned reductions in expenditure but rather from a price level rising faster than the central govenment's revenue, the consequences of decisions about budgetary finance made in earlier years. A similar effect is noted on the expenditure side, falling in real terms despite inflated values in purely nominal terms. Is there a sense in which the Versailles Treaty, as claimed vociferously and frequently in the German press, made bridging this financing gap more difficult? The 40 Milliarden Papermark Compulsory Loan of January 1922 illustrates one of these factors. In commenting on this loan, the *Hildesheimer Allgemeine Zeitung* reported that:

> *Ausserordentlich wichtig sind die Bestimmungen über die Verwendung des Ertrages zur Anleihe. Sie soll nicht etwa einer Ausgleichung des Haushalts für 1922 dienen und in der allgemeinen Defizitwirtschaft verschwinden, sondern für die Bezahlung der Sachlieferungen verwendet werden.... Dadurch aber dass die Anleihe nur der Abdeckung der Sachlieferungen dienen soll, liesse sich vielleicht ein gewisser Ausgleich zwischen der Zeichnung auf die Zwangsanleihe und der Vergebung der Sachlieferungen herstellen.*[1]

> (Of exceptional importance are the regulations about the use of the proceeds of the loan. They are not supposed to balance the budget for 1922 and disappear into the general deficit finance but be used for payment for the deliveries in kind. That the loan must only be used to cover the deliveries in kind makes for a certain balancing

out between the subscriptions to the loan and the handing over of the deliveries in kind.)

Here is one example of the specific financial difficulties caused by the terms of the Treaty of Versailles. The lending capacity of the German economy was to be compulsorily tapped to provide financing for the deliveries in kind required as part of the reparations burden laid on Germany by the Allied Powers. Such financing was thus not available to cover the deficit of 2422 Goldmarks for 1922 shown in Table 6.1.

That Germany was prepared to finance the First World War to a significant degree by essentially printing Papermarks to cover budget deficits is interesting, especially as it went against the received financial orthodoxy of the day. The explanation seems to have been a reluctance to immediately burden the population with taxation levels necessary to finance the war and simultaneously to continue to balance the budget.

> *Die Inflation, das heisst die... Ausweitung der Geldmenge gegenüber der kaufbaren Gütermenge, begann in Deutschland im Kriege mit der Finanzierungsmethode, die – anders als in England – während der Kampfhandlungen die Belastung der Bevölkerung mit Steuern möglichst wenig erhöhen wollte. ‹Wir wollen während des Krieges die gewaltigen Lasten, die unser Volk trägt, nicht durch Steuern erhöhen, solange hierfür keine zwingende Notwendigkeit vorliegt›, hatte Helfferich am 20. August 1915 erklärt, nachdem er zum Staatssekretär des Reichsschatzamtes... ernannt und damit für die Kriegsfinanzierung verantwortlich geworden war.[2]*

(The inflation, that is, the expansion of the money supply in relationship to the quantity of goods available to purchase, began with the method of finance adopted during the war. In Germany, in contradistinction to England, the method of finance did not seek, during the conflict, to burden the population with taxes above the minimum. 'We do not wish to increase the enormous war time burdens on our people yet more by taxation as long as there is no compelling necessity to do so', declared Hefferich on 20 August 1915 after his appointment as Secretary of State of the Reich Treasury and his consequent assumption of responsibility for the finance of the war.)

It seems clear from this quotation that the short-term advantages of inflationary methods of finance during the war were regarded as more important than the recognition of the long-term consequences of inflation, a conclusion that made its own disastrous contribution to the events of 1923.

Compulsory loan and 'crowding out'

The question of the interest rate to attach to the compulsory loan was discussed at some length. The discussion centred around how low the interest rate might be set without any recognition of the importance of the relationship between the interest rate and the rate of inflation. This is interesting because elsewhere in the same article the relationship between the inflation rate and the level of payments is discussed.

> *Bei der Erbschaftssteuer soll die Geldentwertung entsprechend berücksichtigt werden.*
>
> *Zu den einzelnen Bedingungen der Zwangsanleihe, die noch einer Regelung bedürfen, gehört auch die Frage der Verzinsung der Zwangsanleihe. Die Regierung würde Wert darauf legen, dass schon vom ersten Jahre an eine mässige Verzinsung eintrete, etwa in Höhe von 1 Proz. in ersten zwei Jahren und dann steigend auf 2, 3 und mehr Prozent. Die Sozialdemokraten sollen dagegen gestern beschlossen haben, dass sie dem Steuerkompromiss nur zustimmen wollen unter der Bedingung, dass die Anleihe die ersten 5 Jahre unverzinst bleibt.*[3]

(The fall in the value of money will be taken correspondingly into account in connection with the inheritance tax.

One of the few conditions of the compulsory loan that still needs to be settled is the question of the interest rate level of the loan. The Government would favour a moderate rate of interest from the first year onwards, somewhere around one per cent in the first two years and then increasing to two, three or more per cent. The Social Democrats on the other hand are reported to have decided yesterday that they can accept the taxation compromise only on the condition that the loan remains interest free for the first five years.)

The real difference on the question of the level of interest rates to be attached to this loan between the government and the opposition Social Democrats is virtually zero. Given the rate at which the value of money was falling, even as early as January 1922, the effective difference between one per cent and zero was of no significance. The quarrel between the parties in the Reichstag on this point was really an irrelevance compared to the greater current problems of public finance.

The rates of interest discussed would have been in a 'normal' range of values in a period of stable prices: for a period rapidly approaching hyperinflation, they were irrelevant. The loan had some of the characteristics of the 'Post-War Credits' contribution to the finance of government expenditure in the United Kingdom during the Second World War. It was really a question of increased taxation now to meet a particular financial crisis, the payment for deliveries in kind, with a promise to repay in the future an amount rendered relatively worthless by inflation between payment and repayment. The opposition of the Social Democrats was part of a consistent attitude to the compulsory loan. They were keen to protect those in receipt of small pensions from the indexing of contributions to the loan and probably felt that the interest payments would favour the largest contributors to the 'loan', the better-off members of society. Their view is summarized in the *Hildesheimer Allgemeine Zeitung* report as follows:

> *Darf man wohl als selbstverständlich voraussetzen, dass eine der Geldentwertung entsprechende Grenze nach unten gezogen wird und dass nicht den kleinen Rentnern weder Lasten oder auch nur Schwierigkeiten aufgebürdet werden.*[4]

> (One may take it for granted that a lower limit commensurate with devaluation will be established and that those in receipt of small pensions will not be burdened or even inconvenienced.)

The concern expressed is with the relationship between income and the size of the contribution to be made to the compulsory loan. It is not of concern that the small 'saver' may receive an interest rate on his compulsory savings that will be less than the inflation rate.

Some of the concern about the effects of financing deficits by raising loans concerned the possibility of 'crowding out'. Consider this quotation from an article in *Germania* reprinted in the *Hildesheimer Allgemeine Zeitung*.

> *Die ‹Germania› sagt, die Zwangsanleihe solle deshalb niedrig verzinst werden, um den Anleihezeichnern die Möglichkeit zu lassen, ihrerseits Gelder durch Anleihe aufzunehmen.*[5]

> (The *Germania* [newspaper] says that the compulsory loan is intended to carry a low rate of interest to provide the subscribers with the possibility of raising money themselves by way of loan finance.)

The approach to the capital investment decision implied by this quotation would be recognized today. Too attractive an interest rate on this 'loan' by the public sector would prevent the private sector from financing projects estimated to yield around the same rate or less; that is, they would be crowded out by the more attractive higher return on public sector debt. In this sense, unless the rate was kept particularly low, the 'loan' would be a burden working to the disadvantage of the financial flow of funds generally.

At this time, the *Hildesheimer Allgemeine Zeitung* could see bureaucracy spreading its unwelcome tentacles throughout the Reich. Every attempt to reduce the budget deficit by raising new tax revenue was seen as largely self-defeating as additional legions of civil servants were recruited to collect and administer the new tax. The public sector expanded in size, the deficits remained unreduced!

> *Von Berlin aus hat sich über das ganze Reich eine Bureaukratie ausgebreitet, deren Wirken das Unmögliche zu verewigen scheint. Behörden auf Behörden werden geschaffen, und wenn das so weiter geht, ist wirklich bald fast ein Drittel der männlichen Bevölkerung Deutschlands beamtet. Jede neue Steuer zieht einen neuen Beamtenkörper nach sich, und was mit der einen Hand eingenommen wird, wird mit der anderen an Gehältern ausgeben.*[6]

(A bureacracy has spread out from Berlin over the entire country that appears to perpetuate the impossible. Authorities on authorities are created and, if this carries on, then soon practically one-third of the male population of Germany will be an official. Each new tax brings a new authority with it and what is taken in with one hand will be paid out in salaries with the other.)

It was not only the increasing size of the civil service that was cause for comment in the *Hildesheimer Allgemeine Zeitung* during this period. The uncertainty of the programme they were supposed to implement and policy confusion in Berlin also came in for critical comment in the columns of the paper.

> *Zuverlässige Beamte, die aus ihrer alten bewährten Tätigkeit in neue Aemter versetzt worden sind, wissen nicht mehr ein und aus, weil Schema F. allmählich regiert. Order und Konteorder von Berlin sind an der Tagesordnung. Was heute gilt, wird morgen widerrufen, und dabei ginge alles so ungemein einfach vonstatten, wenn die vielen gegeneinander arbeitenden Instanzen sich ihre Tätigkeit nicht selbst auf Schritt und Tritt erschweren würden. Die Klagen darüber reissen nicht ab.*[7]

(Reliable civil servants who have been transferred from their former jobs in which they were tried and tested do not know the ins and outs because scheme X gradually takes over. Order and counter order from Berlin are the order of the day. What applies today will be revoked tomorrow. Everything would work so amazingly well if the many departments working against each other would not themselves make their work more difficult in every way. The complaints about it are endless.)

Wertbeständige Anleihe des Deutschen Reiches[8]

This guaranteed real value loan of the German Reich was introduced in August 1923 in an attempt to finance the Reich's deficits by borrowing. Previous attempts to raise such loans had failed because the terms contained no protection for the lenders against inflation. In the case of this new type of loan, protection against inflation was provided by the arrangement that,

> Zinsen und Rückzahlung reichsgesetzlich sichergestellt durch die Gesamtheit der deutschen Privatvermögen.... Es haften also für Kapital und Zinsen dieser Anleihe anteilig die gesamte Wirtschaft, Banken, Handel, Industrie, Landwirtschaft sowie jeder, der über steuerpflichtiges Vermögen verfügt.... Um den Zinsenbedarf für eine Anleihe bis zu 500 Millionen Mark Gold zu decken, sieht ein von der Reichsregierung den gesetzgebenden Körperschaften vorgelegter Gesetzentwurf die Ermächtigung für die Reichsregierung vor, Zuschläge zur Vermögenssteuer zu erheben.[9]

> (Interest and repayment are legally secured by the entirety of German private assets.... Responsibility for the capital and interest on this loan is placed in due proportion on the entire economy, banks, trade, industry, agriculture and everyone who has taxable assets.... To cover the interest payments on a loan of up to 500 million Goldmarks, the Government has introduced a bill enabling it to levy supplementary taxation on wealth.)

Many subscribers to this loan must have been impressed by these words offering, in effect, the resources of the entire German economy as backing for the loan. The reference to gold backing is misleading. It was in fact to be indexed to the exchange rate between the Mark and the United States dollar. Repayment in 1935 would be dependent on two factors, the value of the Mark in terms of the dollar on that date and sufficient taxable capacity of the German economy to produce the revenue from the proposed wealth tax to repay the loan. It would be the taxable capacity of the institutions and sectors of the economy mentioned and not their assets *per se* that would be important.

The Goldloan of 1923 was publicly advertised as an indispensable prerequisite for achieving price stability.

> *Die Wertbeständige Anleihe des Deutschen*
> *Reiches und der Reichskanzler Stresemann*
>
> ‹An alle Schichten des Volkes richten wir die Aufforderung, diese deutsche Goldanleihe aufs kräftigste zu unterstützen. Sie soll uns eins der Mittel sein, um die Geldinflation zurückzudämmen, die Verhältnisse geschaffen hat, unter denen weite Volksschichten in

Deutschland kaum noch über die notwendigsten Subsistenzmittel verfügen. Wir richten den dringenden Appell an alle Parteien, an dieser für unser Volk so entscheidend gewordenen Frage mitzuarbeiten. In dieser Frage gibt es keine Parteimeinungen, in dieser Frage ist die positive Mitarbeit jedes, der die Verhältnisse zu bessern vermag, vaterländische Pflichterfüllung, die wir dankbar begrüssen.'

Rede in der Sitzung des Reichstags
am 14. August 1923.[10]

(The indexed loan of the German Reich
and Chancellor of the Reich Stresemann

'We call upon all sections of the population to give the strongest possible support to this German indexed loan. It is one of the measures by which we can curb the inflation that has created the conditions in which large numbers of people in Germany barely possess the most necessary means of subsistence. We make an urgent appeal to all political parties to work with us on this most decisive question for the German people. We give thanks to all those who cooperate in improving these conditions from a sense of patriotic duty.'

Speech in the Reichstag on
14 August 1923.)

The ultimate guarantee of real value over the period of a loan was not access to gold. It was never intended that a 'Goldloan' should be redeemed in gold. In essence, the commitment was to use the legal power to tax to ensure that sufficient Papermarks could be handed over at the end of the 12 years to give the same purchasing power that had been invested at the outset.

The desire to borrow to fund the deficit was not embedded within some overall fiscal intent to reduce aggregate demand. It was simply that no money would have been raised without indexing the loan to the Mark value of the dollar. The futility of fixed-interest lending in a period of hyperinflation was well and truly perceived. The loan was simply an attempt to finance the deficit and not generate any inflation-controlling surplus.

One novel feature illustrates just how far from the thoughts of the government of the Reich was the idea of using budgetary finance to reduce the rate of inflation. This loan could either be used by a subscriber as a store of value that effectively index-linked his savings or as a supply of an index-linked means of payment. Instead of the normal certificate with interest coupons as in the 1915 War Loan example discussed above, 'Goldloan coins' were issued as receipts for the sums lent. For each Mark lent to the government, an additional Mark was created and handed back to the investor, thereby increasing the money supply still further in an already hyperinflationary situation. These terms certainly made the issue more acceptable but the purpose of the loan was certainly not explicitly to withdraw purchasing power from the economy. The aim was to meet the pressing need for a stable value form of payment.

This loan was to be no permanent remedy for the hyperinflation. It was at best a palliative for some aspects of the problem. It was an opportunity for the government to get hold of some of the foreign exchange in private hands. It may have had some effect in reducing the velocity of circulation promising a stable purchasing power linked to the dollar. No remedy that did not address the fundamental problem of the government finances would solve the problem.

The appeal would have been largely political. It was an attempt to show the government doing something positive to bring inflation under control. It was an appeal from the government for unity over the heads of the opposition groups in the Reichstag.

Custom and practice would have led one to expect the normal form of presentation of such a loan to be followed. This would have meant a certificate held by the investor and interest coupons attached that would be surrendered in return for each half-year's interest payment, the form in fact of the 1915 War Loan considered elsewhere in this text. But this 1923 loan was novel in its presentation and marked a significant departure from previous practice.

Instead of a certificate, notes were issued in various denominations to the value of the investment. These '*Anleihstücke*' or loan notes were in denominations such that 4.20 Marks = US$ 1, the same rate that was to be set for the November Rentenmark-based stabilization policy. These loan notes could either be saved or spent. The effect on aggregate demand would then depend on the decision whether to save or spend. This gives an insight into the economic thinking behind the form of the loan. The intention was to increase the supply of legal tender or '*Zahlungsmittel*' in the hands of the public that was inflation protected. It was not to drain off purchasing power from the private sector. It had, therefore, no part to play in any concept of controlling an inflationary situation by restricting the growth of the money supply. The comment in the *Hildesheimer Allgemeine Zeitung* on this aspect of the loan is clear enough although it is presented as information without being set in any explanatory theoretical context.

> Sie [die Goldanleihe] ist brauchbar sowohl als Zahlungsmittel, wie als Mittel zur Werterhaltung. Es ist gelungen, sie auf Parität mit dem Dollar zu halten. Die Qualität der Goldanleihe ist in diesen Tagen weiter gesichert worden. Sie hat eine Sachwertfundierung

durch die Bestimmung erhalten, dass jeder Besitzer die Goldanleihe in Rentenmark umtauschen kann. Da die Rentenmark durch eine erststellige hochgedeckte Hypothek auf das deutsche Wirtschaftsvermögen gesichert ist, ist damit auch die Goldanleihe auf Goldwerten fundiert. Im Verkehr sieht die Goldanleihe zurzeit einigermassen kompliziert aus; denn es gibt als Zahlungsmittel:

(a) die endgültigen Goldanleihescheine in Stücken von 1 Dollar aufwärts, und
(b) die Zwischenscheine in Stücken von 1 / 10 Dollar aufwärts,
(c) das auf Goldanleihe fundierte werbeständige Notgeld in Abschnitten von 1 / 10 bis zu 2 Dollars. Dieses Notgeld ist als Teil der Goldanleihe anzusehen und nur eine technisch bedingte vorübergehende Erscheinung.[11]

(It [the Goldloan] may be used both as a means of payment and as a means of preserving value. We have been successful in maintaining its parity with the dollar. The quality of the Goldloan has been further secured in recent days. Its intrinsic value has been strengthened by allowing all holders to change the Goldloan into Rentenmarks. As the Rentenmark is secured by a first-rate well-covered mortgage on the assets of the German economy, the Goldloan is thus also based on gold values. In its circulation the Goldloan appears at the moment to be somewhat complicated; for there are the following methods of payment:

(a) the definitive Goldloan notes in values of 1 dollar upwards,
(b) intermediate notes of 1/10th of a dollar upwards,
(c) the inflation-protected emergency money based on the Goldloan in values of from 1/10th to 2 dollars. This emergency money is to be regarded as part of the Goldloan and as a temporary phenomenon caused by technical circumstances.)

The *Hildesheimer Allgemeine Zeitung* is impressed with the improved backing for the loan derived from its direct link to the Rentenmark, the latter seen as having a real or intrinsic value backing. There is no understanding here of the link between the maintenance of the real value of a currency over time and restrictions on its rate of growth. Reading the newspaper advertisements for the new loan, the loan notes are proposed in multiples upwards from 4.20 Marks to 4200 Marks with the expressly stated provision that there would be no intermediate denominations, '*Zwichenscheine sind nicht vorgesehen*': 'Notes of intermediate value are not planned'. Yet, as the above quotation from the *Hildesheimer Allgemeine Zeitung* makes clear, such loan notes of intermediate value were introduced, thus increasing the likely inflationary impact of the form of the loan chosen.

Both war-time and peace-time expenditure by governments have been financed by raising loans. The most general form has been one in which

Figure 6.3 The inflation-protected loan of the German Reich, August 1923[12]

the receipt for the loan registered in the name of the subscriber attracts interest payments periodically in fulfilment of the obligations of the government under the terms and conditions of the issue. The receipt itself is not normally directly of use as a means of payment. If one wishes to use the security itself, it is normally necessary to sell it on the secondary market for that type of asset at whatever the prevailing market price might be from time to time. In Germany during and after the First World War, there were two notable exceptions to this. One major exception was the *Wertbeständige Anleihe* (Value Protected Loan)

Figure 6.4 The inflation-protected loan of the German Reich, August 1923[13]

issued in 1923 and discussed above. The other notable exception to the normal practice was the way in which the *Darlehenskassen* (State Loan Offices) operated. They took in funds from subscribers to loans including specific War Loans to assist in the financing of the First World War. The receipts they issued were nominal value notes denominated in Marks. They could then be used as a store of value, losing value rapidly as the inflation rate increased or, more effectively, as a means of payment. One of these 'receipts' or *Darlehnskassenschein* is illustrated in Figure 6.5.

The effects of this form of finance were predictable. For each Mark lent to the government in this fashion, another was created. Purchasing power was created for the government at no loss in purchasing power to the subscriber. Certainly, the avowed aim of these issues was to ensure an adequate supply of a suitable payments medium but it could only be achieved by increasing the rate of inflation as total expenditure rose. The very essence of non-inflationary lending to governments to finance war expenditure is that purchasing power transferred from the private sector is not replaced by a device such as that used in these examples.

Figure 6.5 Five-Mark *Darlehnskassenschein* note, Berlin 1917

The way in which the *Darlehnskassen* operated is described by Heinz Pentzlin in his work on the life of Hjalmar Schacht.[14]

> *Um den Kreditbedarf der Wirtschaft, der sich mit der Umstellung auf Kriegswirtschaft ergab, leichter zu decken, wurden von der Reichsbank kontrollierte Darlehenskassen geschaffen, die Darlehen gewährten und Darlehenskassenscheine ausgaben, die als Zahlungsmittel benutzt werden konnten, also ein zusätzliches Geld darstellen. Die Darlehenskassen beliehen auch Kriegsanleihen, so dass die Zeichner dieser Anleihen für den grössten Betrag, den sie für die Anleihe einzahlten, wieder ein Zahlungsmittel zurückhielten.*

(In order to more easily meet the credit needs of the economy arising from the changeover to a war economy, the Reichsbank established and controlled State Loan Offices. These gave loans (to the state) and issued State Loan Office Notes that could be used as a form of payment and thus constitute an additional form of money. They lent money in the form of War Loans in such a way that the subscribers to these loans received back a form of payment for the largest sum that they had paid in.)

City finance

The framework for city budgets in Germany was set by the centrally determined policy of the Reich government in Berlin. As the government in Berlin struggled to balance its own budget, so it diverted tax revenues away from the cities into the central Exchequer and transferred responsibility for certain classes of expenditure down to the cities. There were no extra grants-in-aid for this transferred expenditure (*Reichsbesoldungszuschüsse*) nor a legal framework that allowed the local authorities to raise additional finance. For the city of Hildesheim, these extra burdens in June and July 1923 raised the deficit faced by the council from 151 million to 3.5 thousand million Marks. As the editorial comment in the *Hildesheimer Allgemeine Zeitung* summed up the situation,

> *Als wir vor vier Wochen im Finanzausschuss in die Etatberatungen eintraten, schloss der Haushaltsplan mit einem durch Steuern zu deckenden Fehlbetrag von 151 Millionen ab. Innerhalb dieser vier Wochen ist dieser Fehlbetrag . . . infolge der durch die Markentwertung notwendig gewordenen Gehalts- und Lohnerhöhungen auf sage und schreibe 3.5 Milliarden angewachsen.*[15]

> (Four weeks ago when we began to consider the budget in the finance committee, we planned for a deficit of 151 million Marks to be recovered by taxation. In these four weeks, the deficit has risen, as a result of increases in salaries and wages necessitated by the depreciation of the Mark, to an unbelievable 3.5 thousand million Marks.)

Strategies at the local level to maintain real expenditure

The City of Hildesheim faced a budget deficit of some 3.5 thousand million Marks in July 1923. What strategies were recommended in the Oberbürgermeister's address to the Council to cope with this shortfall? Particular attention would have to be given to the strengths of the various claims on city funds and the political acceptability of various proposals to the electorate. The equivalent of 'rate-payers candidates' were coming to the fore in Hildesheim in July 1923. As the local newspaper headlined in its edition of Thursday, 12 July 1923: '*44 Bürgervorsteher sollen im November gewählt werden*' ('44 representatives are to be elected in November'). Any proposals would have to be clearly framed within narrowing political constraints.

One of the consequences of the hyperinflation was the fall in the real resources commanded by the City budget. This was explicitly referred to by the Oberbürgermeister in his budget speech.

> *Der Haushaltsplan ergibt, wie aus dem Nachtrag zu ersehen ist, eine Gesamtausgabe von 11.7 Milliarden gegen 78 Millionen im Vorjahre, d. h. eine Steigerung auf das 150 fache, während die Reichs-Indexziffer für die Lebenshaltung vom Juni 1922 von 38 bis auf 7650 im Juni 1923, also auf das 200 fache geklettert ist. Sie erkennen daraus schon, dass wir uns stark eingeschränkt haben.*[16]

(The budget plan shows in the appendix total expenditure of 11.7 thousand million Marks compared to 78 million the previous year, i.e. an increase of 150 fold, whereas the Reich Cost of Living Index from June 1922 to June 1923 rose from 38 to 7650, a 200-fold increase. You will realize from this that we have made severe cutbacks.)

The very inflation itself makes precise intertemporal comparisons difficult. The general point is, however, sufficiently well made. A 150-fold increase in nominal expenditure represented a substantial fall in real terms when faced with a 200-fold rise in the general level of prices. With such a reduction in real expenditure was associated a fall in the level of employment. No wonder that local authorities in these situations felt compelled to make large and frequent issues of emergency money to fill the 'gap in the housekeeping'.

With such rapidly rising prices, the very basis of such comparisons is called into question as well as the very meaning of the budget figures presented to the council. The actual figures described the budget position often for no more than a brief interval of time: '*Alles ist ständig im Fluss, und die Zahlen verändern sich von Woche zu Woche, ja von Tag zu Tag*' ('Everything is constantly changing and the figures change from week to week, indeed from day to day').[17] The editorial comment on the figures presented to council was even more pessimistic: '*die Zahlen des Etats ändern sich ... fast stündlich*' ('the figures in the budget are changing practically hourly').[18]

One major time-honoured device for a city or country faced with a budget deficit is, of course, to reduce expenditure. For Hildesheim to reduce expenditure in 1923 would simply have been to reinforce the real losses already caused by the hyperinflation. However, the Oberbürgermeister felt obliged to review the city's expenditure commitments and to consider if a larger surplus could be generated from its trading operations.

There was the commiment to youth and sport. The very future of the race depended on sport! The speech stresses, '*die hohe Bedeutung, die der Stählung und geistigen Förderung unseres heranwachsenden Ges-*

chlechts zukommt' ('the great importance attached to the physical toughening and spiritual development of the rising generation').[19] Besides, the 12 million Marks devoted to this head of expenditure represented only 4.36×10^{-7} per cent of the then-current deficit! Not much of an inroad into the deficit by reducing expenditure on sport was possible!

A popular theme in our own day that the public sector is inefficient and employs too many people very well paid for doing very little was sufficiently strongly held in Hildesheim in 1923 for the Oberbürgermeister to devote some time to detailing attempts to ensure that Hildesheim possessed a slimmed-down, cost-effective administration. Further reductions should be made if possible but don't expect 'time and motion' study to produce savings that would be likely to make a significant contribution to the deficit considering that we have always looked for cost-effectiveness from our employees.

> *Wir haben seit Jahren in der Verwaltung abgebaut und seit 1918 über 10 Proz. unserer Beamten und Angestellten entlassen, obgleich wir durch die Reichsgesetze in erheblichen Masse mit neuer Arbeit belastet worden sind.... Obgleich unsere Beamten fast ständig Ueberstunden leisten müssen, sind wir trotzdem nochmals in eine erneute Prüfung der Frage, ob noch Ersparnisse in der Verwaltung gemacht werden können, eingetreten. Seit Monaten ist ein Bureaurevisor tätig, der eingehend in allen Bureaus nachprüft, ob überflüssige nicht mehr zeitgemässe Arbeiten geleistet werden, ob Beamte noch entlassen werden können.... Auch eine Vereinfachung unseres Rechnungs- und Kontrollwesens führen wir zurzeit durch.*[20]

(For years we have been reducing the size of the administration and since 1918 we have shed more than 10 per cent of our officers and employees, despite the increased work load as a result of new laws passed by the Reich government.... Although our officers are almost permanently on overtime we have nevertheless started reviewing the position again to see whether cutbacks can be made in the administration. An inspector has been busy for months checking in all offices thoroughly for superfluous and no longer appropriate work and seeing if still more officers can be dismissed. At the moment we are also simplifying our payments and control systems.)

What about cutting welfare payments? Is social security expenditure too high? Are we really getting value for money? These questions, common in our own day, were asked in Hildesheim in 1923. In Hildesheim in 1923, poverty was widespread and absolute in many cases. A growing number could not afford to bury their dead, pay hospital bills, buy milk for their families or coal for winter heating. As the Oberbürgermeister reported,

LOANS AND PUBLIC SECTOR FINANCE

Die Zahl derer, die die Beerdigungskosten nicht mehr aufbringen, die Kosten im Krankenhause nicht mehr tragen, die die teure Milch oder die Kohlen für den Winter nicht mehr einkaufen können, wächst von Tag zu Tag, in immer mehr Fällen ist ein Eintreten der Stadtverwaltung nötig.[21]

(The number of those who cannot afford funeral costs, who cannot meet hospital costs, who can no longer afford the expensive milk nor buy coal for the winter is growing daily, necessitating municipal assistance in an increasing number of cases.)

Not much scope for reducing expenditure in this direction!

There was a qualified success to report in the provision of council homes for the homeless (*Sozialwohnungen für die Wohnungslosen*). A steady rise in the number of completed homes from 53 in 1921, 65 in 1922 to 47 in the first half of 1923. The problem here was the sharp rise in demand for such accommodation. There were 624 marriages in Hildesheim in 1922 compared to an average of 350 since the end of the war. Did this mean that there had been some increase in prosperity since 1918?

We find yet another problem that is common in some areas in our own time in debates about the provision of council housing, the supply of single-person accommodation to free larger homes for families.

Wir werden weiter dazu überheben, noch einige Rentnern oder Damenheime zu schaffen, in denen Einzelpersonen, die zurzeit noch übergrosse Wohnungen inne haben und deren Mietausgabe auch nicht mit ihren Einkommensverhältnissen mehr in Einklang steht, untergebracht werden können. Auf diese Weise, hoffen wir noch manche Wohnung für die Wohnungslosen frei machen zu können.[22]

(We will build a few homes for pensioners or ladies to accommodate single people who are living in homes at the present time that are too large and whose rents are no longer in line with their incomes. In this way, we hope to free several houses and make them available for the homeless.)

A cost-effective strategy within the stringent constraints of the time designed to make as effective a contribution to the housing problem as possible but certainly not a significant contribution to the overall deficit.

The income from municipal enterprises was reckoned in millions but the deficit was in thousands of millions. Useful contributions to the City's income could be expected from the municipal electricity works, 300 million, forestry 200 million, gasworks 150 million, and 35 million from the waterworks. Nothing could be expected from the municipal abattoir, the milk marketing activities of the city and the municipal pawnshop.

The fall in real incomes caused a drop of 50 per cent in the number of animals slaughtered to supply the demand for meat: *'der Schlachthof ist bei dem Rückgang der Zahl der Schlachtungen, die etwa auf die Hälfte der Friedenszeit gefallen ist'* ('the slaughterhouse is affected by the reduction in throughput to about 50 per cent of the peace-time level').[23] No decent surplus could for welfare reasons be generated by the City's milk marketing. At best, only a small contribution towards administrative expenses could be expected: *'Alle übrigen Gewinne werden zur Verbilligung der Milch für Kinder, Säuglinge und Kranke dem Wohlfahrtsamt überwiesen'* ('All remaining earnings will be used to reduce the price of milk supplied to children, babies and the sick, and transferred for this purpose to the welfare office').[24] And as for the municipal pawnshop! It also could only decently be expected to cover its administrative costs: *'in gleicher Weise soll auch das Leihhaus keine Ueberschüsse bringen. Es trägt sich aber jetzt selbst'* ('In the same way, the pawnshop will produce no surplus. It now covers its own costs').[25]

A survey of welfare constraints, commitments to the distressed of the city and the use of efficiency audits to make possible savings led to only one possible conclusion: the City of Hildesheim, in common with others throughout Germany in 1923, could not balance its budget. Towards the end of his speech came his suggestion to meet the deficit, a suggestion he must have known could not be accepted or implemented. The proposal was that all council expenditure and income be indexed monthly to the declining value of the Mark. From rejecting what he had discussed previously, he passed to his indexing of all payments proposal.

> *Allein diese kleinen Ersparnisse, die wir noch erzielen können und natürlich erzielen müssen, können uns nicht retten.... Helfen kann uns nur eine starke Erhöhung der Einnahmen, die wir bisher im Interesse unserer Bürgerschaft ... nicht der Geldentwertung entsprechend durchgeführt haben oder infolge des Widerstandes in Bürgerschaft nicht durchführen konnten.... Bei der schnell fortschreitenden Geldentwertung müssen wir auch alle Einnahmen ... der Geldentwertung automatisch anpassen.... Wir müssen monatlich fliessende der Geldentwertung sich anpassende Steuern haben.*[26]

(Yet these small savings, which can and of course must be made, cannot save us. The only thing that can help us is a large increase in income, which in the interests of our citizens we have so far not exacted in line with the depreciation in the value of the money, or could not exact because of the opposition of the citizens. With rapidly increasing depreciation in the value of money we must also ... automatically adjust all income in line with the depreciation. We must have taxes which change monthly or adjust to the depreciation.)

Interest groups would oppose such a proposition. In general, such increases in taxation would be seen as not so much a remedy but more of an additional burden on an already impoverished citizenry. Those using municipal services would have a direct interest in opposing increased charges for supplies of gas, electricity and water.

Such linkage would form part of the Reich government's stabilization policy later in 1923. It was not to happen in Hildesheim in July of that year. The attitude of Council to the Oberbürgermeister's proposal is neatly encapsulated in a sentence of editorial comment on the proceedings.

> *Nur die Hundesteuer wurde verdoppelt, die Mehreinnahme von 40 Millionen Mark wird aber möglicherweise schon im Verlauf der fünfstündigen Sitzung durch die sprunghaft Geldentwertung ausgeglichen sein.*[27]

(Only the charge for dog licences was doubled. However, the increased 40 million Marks may very well be cancelled out even in the course of the five-hour meeting by the galloping depreciation of money.)

The restoration of financial stability to Hildesheim would not lie in these proposals for index-linked taxation but would begin four months later with the currency reforms to be introduced nationwide in November 1923.

Borrowing in normal times may be a significant way of raising finance to support local expenditure by postponing the burden of the expenditure to the future. In a hyperinflationary situation, this is not possible at any level of government, central or local.

The *Hildesheimer Allgemeine Zeitung* of 12 July 1923 could headline that: '*Fast alle Schulden der Stadt getilgt*' ('Practically all the City's Debts Paid Off'). A debt-free city during a period of hyperinflation does not indicate new borrowing possibilities in the normal way; it simply means that existing debts were easily paid off in devalued paper money. New loans would of course be heavily undersubscribed.

Yet there was a way for cities to borrow and thus to acquire the use of real resources at zero interest charge and zero capital repayment obligation. This was simply to print their own Emergency Money (*Notgeld*). Thus, positive feedback forces were reinforced. An apparent shortage of money to meet the ever-rising price level led to cities printing their own monies and hence driving the price level yet higher still.

Notes

1. *Hildesheimer Allgemeine Zeitung*, Thursday, 26 January 1922. *Zwangsanleihe von 40 Papiermilliarden*: Compulsory Loan of 40 Thousand Million Papermarks.
2. Heinz Pentzlin, *Hjalmar Schacht, Leben und Wirken einer umstrittenen Personlichkeit* (Ullstein Books 1980), p. 33.
3. *Hildesheimer Allgemeine Zeitung*, Thursday, 26 January 1992. *Zwangsanleihe von 40 Papiermilliarden*: Compulsory Loan of 40 Thousand Million Papermarks.
4. Ibid.
5. Ibid.
6. Ibid.
7. Ibid.
8. *Wertbeständig* translates as 'of fixed value', 'lasting in value' or 'stable'. A '*wertbeständige Anleihe*' is thus a loan, the purchasing power of which will be maintained so that the lender suffers no real loss due to inflation. The protection will be in the form of some indexing. In this case, as in so many others at this time, protection took the form of indexing the repayment to the change in the exchange rate between the Mark and the dollar over a stated period of time. In the case of this loan, the relevant period was between the issue of the loan in 1923 and its redemption in 1935.
9. *Hildesheimer Allgemeine Zeitung*, Tuesday, 14 August 1923. *Wertbeständige Anleihe des Deutschen Reiches*: Inflation Protected Loan of the Reich.
10. *Cuxhavener Zeitung*, Friday, 24 August 1923.
11. *Hildesheimer Allgemeine Zeitung*, 2 November 1923, *Unser tägliches Geld*: Our daily money.
12. *Hildesheimer Allgemeine Zeitung*, 13 August 1923.
13. Ibid.
14. Pentzlin Heinz, *Hjalmar Schacht, Leben und Wirken einer umstrittenen Persönlichkeit* (Ullstein Books 1980), p. 33.
15. *Hildesheimer Allgemeine Zeitung*, 12 July 1923.
16. Ibid. Extract from the Oberbürgermeister's speech to Council.
17. Ibid. Extract from the Oberbürgermeister's speech to Council.
18. Ibid. Editorial comment on the Oberbürgermeister's speech.
19. Ibid. Oberbürgermeister's speech.
20. Ibid.
21. Ibid.
22. Ibid.
23. Ibid.
24. Ibid.
25. Ibid.
26. Ibid.
27. Ibid. Editorial comment.

CHAPTER SEVEN

Emergency Money – Notgeld

Did the rapidly expanding note issues primarily cause the hyperinflation in Germany during these years? Did not perhaps other factors force monetary expansion in a situation where possible alternative non-inflationary financing possibilities were not available as realistic policy choices? On this view, the deeper political, social and economic problems of Germany were the more fundamental causes of inflation with monetary expansion allowing them to be expressed in price increases. This view was certainly commonly held at the time.

On 22 June 1922, Hugo Stinnes the industrialist was invited by the Foreign Minister, Walther Rathenau, to express a view on aspects of the reparations problem. It was Stinnes' expressed view that the monetary expansion after 1918 was the only policy in the circumstances that would permit some four million soldiers to find work on demobilization. Inflation would be the unavoidable concomitant of providing the population with work. Stinnes saw inflation as the means of preserving the economic and political life of the nation hemmed in by military occupation, internal political difficulties and the failure of international trade to quickly re-establish itself after 1918.[1]

Rudolf Havenstein, Schacht's immediate predecessor at the Reichsbank, took essentially the same line in an address to the Executive Committee of the Reichsbank on 25 August 1923. In his opinion, the fundamental immediate cause of the inflation was the growth of paper money caused by the discounting of Reich Treasury bills to cover the deficits arising from reparations payments, and the failure to generate sufficient income from taxation to meet the ordinary expenditure commitments of the Reich. The Reichsbank, according to Havenstein, simply could not refuse to discount Treasury bills as long as no other means existed to finance its deficit. On justification such as this, the note issue rose as the direct consequence of being the only means available to finance the Reich's expenditure.[2]

These views of the causes of hyperinflation were supported in a retrospective analysis by Carl-Ludwig Holtfrerich.[3] In summary, he argues that the depreciation of the currency was not directly determined by the money supply but was certainly accommodated by money supply changes.

Langfristig wurde die Entwicklung des Entwertungsprozesses von

> *der Entwicklung der Geldmenge zwar nicht unmittelbar determiniert, aber auf jeden Fall ermöglicht.*[4]

(The long-term process of currency depreciation was not directly caused by trends in the money supply but was certainly made possible by them.)

The view is very much that price stabilization was not only not possible at this time but arguably not even desirable because of the costs it would impose in other directions. The weakness of the Reich in relation to the provinces, new levels of expenditure on social service provision after 1918, the burden of reparations and the need to facilitate mobilization in 1914 and demobilization in 1919 were factors that contributed to large Reich budgetary deficits. In such a situation,

> *eine Stabilisierung des Geldwertes nicht nur kaum durchsetzbar, sondern auch kaum nützlich gewesen wäre.*[5]

(A stabilization of money values would not only have been difficult to implement but also of little use.)

Havenstein and Stinnes would not have disagreed with this analysis.

Emergency Money

The relationship between the money supply and the total expenditure thereby financed may be examined using the equation below:

$$MV = Y$$

where M = money supply, V = velocity of circulation or the average frequency per period of time that each unit of the money supply is used, and Y = total expenditure

As long as V remains constant, there will be a constant proportional relationship between increases in M and increases in Y. As the 'flight from money' that is characteristic of hyperinflation takes place, this is reflected in an increase in the velocity of circulation. The actual number of transactions may well fall as, for example, during the widespread strike by the Germans against the French and Belgian Occupation of the Ruhr in 1923. Output falling on the supply side, and an increased demand for goods mirroring the flight from money on the demand side, both drive up the general level of prices. The result is that the ratio of the price level to the money supply ($\Delta P/\Delta M$) rises at an increasingly rapid rate.[6]

So much may be deduced by an observer from outside studying time series data on these variables. The process may, however, be perceived quite differently by those caught up in the process. They may be convinced that money is in short supply as evidenced by their own manifest inability to obtain enough currency to maintain previous real consumption levels. The rapid rise in the velocity of circulation creates a world in which insufficient money is available to enable everyone to pay the high prices or so is the picture perceived from within the economy by large numbers of those affected by the process.

Thus, a positive feedback mechanism may be created as additional monies are printed to alleviate the perceived shortage. The Notgeld issues in Germany, especially those in 1923, may be viewed in this way. How could the note issue cause inflation if people are aware of a shortage of money and not an excess? That there was a widespread feeling that this was so is clear from the press quotations considered elsewhere. One of the clearest statements of this view is the following:

> *Die letzte Rede Poincarés hat gezeigt, dass dieser noch immer an der Auffassung festhält, die Entwertung der deutschen Mark sei durch die Vermehrung der deutschen papieren Zahlungsmittel verursacht worden. Wir wissen aber längst, dass der innere Zusammenhang umgekehrt liegt. Durch die Entwertung der Mark, infolge übermässiger Reparationszahlungen, und da kein entsprechender Produktionsüberschuss in der deutschen Wirtschaft gegenüberstand, ist Vermehrung der Papiernoten notwendig geworden.*[7]
>
> (Poincaré's last speech showed that he is still convinced that the devaluation of the Mark was caused by the increase in German paper money. But we have known for a long time that the real connection is the other way around. The devaluation of the Mark as a result of excessive reparations payments, without a corresponding production surplus in the German economy, necessitated an increase in paper notes.)

The need for more money to meet the high prices was enthusiastically responded to in Germany by recourse to large issues of Notgeld or Emergency Money. It was a serious development in that it meant that Reichsbank control over the money supply virtually ended. One source identifies over 4 thousand points of issue of Emergency Money in Germany issuing an estimated nominal value totalling one trilliard Marks (10^{21}). Such vast issues played a major role in the final destruction of the Mark in 1923.[8]

The more rapidly the price level rose, the more apparent the shortage of money became and the greater the nominal value of the notes issued by individuals, companies and the various levels of local and regional government. No longer were Notgeld issues confined to small change units of a few pfennigs. This was the era of the increasingly large denomination notes.

Figure 7.1 Example of a small value note issued by a bookseller as a remedy for the shortage of small change in Germany

Figure 7.2 Notes that made a significant contribution to inflation: a three-million Mark note issued in 1923 by a lignite mining group. As the note makes clear, these were issued with the express permission of the government

The origins of Notgeld

A shortage of small change was particularly noticeable in Berlin immediately after the outbreak of war in 1914. Shops were particularly affected. The shortages arose for a number of reasons. Coins containing precious metals had been withdrawn from circulation to prevent them falling into the hands of the enemy. Many of those not withdrawn from circulation had been hoarded. Various substitutes were used to replace the withdrawn or hoarded gold and silver coins.

Shops could acknowledge debts to customers by signing a bit of paper together with the official stamp. On a subsequent visit, the signed bit of paper could be handed over by the customer as cash. As they were normally a form of bearer security, the bits of paper could also be used to settle debts between third parties. The normal value would be for a few pfennigs at most and no great inflationary consequences would be expected from this substitution of paper for metal coins.

The cities organized the minting of base metal replacements for the now vanished precious metal coins. Issues of base metal War Money (*Kriegsgeld*), City Money (*Stadtgeld*) and Emergency Money (*Notgeld*) became commonplace.[9]

No great significance was apparent at this stage in the Notgeld issues. They were merely substitute paper and base metal currency to replace precious metals needed for the war effort. The shortage of money was obvious as coins had been withdrawn from circulation.

The scene was being set, however, for a significant contribution from Notgeld to the inflationary spiral in the following years. Cities, companies and individuals had had the experience of printing and minting their own monies to remedy the lack of notes and coins from the Reichsbank. A process of 'monetary disintegration' was at work. With the integration of regions into a cohesive nation state, monetary control normally passes into progressively fewer hands culminating in the establishment of one central bank with the monopoly over the creation of notes and coins. Allowing the process to work in reverse was to prove disastrous after 1918.

Another 'shortage of money' was noticed after 1918! During hyperinflation, the price level, whether measured by the decline in the external value of the currency as was most frequently the case in Germany at this time or by a general price index, rose at a faster rate than the money supply. This was achieved as a consequence of a rapidly increasing velocity of circulation (*Geldumlaufgeschwindigkeit*). This was often recorded by contemporary observers such as Friedrich C.A. Lange, Mayor of Berlin as a rush into real assets (*Flucht in die Sachwerte*).

This was the physically obvious counterpart to a decline in the demand for money to hold.[10]

There are a number of ways in which an increase in the velocity of circulation may be identified. A commonly found way of doing this in newspaper reports in Germany in the 1920s was to deflate the nominal money supply either by using exchange rates or price indices as deflators. This effectively meant measuring real as opposed to nominal changes in the money supply. An example of this sort of analysis is to be found in the *Cuxhavener Zeitung*.

Die Währungsreform

... *Während im Frieden der Geldumlauf rund 5 Milliarden betrug, stellt sich der heutige Papiergeldumlauf in Gold umgerechnet auf etwa 100 bis 150 Millionen Mark. Dass die deutsche Wirtschaft mit diesem minimalen Betrag heute auskommt, ist darauf zurückzuführen, dass der Umlauf im schnellen Tempo vollzieht.*[11]

(Currency Reform

... Whereas in peace time the money in circulation amounted to about 5 thousand million Marks, paper money in circulation today amounts to 100 to 150 million Goldmarks. That the German economy manages today with this small amount is explained by the speed of the circulation of money.)

The reference to calculating the change in the real money supply in gold means that exchange rate data was used for this particular calculation. Such an analysis can lead to confusing conclusions. The use of such words as 'minimal amount' (*minimalen Betrag*) and noting that 150 million is only three per cent of five thousand million might well convince the reader that there really was a money shortage and that, confusing real and nominal magnitudes, the money supply was not responsible for the inflation he was experiencing.

A better picture of inflationary pressures would have been conveyed if the article had given the money supply data in nominal terms. The 100 million Goldmarks would convert to 10^{20} Papermarks when multiplied by the conversion rate to be used in the November 1923 stabilization of the Mark.[12] This would have given a more dramatic impression of the flow of paper needed to finance the Reich deficits. A certain sophistication would be required of the non-specialist reader to understand that an increase in the velocity of circulation is required if the price level rises by a higher percentage than the supply of money. The average citizen might still be left wondering how the money supply could shrink in real terms and still be the cause of hyperinflation!

The individual would certainly have regarded himself as short of money! The failure of daily indexing of his income would have been sufficient to achieve this!

Local authorities would have felt themselves short of money for a number of reasons. Just as for the individual, a failure of local authority income to rise in line with inflation would have given them a feeling of being unable to buy as much in real terms as previously had been possible because they did not have enough money, that is, money was in short supply. The poverty in Germany at this time suggests a low real tax base and the prospect therefore of limits on increasing yields by increasing tax rates.

The debate in Hildesheim over the budget in July 1923 has been discussed in some detail (see pp. 108–14). Other cities and towns were in much the same position for the same reasons. Additional examples of pressures on civic budgets are quoted below from the diary of Friedrich Lange and relate to the capital of the Reich, Berlin. Faced with these pressures, the temptation to issue Notgeld must have been irresistible if only to keep some semblance of civic activity going in the face of overwhelming financial difficulties. Lange's diary notes some of the increased financial burden falling on Berlin during the years 1922 and 1923. On 12 July 1922, he wrote that,

> Ein Opfer der Inflation ist die Emilie-Rudolf-Mosse-Stiftung geworden, Erziehungsheim für Knaben und Mädchen in Wilmersdorf, deren Angebot, das umfangreiche Heim nebst Zubehör der Stadt zu 'schenken', vom Magistrat angenommen worden ist. Die Stadt hat beschlossen, die Anstalt mit ihrer merkwürdig lieblosen Einrichtung in ein Haus der Jugend umzuwandeln und unter dem Namen Emilie-Ruldolf-Mosse-Heim weiterzubetreiben.

> (The Emilie-Rudolf-Mosse Foundation, a home for boys and girls in Wilmersdorf, has become a victim of inflation. The city council has accepted the foundation's offer to 'donate' this extensive home with all its fixtures and fittings to the city and has decided to convert the strangely inhospitable establishment into a meeting house for young people, renaming it the Emilie-Rudolf-Mosse Home.)

Expenditure commitments were not only rising in areas of welfare but also to maintain the infrastructure provision of the city. On 10 September 1923, he wrote that,

> Die Wirtschaftsführung der Berliner Strassenbahn wird dadurch erschwert, dass sie im Gegensatz zu anderen Städten gezwungen ist, infolge der scharfen Konkurrenz mit den anderen Verkehrsunternehmungen ständig mit entwerteten Tarifen zu fahren. In den letzten Wochen hat sich die wirtschaftliche Krise bei der Strassenbahn

gesteigert. Sie fuhr zuletzt mit einem Fehlbetrag von 90 Milliarden Mark, so dass der Magistrat sofort handeln musste. Er legte vorgestern im Einvernehmen mit der Verkehrsdeputation den Betrieb still, nahm die erforderlichen Kündigungen von Angestellten und Arbeitern vor und gründete eine Berliner Strassenbahn-Betriebs-GmbH., die heute den Betrieb wieder begonnen hat.

(In contrast to other cities, the management of the Berlin trams has been handicapped by the fact that it is constantly forced to operate with reduced fares because of competition from other transport companies. The financial crisis of the trams has worsened over recent weeks, to the tune in the end of a 90 thousand million Mark operating loss, so that the council had to take immediate action. The day before yesterday, in agreement with staff representatives, it closed operations down, gave the necessary notices to its staff and workers, and formed the Berlin Tramway Operating Company Ltd., which re-started services today.)

City deficits were already large. Taking on a children's home and municipalizing loss-making tramway services merely added to an already substantial problem. Pressures to find alternative sources of finance were increasing continuously. The solution for most German cities was to print their own notes!

Recognition of the falling value of money sometimes gave rise to expressions of ironic humour. An example of this is to be found on the 500,000 Mark note issued in August 1923 by an industrial group of companies in Regis-Breitingen.

The inscription on the note recognizes one of the consequences of hyperinflation.

Sollt' ein Brikett noch teurer sein
Steck' mich ruhig in' Ofen rein!

Ohne Fleiss kein Preis

(If the price of coal gets higher,
Go and stick me in the fire!

No Pain, No Gain.)

If the price of coal continues to rise, the note informs us that the 500,000 Mark note would have greater value as fuel than as a note used as a form of payment.

The note also illustrates a not infrequently found community of interest between a city and its business community. A grouping of local companies issued the notes as a remedy for their own cash shortage and they were then accepted by the local council in settlement of debts thereby enhancing its own cash flow.

> Sollt' ein Brikett noch teurer sein
> Steck' ruhig mich in' Ofen rein!
>
> **500000 Mark**
>
> Regis-Breitingener Industrie:
> Deutsche Erdöl-Aktiengesellschaft — Brikett, Öle ~,
> Vereinigte Flanschenfabriken und Stanzwerke A.-G.,
> Regiser Glaswerk A.-G. — i. E. ~,
> Mühlen und Sodafabrik, Elektrotechnische Fabrik
> und Installationen Semmler & Ahnert.
>
> Ohne Fleiß kein Preis.

Figure 7.3   A 500,000 Mark note

The idea that a note may be worth more in direct use as fuel than as a medium of exchange is explored by Erich Maria Remarque.

> *Zum Glück brennt ein kleines Feuer im Ofen. Ich rolle einen Zehnmarkschein zusammen, halte ihn in die Glut und zünde mir damit die Zigarre an.... Ich werfe den Rest des Zehnmarkscheins in den Ofen.*[13]

(Luckily a small fire is burning in the oven. I roll up a ten Mark note, stick it into the flame and light a cigar with it.... I throw the remains of the ten Mark note into the oven.)

Remarque's hero is portrayed as having a certain cynicism towards events. In his fictional account of aspects of the inflation based on his real experiences of having lived through the process, he reflects the tone of some of the contemporary newspaper reports of the day. Consider the following report on the introduction of the million Mark note.

Die Millionen-Note

Die Geldmaschine wirft nun ihren neuesten Trumpf auf den Tisch:

> *der Millionenschein ist auf dem Marsch. Als kleiner Vorläufer kommt die Halbmillionennote am Freitag heraus. Es sind hübsche runde Summen. Glatte Einzahlen mit entsprechenden Nullenbehang. Man wird die neuen Erzeugnisse staatlicher Drucktechnik kaum sonderlich bestaunen oder als einzigartige Phänomena betrachten. Sie sind nur neue Etappen auf der Dezimalstufenleiter der deutschen Währung, keine Endstation. Man ist an die ‹gleitende Skala› der Notendruckwalze schon so gewöhnt, dass man nicht weiter in Ekstase gerät, wenn sie siebenstellige Ziffer erreicht. Die Million hat längst ihre imponierende Grösse verloren. Sie ist zum alltäglichen Rechnenfaktor geworden.... Die Billion und die Trillion sind keine märchenhaften Begriffe mehr. Der Absturz der deutschen Mark ist unabsehbar. Niemand weiss, wo der rasende Fall endet.*[14]

> (The Million Mark Note
> Now the money machine is throwing its latest trump card on the table: the million Mark note is on the way. Its smaller forerunner, the half million Mark note, makes its appearance this Friday. Nice round sums of money, single figures with the appropriate number of zeros. People will hardly marvel at the new products of state printing technology or regard them as unique phenomena. They are just new rungs on the decimal ladder of the German currency and are certainly not the end of the line. We have become so accustomed to the 'sliding scale' of the note printing press that its arrival at a seven-figure number is no longer greeted with ecstasy. The million has long since lost its impressive grandeur and has become just another number in everyday calculations.... The billion and trillion are not fairytale notions any more. The German Mark is plunging to unfathomable depths, and nobody knows where its headlong fall will end.)

As well as cynicism and an air of resignation about the depreciation of the currency, there was also anger to be detected in attitudes to its fall in value and the related appreciation in value of foreign currencies. The following report reflects anger at foreign contempt for Germany and its depreciated currency.

> *Was sich Ausländer bei uns leisten*

> *Der ‹Frankfurter General-Anzeiger› erzählt folgende wahre Geschichte, deren Augen- und Ohrenzeuge ein Frankfurter auf der Rückfahrt nach Frankfurt war.*
> *An der Zollstation musste alles aus dem Zug heraus. Beim Wiedereinsteigen waren aber die alten Plätze besetzt, und jeder musste sich neue suchen. Ein Frankfurter Ehepaar konnte aber nur noch in einem Abteil erster Klasse Platz finden, ebenso mehrere andere Passagiere. Kaum hatten diese ihr Gepäck verstaut, da kamen drei Amerikaner herein – zwei Herren und eine Dame – und reklamierten das ganze Abteil für sich – die Sitzenden aber weigerten sich,*

zu räumen. Hierauf nahmen die Amerikaner das Gepäck der anderen und warfen es auf den Gang. Der Frankfurter Herr verbat sich das, und es gab ein wüstes Geschimpfe von Seiten der Amerikaner – wie verfluchte ‹Dutchmen' und ‹Bosch' – kurzum im schlimmsten Kutscher und Dockarbeiteramerikanisch – und schliesslich war ein allgemeines Handgemenge im Gang, als endlich Zugpersonal erschien.

Sogar das Personal wurde beleidigt, und als sich der Zug in Bewegung setzte, streckten die fremden Herrschaften dem Stationsvorsteher draussen die Zunge heraus, drehten eine Nase und – was abscheulichste war – zerissen zum Fenster hinaus ein Bündel Tausendmarkscheine.

Es war keine angenehme Situation im Wagen für alle Beteiligten, das kann man wohl sagen. Da geschah an der nächsten Station etwas Unerwartetes. Es erschienen mehrere Beamte im Wagen, deren Führer die Amerikaner wegen ihres ungebührlichen Verhaltens auf der letzten Station zur Rede stellte und zehn Dollar Strafe verlangte.

Die Herrschaften gingen in die Luft – aber der deutsche Herr war auch nicht nachgiebig und schrie nur immer: ‹10 Dollar! 10 Dollar! Oder Sie bleiben hier!' ‹Wir haben keine Dollars', erklärten nach Hängen und Würgen die Amerikaner.

‹Dan zahlen Sie drei Millionen Mark!'

Kurzum, sie mussten die drei Millionen zahlen (Notabene war der Tageskurs dafür nur etwa zwei Millionen). Aber nun trat ein, was man kaum noch zu hoffen gewagt hatte: die Amerikaner wurden ganz zahm und kleinlaut, und der eine fragte in gebrochenem Deutsch, ‹War das die deutsche Polizei?' Und als ihm das bejaht wurde, fragte er weiter: ‹Kommen die jetzt auf jede neue Station wieder?'

Man sieht, die Sache bog am Schluss ins komische Fahrwasser ab. Einen ersten tiefbedauerlichen Hintergrund hat sie aber deshalb doch, dass man nämlich heute als Ausländer mit den Deutschen alles machen darf. Es sei ferne von mir zu behaupten, dass man deshalb den Amerikanern im allgemeinen daruas einen Vorwurf machen dürfe. Die drei Exemplare hier waren sicherlich nur eine Ausnahme und eine Sorte von Reisenden mit einem Auftreten, das die überwiegende Mehrzahl ihrer Landsleute sicher genau so verdammt wie wir.[15]

(What foreigners are getting up to in Germany

The *Frankfurter General-Anzeiger* relates the following true story seen and heard by a resident of Frankfurt returning to that city.

Everybody had to get out of the train at the customs. On returning to the train, all the old seats were occupied and everybody had to look for alternatives. A married couple from Frankfurt could only however find seats in a first-class compartment as could many other passengers. Hardly had they stowed their luggage when three Americans, two gentlemen and a lady, appeared and *claimed the entire compartment for themselves.* Those with seats refused to move. The Americans took the Germans' luggage and *threw it into the corridor*. The gentleman from Frankfurt refused to tolerate this behaviour and this was followed by filthy abuse from the Americans with such word as 'bloody Dutchman' and 'Boche' in the worst possible cab driver and docker language. Finally, there was a general set-to in the corridor as finally train staff appeared.

Even the staff were insulted. As the train started to move, the foreign gentlemen stuck out their tongues and stuck up their noses at the Station Master outside. The most disgusting thing was that they threw out of the window a *bundle of torn-up thousand Mark notes.*

One can certainly say that it was not a pleasant situation for all those on the train. Something unexpected happened at the next station. Several officials got on the train. Their leader took the Americans to task on account of their uncivilized conduct at the last station and demanded a fine of ten dollars.

The gentlemen exploded but the German did not give way and repeatedly shouted, 'Ten dollars! Ten dollars! or you stay here!' 'We don't have any dollars', explained the Americans, only with the greatest difficulty.

'Then you can pay *three million Marks*!'

To cut a long story short, they had to pay the three million [note that, based on the day's rate of exchange, the equivalent was only about two million Marks]. But then something happened that one could not possibly have hoped for. The Americans were very subdued and meek and one of them asked in broken German, 'Was that the German police?' As the reply was in the affirmative, he again asked, 'Are they going to repeat this at every station down the line?'

One can see that this affair took a comical turn in the end. Deeply to be regretted, however, is the background to this in that foreigners today can do anything to Germans. It is remote from my intention to claim that one should make such complaints against all Americans. The three examples here were certainly an exception and a type of traveller that the majority of their countrymen would certainly condemn as severely as we would.)

This report in the *Deutsche Allgemeine Zeitung* is not just about the behaviour of three Americans on a train: it contains much more that would have been recognized by the readers in 1923. The passengers had been obliged to leave the train because the customs were between the Occupied and Unoccupied areas of Germany. The headline news in most newspapers virtually every day in 1923 was connected with one aspect or another of the French and Belgian occupation of the Fatherland. Not content apparently with insulting German passengers on a train in Germany, the travellers even had the temerity to insult officials of the Reich in the course of their duty! It also illustrates just how important a knowledge of exchange rates could be in a country beset with hyperinflation, a knowledge of which in this particular example enables the officials to turn the tables on the troublemakers. National pride is of course tied up with the value of the currency. What greater insult, therefore, than to have thousand Mark notes torn up and thrown at you out of the window – notes so recently valuable, now worthless!

There was recognition that issues of Notgeld represented interest-free loans of real resources from those prepared to accept them in payment for goods and services. For some, there was also the hope that the loans would never have to be repaid. This could arise because of the rapid erosion of the real value of the issue by further inflation. It could also arise if the lavish decoration of the issues attracted collectors and they were never presented for redemption. An example of an explicit statement of the second point is to be found on a Notgeld issue of the community of Pram-Oesterreich ob der Enns in Austria (Figure 7.4). Although this is an Austrian example, the same idea was well understood in Germany.

So zieh' hinaus ins weite Land,
mach' deinen Weg mit Glück,
fall' einem Sammler in die Hand
und kehre nicht zurück!

So go off far away,
On your way with luck,
Fall into the hands of a collector,
And don't come back!

Figure 7.4 A Notgeld collector's item!

By 26 October 1923, the city of Heilbronn was in deficit on the city budget to the extent of some five to six trillion Marks (5 or 6 × 10^{18} Marks). The Reich government had only given permission for one trillion Marks in Notgeld to be printed or minted! The city went ahead and printed its requirements in denominations ranging from 10 to 50 milliard Mark notes, that is, from 10 to 50 × 10^9 Marks. By 22 November 1923, collector interest was very much in the mind of the city fathers as they made their Notgeld decisions. They minted coins in values of 1, 2 and 3 Goldmarks.

> *Die Stadt gibt gemünztes Notgeld aus, zunächst eine Arbeiter- und Kleinrentnermünze, beide nach Entwürfen des Bildhauers Prof. Heinrich Jobst (Darmstadt), geprägt von der Fa. Peter Brückmann & Söhne AG. Später folgt eine Münze ‹Der Tanz um das Goldene Kalb› nach einem Entwurf von Bildhauer Josef Michael Lock bei der Fa. Brückmann. Der Reinertrag soll wohltätigen Zwecken dienen. Die als Erinnerungsstücke an die schwere Zeit gedachten Münzen sind in Bronze hergestellt, versilbert oder vergoldet. Sie kosten 1, 2 und 3 Goldmark und sind in erster Linie für Sammler gedacht.*[16]

(The city is issuing Notgeld in the form of coins. First of all, a coin depicting a worker and a pensioner after a design by the sculptor Prof. Heinrich Jobst of Dearmstadt and minted by Peter Brückmann & Co. This will be followed by a coin entitled 'The Dance around the Golden Calf' designed by the sculptor Josef Michael Lock and minted again by Brückmann & Co. The proceeds will be totally used for charity. The coins, intended as memorials to these difficult times, have been produced in bronze, silver or gold plated. They will cost 1, 2 and 3 Goldmarks and are principally intended for collectors.)

These were not the small value bits of paper issued in Pram and throughout Germany and Austria around 1920 but very large value issues towards the end of the hyperinflationary period. The Goldmark pricing is interesting. It would allow the coins to be issued over a period of time at whatever Papermark equivalent was read off from the latest exchange rate information from Berlin.

Some of the great German industrialists enhanced personal fortunes by the use of large denomination Notgeld issues. One of these was Hugo Stinnes. Consider the five-million Mark issue of one of his companies, Hugo Stinnes Linien, on 10 August 1923 and illustrated in Figure 7.5.

This note could be redeemed at its face value from 15 September. The exchange rate between the Reichsmark and the United States dollar was

Figure 7.5 Five-million Mark note of Hugo Stinnes' Shipping Company

one of the major ways of measuring not only the exchange rate movement but also the decline in the internal purchasing power of the currency. The exchange rate on 8 August 1923 in Berlin stood at 4,700,000 RM = US$1. By 14 September 1923, this had declined to 106,000,000 RM = US$1. Thus, this particular debt of Hugo Stinnes Linien had declined in real terms both externally in relationship to the US dollar and, using the exchange rate movement as a proxy for internal inflation, by a similar amount in terms of Reichsmark-denominated purchasing power within Germany. A decline from 5,000,000 RM to 221,698 RM, a real value loss in just over a month of some 95.6 per cent. Quite a bargain for the debtor! An interest-free loan repayable at the most by an amount in real terms some 95 per cent less than the sum borrowed only one month before. But was this purely the unforeseen consequences of spiralling inflation? Or was this particular debtor fully aware of the opportunities presented by the monetary collapse of 1923 to obtain control of real resources virtually at zero cost? There is evidence to suggest the second interpretation of the motives of Hugo Stinnes' Companies for issuing their own Notgeld!

Hugo Stinnes 1870–1924

Hugo Stinnes was one of the most significant figures in German industry during the period of hyperinflation. He established a large industrial empire by astute use of the opportunities presented by the depreciating currency. The rapid erosion of debts due to the inflation and the printing of his own Notgeld or Emergency Money helped to create his industrial empire. The following list[17] gives an impression of the industrial empire that he created.

Deutschland Vergeht
Stinnes Besteht

Hugo Stinnes G.m.b.H.

Handel, Schiffahrt, Transport
Hugo Stinnes Linien
H.S. Seeschiffahrt Hamburg
H.S. Transport Oel Rotterdam
Oeresund Werft Schweden
H.S. Reederei und Kohlenh.
Industrust A.G. Wien
Ostsee Reederei Flensburg
H.S. G.m.b.H. Abteilung
  Russland
H.S. Eisen A.G. Mülheim
Hamburger Verkehrs A.G.
  Hamburg
'Ferro' Ver. Eisen u. Erzh. A.G.
Oesterr. Alp. Montan Ges.
  Wien

Metallwerke,
  Maschinenfabriken
Metallurg. Werke Briansk
Aluminiumfabrik in Neapel
Liptak & Co Eisenindustrie
  Budapest.
Rima-Muran Salgo Carjaner
  Eisenwerke.
Autom.werke H. Büsing
  Braunschweig
Maschinenfabrik Herrenberg
Rhein Westf. Kupferwerke
  A.G. Olpe
Erzwerk A.G.Alumin. Köln
Aluminiumerzwerke A.G.
Waggon u. Schillabr. Danubius
Dines Automboilwerke Berlin
Ostd. Emaill. u. Stanzwerke
  Küstrin

Holz, Zellstoff, Zeitungen
Nordische Holzhandels
  G.m.b.H.
Standard A.G. für
  Forstindustrie
Siebenbürger Grödel
  Holzwerke
Koholyt A.G. Berlin
Nordd. Buchd. u. Verlagsanst.
  Berlin
Lohndruckerei Büxenstein
  Berlin
Buch u. Zellstoffgewerbe
  Stinnes
Elbe Papier Mühlen
  Oesterreich
R. Hobbing Verlagsbuchh.
  Berlin

Banken
Barmer Bankverein
Berliner Handelsges.

Kohle
Zeche Carolus Magnus
Vereinigte Wilhelm I u. II
  Bottrop
Zeche Schw. Junge Dahlhausen
Zeche Math. Stinnes I, II, III &
  IV Carnap
Nordd. Braunkohlenwerke
  Helmstedt
Harbker Kohlenwerke
Braunschw. Kohlenbergw.
  Helmstedt
Mulheimer Bergwerks Verein
Bergw. Ges. Diergardt

Oelinteressen
H.S. Riebeck Montan u.
 Oelwerke A.G. Halle a.S.
Petroleum Ind. Berlin
Hanseastische Mühlenwerke
 Hamburg
Mineralöl Handels und Betell
 Ges.
Roth u. Paschkis Stuttgart
 Mannheim
Oel u. Benzin Import Ulm
Nordd. Oelmühlenwerke
 Hamburg
Tankanlagen der Reichsmarine
Petroleumkonzessionen
 Argentinien
Olen Werke Frankfurt am
 Main.

Sonstige Unternehmungen
Filmunternehmen in Postdam
Rittergüter
Zuckerfabrik Rombach
Kalkwerke Königsberg
Rhein Weser Elektr. Werk
 Essen.
Hoch u. Tiefbauten Frankfurt
 Essen
Dührkop Lohgerberei Oldesloe

Britain also had its own Emergency Money in the form of Treasury Notes issued between 1914 and 1927, intially on the authority of Lloyd George, on the outbreak of war in August 1914. The prime motivation behind the issue of these notes was to replace gold and, shortly afterwards, silver coins. Gold coin note substitutes were put into circulation but silver substitute notes were destroyed because of the fear that they would contribute towards an unacceptably high rate of inflation. The motivation was similar to that in Germany that led to the issue of base metal '*Kriegsgeld*', '*Ersatzgeld*' or '*Stadtgeld*' Emergency Money. Paper monies could be safely introduced as the right to demand redemption in gold had been suspended in both countries on the outbreak of war. Both countries were likely to need the gold content of its coinage to pay for imports of supplies from neutral countries to continue fighting. As British and Allied armies were fighting on the mainland of Europe, the Germans had the added reason of not wanting its gold coins to fall into enemy hands. The English substitutes for gold, Bradburys as they were nicknamed after the Secretary of State to the Treasury, John Bradbury, whose signature appears on the earlier notes, were issued not by the Bank of England but by the Treasury. This may be viewed as a weakening of the power of the former in relationship to the latter somewhat arguably akin to the loss of authority over the note issue of the Reichsbank in Germany in the face of the flood of alternative monies such as Emergency Money, Notgeld, and Darlehnskassenscheine to mention but a few of the flood of various issues.[18]

Figure 7.6 An example of a Treasury Note: a Bradbury, issued in 1917, part of Britain's Emergency Money of the Great War, under the control of the Treasury and not the Bank of England

Production of the new Treasury Notes remained centralized and, unlike Germany, the cities and individual companies of the United Kingdom did not 'get in on the act'. Centralized control ensured that a vast expansion of these new issues did not take place. The unchallenged nature of the unitary state also ensured more effective lines of control than existed in Germany.

Schacht was clearly aware of the abuses of money and credit practised by leading industrialists. Some of the leading figures of the day were to exploit their power over the banking system to gain control over resources and to speculate against the Mark.

> Herr Schlittler, Manager of the Deutsche Bank, travelling with August Thyssen.
> 'Herr Thyssen, we have a quantity of your Emergency Money in our safes. What shall we do about it?'
> Thyssen was silent, deep in thought for a moment and then replied,
> 'You are quite right, Herr Schlittler, what shall we do about it?'[19]

Much emphasis is rightly placed on the inflationary impact of the Reichsbank being obliged to discount the securities issued to finance the budget deficits of the Reich. Examples of 'credit abuse' could also be found in the private sector. Consider the use of the financial or accommodation bill. This could be used to provide capital for a new industry. A specific example quoted by Schacht was the creation in 1911 by August Thyssen, Hugo Stinnes and the Dresdner Bank of the Saar-

und-Mosel-Bergwerkgesellschaft Mining Co. to convert coal in the Saar into coke. Thyssen and Stinnes were each to contribute 10 million Marks with 1 million from the Dresdner Bank.

> *Thyssen to Stinnes: 'Now, Herr Stinnes, we must each pay in the ten million Marks we have taken up. So I'll make you a proposition. I will issue bills to the value of ten million Marks to you which you will accept and the Dresdner Bank will discount those bills.'*
> *Stinnes to Thyssen: 'But Herr Thyssen, I have never yet put my name to an accommodation bill!'*
> *Thyssen to Stinnes: 'Then I'll make you another proposition, Herr Stinnes. You issue bills to the value of ten million Marks to me and I will accept them.'*[20]

These were early signs of what was to play a significant role in creating inflationary conditions in Germany after 1918. Large commercial and industrial companies such as these were in effect playing a significant part in determining the rate of increase of the money supply. In the case above, the Dresdner Bank credited the discounted amounts of the above bills. The large Notgeld issues of these and other companies and cities and towns were to be regarded by Schacht as a 'widespread nuisance', causing difficulty for the stabilization programme.

There are interesting examples of German nationalism to be found in the Notgeld issues. The use of the plebiscite to enable self-determination of citizenship aroused much bitterness. Schacht was particularly offended that the plebiscite was denied to Germans but allowed to others.[20] Such a plebiscite took place in North Schleswig in 1920 to determine a new border between Denmark and Germany. The further north in the plebiscite area, the greater the vote for Denmark. The area seceded to Denmark had in the main voted over 75 per cent in favour of the new national allegiance. Despite this, nationalist sentiment in Germany looked forward to a future reincorporation of the lost territory within the Reich. An example of such sentiment is shown on the one-Mark Notgeld issue by Aventoft in 1921 shown in Figure 7.7.

There was an explicit prohibition of the use of the plebiscite to determine the question of the unification of Austria and Germany. The two German-speaking nations were not to be joined together irrespective of the will of the people. The Notgeld 75 heller issue of 1919 from Fieberbrunn in Austria expresses sentiments that were echoed on the German side of the frontier, Germans and Austrians working together to defeat the provisions of the Versailles Treaty banning their union.

From far off we see the flag in New Denmark [the seceded area]
It greets you, our lost brothers,
When we are once again healthy and strong,
You will be united with us again.

Figure 7.7 An example of a political message: the one-Mark Notgeld issue of Aventoft

Redemption of Notgeld

Notgeld issues were, of course, liabilities of those cities, companies and individuals responsible for them. A notice would normally be placed in the local newspapers announcing the recall of the issue currently in circulation. The following is a more complete statement than would normally be found on Notgeld issues.

> *Zur Behebung der herrschenden Hartgeldnot gibt die Gemeinde Pennewang auf Grund des Gemeindeausschuss-Beschlusses vom 23. Mai 1920 Gutscheine bis zu einem Gesamtbetrage von 100,000 Kronen aus. Diese Gutscheine werden in der Zeit vom 1. bis 31. Dezember bei der Gemeindekasse in gesetzlichem Bargelde eingelöst.*[21]

> (The local council of Pennewang, acting on a resolution passed in committee on 23 May 1920, will seek to relieve the prevailing shortage of hard currency by issuing vouchers to a total value of

Figure 7.8 An example of Austrian Notgeld: the 75 heller issue of Fieberbrunn

100,000 crowns. These vouchers may be exchanged for legal tender at the council cash office from 1 to 31 December.)

Redeeming these notes in a period of accelerating inflation would never be a problem. That so many examples survive today is probably due in large part to the fact that they were virtually worthless at redemption and simply not worth the bother of a visit to the *'Gemeindekasse'*. Although legal tender is promised at redemption in exchange for the Notgeld, this might well have simply been yet another issue of Notgeld itself.

Collector interest and the effects of inflation over the life of a Notgeld issue effectively meant that such issues were a way to acquire real resources at zero cost. Substantial transfers of resources between debtors and creditors were achieved in this way. Creditor resistance grew as inflation rates increased and it became necessary to issue indexed Notgeld (*wertbeständiges Notgeld*), a form of Goldmark notes. These issues gave the creditor a substantial measure of protection against inflation. The example illustrated on p. 82 meant that the holder always had control over Papermarks equal in value to 1/42 of a dollar. He could afford to hold on to money for somewhat longer. The exchange rate or a prices index would not remind him of yet more real losses. The issue of such notes would slow the flight from money.

Such *'wertbeständiges Notgeld'* did, however, create a problem towards the end of 1923 after the stabilization of the Mark. Notgeld issues had to be withdrawn as part of the reforms designed to restore control over the money supply to the Reichsbank. The issuing authorities had to redeem the Notgeld that they had printed and circulated. But how and with what? The credit standing of most issuers meant that considerable time would elapse before all Notgeld issues could be withdrawn from circulation.

Outrage and despair at the experience of living through hyperinflation are often expressed on Notgeld issues of the time.

As the flood of large denomination notes issued by local authorities towards the end of 1923 was at its height, there was explicit recognition on the notes themselves that the flood of paper money was responsible for the destruction of the financial system and of the economy. This is to be found nowhere more explicitly stated than on the 500 million Mark note of Vohwinkel issued on 15 October 1923. It is significant that the nominal value of the note and the illustrative prices prevailing on the day of issue are printed in red.

Figure 7.9 Commemorating the inflation – the 500 million Mark issue of Vohwinkel

> Prices on 15 October 1923. A litre of water 98 thousand Marks, a pound of salt 42 million Marks, an egg 75 million, a litre of milk 152 million, a pound of potatoes 40 million, one herring 50 million, a pound of bread 210 million, a pound of lard 1.25 thousand million, a pair of shoe soles 6 thousand million, a death certificate from a doctor 600 million, a coffin 45 thousand million.

EMERGENCY MONEY – NOTGELD

Figure 7.10 Commemorating the deliveries in kind – the 1000 Mark issue from Bielefeld

Outrage is well expressed on the 1000 Mark note issued in Bielefeld in 1922. The financial burdens placed on Germany by the Treaty of Versailles are listed in detail. Exhortations to work and save in the belief that God helps those who help themselves are expressed on the note. Import substitution is urged in a buy German goods campaign, 'German hens lay not dollars but German eggs!' With the note virtually worthless soon after it was issued, it was provided with an inflation proof value of direct use in the form of a printed calendar for 1923.

Notes

1. F.K. Ringer, *The German Inflation of 1923* (Oxford University Press 1969), p. 90.
2. Ibid., p. 93.
3. Carl-Ludwig Holtfrerich, *Die deutsche Inflation* (de Gruyter 1980).
4. Ibid., p. 327.
5. Ibid., p. 328.
6. 'Δ' represents 'change in' price/money supply.
7. *Hildesheimer Allgemeine Zeitung*, Friday, 25 August 1922. *Der Dollar an 2300!*: The Dollar near 2300!
8. M. Pick, *Der Notgeld Kompass. Ausgabeorte der deutschen Notgeldscheine*

geordnet nach Ländern und Zeitspannen (Druckschnelldienst Nürnberg 1975).
9. H.J. Kurtz, *Für Gold und Silber Nimm den Schein*. Aus einem Kapitel norddeutscher Geldgeschichte (Lübeck: LN Verlag 1981), *passim*. A. Peisker, *Das Berliner Notgeld 1914 – 1924*. Band 16 aus der Schriftenreihe Die Münze' (Berlin: Buchdruckerei Erich Pröh 1972), pp. 1–15. M. Pick, *Der Notgeld-Kompass* (Schwalbach: Hoffmann 1975), *passim*.
10. F.C.A. Lange, *Gross-Berliner Tagebuch 1920 – 1933*, *passim*. There were movements noted both ways, i.e. into and out of real assets. Hoarding purchases are noted in the diary as are sales of real assets by the poor, desperate to find enough immediate cash to survive.
11. *Cuxhavener Zeitung*, Wednesday, 19 September 1923.
12. 1 Goldmark = 10^{12} Papermarks, therefore 10^8 Goldmarks = 10^{20} Papermarks.
13. Erich Maria Remarque, *Der Schwarze Obelisk* (Frankfurt/M, Berlin, Wien: Ullstein Books 1978), pp. 7–8.
14. *Deutsche Allgemeine Zeitung*, 6 July 1923.
15. *Deutsche Allgemeine Zeitung*, 31 July 1923.
16. *Chronik der Stadt Heilbronn 1922 – 1933* (Stadtarchiv Heilbronn 1986). Entry for 23 November 1923.
17. S. Grossman 'Tagebuch der Wirtschaft', *Das Tage-Buch*. Heft 37. Jahrg. 4. S. 1531 (Berlin: Athenäum Verlag 1923). A publication of data on Stinnes originally published by Dr Norbert Einstein and the Organization of German Metal Workers Unions. Practically 100 pages are devoted to a detailed consideration of the Stinnes empire and its linkages. The summary table simply indicates something of the size of that empire as measured by the number of significant companies controlled by Stinnes. The column headings are translated below.

Germany's decaying
Stinnes is staying

Hugo Stinnes G.m.b.H.

Commerce, Shipping Companies, Transport	*Timber, Pulp, Newspapers*
Metal Works, Factories	*Banks*
Oil Interests	*Coal Production*
	Other Undertakings

This was a vast network of companies linked by vertical and horizontal integration advantages. A network that was to collapse after the death of Stinnes in 1924 and the end of the period of hyperinflation. The collapse was to require the active participation of the Reichsbank to introduce a rescue plan.

18. The story of British Emergency Money of this period is summarized in *Collectors Bank Notes Treasury and Bank of England* (Rotographic Publications, 3rd Edition 1990). Richards Pocket Reference and Price Guide, *passim*.
19. This story is repeated twice by Hjalmar Schacht. *My First Seventy-Six Years*, p. 145 and *Account Settled* or *Abrechnung mit Hitler*, p.12.
20. Hjalmar Schacht, *The Stabilisation of the Mark*, ch. 10 'International Cooperation'.
21. 50 Heller Voucher of Pennewang. Issued 23 May 1920.

CHAPTER EIGHT

The Views of Hjalmar Schacht, President of the Reichsbank

Schacht's views on the cause of inflation and the cure for it are detailed extensively in Chapter 4 of his book, *The Stabilisation of the Mark*, the chapter having the same title in essence as the book, 'Die Markstabilisierung'.

Inflation on the scale experienced in Germany in 1922 and 1923 was explained by him as arising from a vast increase in the note issue; stabilization of the price level and the exchange value of the Mark could only be achieved by a reduction in the size of the note issue. Consider the following statements by Schacht to this effect:

> *Die Überlegungen, wie ein solches Festhalten zu erreichen sei, endeten alle in dem einen Punkt, dass nur eine Kontraktion der Umlaufsmenge des gesetzlichen Zahlungsmittels zum Erfolg führen könnte.*

(Deliberations on how to achieve such a stabilization always came to the same conclusion, that only a contraction of the amount of legal tender in circulation could lead to success.)

> *das Mittel zur Durchführung dieses Versuches immer nur das gleiche blieb, nämlich die Kontraktion des gesetzlichen Zahlungsmittel, der Papiermark.*

(The means of effecting these attempts at stabilization always remained the same; namely, the contraction of the legal tender, the Papermark.)

> *In die Strategie der Papiermark-Kontraktion fiel neben der Heraufsetzung des Dollardivisors ein weiteres Moment, nämlich der Kampf um das umlaufende Notgeld. Die ganze Geschichte des sogenannten Notgeldes während des Krieges sowohl wie nach dem Kriege und insbesondere in der Zeit des Ruhrkampfes sieht sich wie ein Satyrspiel an angesichts des tragischen Ablaufes der sonstigen Ereignisse. Es ist die einfache technische Unmöglichkeit, den Verkehr mit der genügenden Menge von bunt bedruckten Papierzetteln zu versehen, die die Reichsbank wiederholt zwingt, selber die Anregung dazu zu geben, dass Länder, Provinzen, Kommunen und selbst private Unternehmungen Notgeld für sich drucken und in Verkehr setzen. Die Ressortberichte der Reichsbank über die technische Bewältigung*

der Aufgabe, genügend Geldscheine herzustellen, lesen sich wie eine Groteske. Da die Reichsdruckerei, die in Friedenszeiten allein den Notendruck für die Reichsbank versieht, die Zahl der angeforderten Geldscheine zu drucken nicht in der Lage war, so mussten Privatdruckereien zum Druck von Geldscheinen mit herangezogen werden. Die ständig und immer rascher sich vollziehende Entwertung machte immer wieder neuen Druck erforderlich. Annähernd zweitausend Beamte und Angestellte der Reichsbank waren schliesslich im Aufsichtsdienst in den Druckereien und Papierfabriken, sowie als Begleiter bei Papier- und Geldscheintransporten erforderlich. Im Jahre 1923 arbeiteten in der Geldscheinherstellung für die Reichsbank beziehungsweise für die Reichsdruckerei 133 Druckereien mit 1783 Maschinen. Über dreissig Papierfabriken arbeiteten im vollen Betrieb lediglich für die Reichsbank. So grotesk sich diese Zahlen ausnehmen, so ist doch andererseits die rein technische Bewältigung einer solchen Arbeit auch wieder anerkennenswert, und es ist nahezu ein Wunder, wenn nach dem Abbau dieser ganzen Ungeheuerlichkeit konstatiert werden konnte, dass nennenswerte Verluste durch Veruntreuungen und dergleichen der Reichsbank aus diesem ganzen Appartat nicht erwachsen waren. Ich habe diese Ziffern angeführt, um daran anknüpfend festzustellen, dass selbst mit einem so ungeheuren Hilfsapparat die Reichsbank nicht imstande war, eine ausreichende Menge von Geldscheinen für den Verkehr zu liefern. Infolgedessen setzte der Druck kommunalen und privaten Notgeldes von Zeit zu Zeit immer wieder ein.... Ende 1922 dürften schon etwa zwanzig Milliarden Mark solchen Notgeldes im Umlauf gewesen sein bei einem gleichzeitigen Umlauf von 1280 Milliarden Reichsbanknoten. Im Laufe des Jahres 1923 hat sich der Betrag des von unzähligen Stellen ausgegebenen Notgeldes ganz ausserordentlich erhöht und im Verhältnis zum Reichsbanknotenumlauf eine sehr viel grössere Bedeutung gewonnen. Auch wurde die Deckungsvorschrift mehr und mehr missachtet. Der Betrag des meist ohne Deckung ausgegebenen nicht wertbeständigen Notgeldes dürfte sich Ende 1923 auf etwa vierhundert bis fünfhundert Trillionen belaufen haben, das heisst rund eine halbe Milliarde Goldmark, also ebensoviel wie der Goldwert des gesamten Reichsbankumlaufes zur gleichen Zeit betrug, während daneben noch einmal ein gleich hoher Betrag von wertbeständigem Notgeld umlief. Insgesamt also zirkulierte doppelt soviel Notgeld als Reichsbankgeld. Est ist ganz selbstverständlich, dass in der wilden Geldentwertung des Jahres 1923 das Notgeld nicht lediglich Abhilfe gegen die unzulängliche Belieferung mit Geldscheinen durch die Reichsbank darstellte, sondern eine höchst willkommene Quelle der Kreditversorgung und Geldmacherei war. Die Ausgabe von nicht wertbeständigem Notgeld war eines der bequemsten Mittel, Inflationsgewinne zu machen, und wurde deshalb nicht nur von Kommunen sondern vor allem auch von grossen Privatbetrieben reichlich und gern gehandhabt.[1]

(In addition to raising the dollar divisor there was another factor in the strategy of Papermark contraction – viz. the battle over the

Emergency Money which was circulating. In view of the tragic course of other events, the whole business of this so-called Emergency Money, both during and after the war and especially during the struggle for the Ruhr, resembles some kind of comic epilogue. It is the simple impossibility technically of supplying sufficient quantities of pretty bits of paper which repeatedly forces the Reichsbank itself to encourage states, provinces, local councils and even private firms to print their own emergency notes and put them into circulation. Reichsbank departmental reports on the technical aspects of this job make grotesque reading. Since the Reich press, which in peacetime has sole responsibility for the production of paper money for the Reichsbank, was incapable of meeting the demand for notes, private printing firms had to be engaged. The continual and ever accelerating depreciation meant that new printing was constantly necessary. Nearly 2000 officials and employees were needed as supervisors in the printing works and paper mills or as escorts during the transport of paper and notes. In 1923 there were 133 printing works with 1783 machine working on banknote production for the Reichsbank or for the Reich press. More than 30 papermills were working flat out solely for the Reichsbank. As grotesque as these figures appear, one cannot help but acknowledge the purely technical achievement in managing a task of these proportions, and it is almost a miracle that, after this monstrosity had been removed, no significant Reichsbank losses were recorded through embezzlement and the like. I have cited these figures in order to establish the fact that, despite having such an enormous supporting organization, the Reichsbank was incapable of supplying a sufficient quantity of notes. The result was that printing of local council and private Emergency Money started up again and again from time to time.... By the end of 1922 there must have been about 20 thousand million Emergency Money notes in circulation, accompanied by 1280 thousand million Reichsbank notes. During 1923 the amount of money issued by countless sources increased to an extraordinary extent and gained much more importance in relation to the circulation of Reichsbank notes. The backing regulation was increasingly ignored. At the end of 1923 the amount of Emergency Money issued without backing and without inflation-protected value must have been between 400 and 500 trillion, that is around 0.5×10^9 Goldmarks (milliard), which equates to the gold value of all the Reichsmark notes in circulation at that time, while in addition an equally large amount of inflation-protected Emergency Money was in circulation. In total, then, the amount of Emergency Money in circulation was double that of Reichsbank money. It goes without saying that during the chaotic days of money depreciation in 1923 Emergency Money did not just constitute a remedy for the inadequate supply of notes by the Reichsbank, but was rather a highly welcome source of raising credit and making money. The issuing of Emergency Money without inflation protection was one of the most convenient ways of making a profit out of inflation and was therefore widely and gladly practised, not only by local councils but above all by large private companies.)

In these extracts, there are both qualitative judgements and quantitative estimates of what went wrong in this area of monetary policy during these years. The stabilization policy rested on the ability of the authorities to reduce the note issue. Yet, during these years, control over the note issue had not only not been exercised by the Reichsbank in the interests of price level and exchange rate stability but it had allowed the production of notes to be determined elsewhere than within the Reichsbank itself. Countless numbers of individuals throughout the Reich could by 1923 make the decision to print money, Schacht's 'pretty bits of paper' in the quotation. Not only that, but the Reichsbank would, until the stabilization policy was introduced in November 1923, actually accept the privately printed monies in exchange for Reichsbank notes, effectively a way of laundering less acceptable Emergency Money notes (Notgeld) into the more acceptable Reichsbank notes. This provided a way to acquire foreign exchange. Foreign monies could only be purchased on the foreign exchange market against Reichsbank notes. What could be more simple therefore than to take Emergency Money to the nearest branch of the Reichsbank, send it to another branch by Giro and withdraw it in the form of Reichsbank notes and then use the proceeds to buy foreign currency, thus contributing to driving down the external value of the Mark still further. For some prominent individuals such as Hugo Stinnes, the process could be further shortened. He was simply able to exchange his own Emergency Money directly for Reichsbank notes without bothering with the Giro!

It was a process that put the development of central banking into reverse. Over the previous century, lines of control and influence in monetary matters had gradually favoured the centre at the expense of the regions. For example, the note issue had become concentrated in the hands of the central bank and gold standard disciplines had ensured a restriction in the overall growth rate of this medium. The events of 1922 and 1923 in particular threw this process into reverse, creating innumerable note printing points throughout the country and removing the restrictions of the gold standard rules. On Schacht's estimates, by the end of 1922, some 20×10^9 (milliard) Emergency Money (Notgeld) was in circulation alongside 1280×10^9 (milliard) Reichsbank notes – the so-called Papermarks, that is, Emergency Money, amounting to some 1.6 per cent of the Reichsbank issues. The inflationary consequences of this small addition to the total were probably insignificant over and above the contribution of the rapidly growing Reichsbank issues. 1923 was, however, a different story! Schacht's estimate for 1923 is that the total Notgeld issue amounted to between 4 and 5 hundred trillion, that is, between 4 and 5×10^{18}, and this was only the nominal value Emergency Money approximately equal to the total circulation of Reichsbank notes.

This one factor alone had doubled what otherwise would have been the total note issue. Taking 'value-protected' Emergency Money into consideration, Schacht informs us that the total amount of Emergency Money in circulation was double the amount of Reichsbank notes, that is, two-thirds of the total money supply. Put another way, as a result of Emergency Money, the note issue at the end of 1923 was 200 per cent greater than it might otherwise have been.

It was, of course, a process that in itself was not equilibrium seeking but rather one that contained strong, positive feedback forces, in other words, those forces that operate in an initial disequilibrium situation to make subsequent related disequilibria even greater. A price increase takes us above the threshold at which the flight into goods away from money begins. The rise in the velocity of circulation causes a price rise greater than the increase in the note issue causing the perception of a shortage of money. This is responded to say by an increase in either Reichsbank notes or Emergency Money. It is not a static world, there is no absolute once and for all shortage that such an issue of fresh notes would solve. The 'shortage' appears yet again at a yet higher level of prices and so on indefinitely, or until a radical stabilization policy is introduced. This is why Schacht realizes that the Reichsbank, with the 'support team' from the private sector could not hope to close the apparent gap between a given level of note issue and an apparent greater need.

Lack of control over the note issue in Germany 1923

At this time in Germany, there was no independent central bank charged with the job of stabilizing the internal and external value of money. As Schacht points out, the Reichsbank was not unaware of the consequences of a rapidly rising note issue but powerless to make its views influence monetary policy. It was in effect an office of the central government and worked according to the instructions of the Chancellor of the Reich. He could simply instruct the Reichsbank to give him the credits he needed to balance his budget.

> Bis zum Erlass des Autonomiegesetzes vom 26. Mai 1922 war die Reichsbank nichts anderes als eine nach den Anweisungen des Reichskanzlers arbeitende Reichsstelle.[2]

> (Until the enactment of the Autonomy Law of 26 May 1922, the Reichsbank was nothing more than one of the central government offices working according to the instructions of the Chancellor of the Reich.)

> *So lange auch nach der Revolution dieses Verhältnis bestand, konnte der Reichskanzler dieses Beamtengremium jederzeit einfach anweisen, die von ihm gewünschten Kredite zu geben.*[3]

(For as long as this relationship existed after the Revolution, the Chancellor of the Reich could, on every occasion, simply instruct this body of civil servants to give him the credits he wanted.)

So here we have a statement about the major initial cause of the hyperinflation and its growing intensity through 1922 into 1923, the year that witnessed the culmination of the process with the total devaluation of the Papermark. The financing of the budget deficit was largely undertaken with credits supplied by the Reichsbank. In Germany at this time, there is a direct link between the deficit and the growth of the note issue. This close link is the product of a particular set of historical circumstances working together involving principally a Chancellor taking the relatively easy way out of the problem of financing a budget deficit by issuing instructions to a totally dependent central bank to supply him with the necessary notes.

Stabilization of prices and the exchange rate

The relationship between Chancellor and the Reichsbank had effectively operated as if the former had had a note-printing press in his own office. Two important and absolutely essential steps were involved. The budget had to be financed by means other than the use of the printing press and the Reichsbank had to be given greater independence from the Chancellor both in terms of the constitutional relationship between them and in the willingness of the former to resist demands from the latter for credits to finance the deficit. The Autonomy Law of 26 May 1922 established the Reichsbank as more of an independent institution. The directorate of the bank could now resist the government's demands without the threat of being removed from office. It could not of course of itself remove any moral obligation the directors might feel to go along with the wishes of the government, to support it in a hostile political world, particularly in its struggle with the French.

The use of its newly acquired legal independence must await a test of its willingness to put the interests of moving towards monetary stability before its desire simply to do the government's will. That test came towards the end of 1923 when it looked as if the government might not be able to pay the salaries of the civil servants without additional credits from the Rentenbank over and above those allocated as an integral part of the stabilization policy; that is, pressure to return to the old ways! At a meeting on 20 December 1923, this request for a return to the printing press was rejected. The importance of this decision was stressed by Schacht,

> *Es ist ein historisches Verdienst des Verwaltungsrates der Rentenbank, dass er in seiner Sitzung vom 20. Dezember 1923 das Ersuchen des Reichsfinanzministers ablehnte und damit den Zwang, aus eigener Kraft zur Budgetkonsolidierung zu kommen, für das Reich verstärkte.*[4]

(It is to the historic credit of the Administrative Council of the Rentenbank that, in its meeting of 20 December 1923, the request of the Finance Minister of the Reich was rejected and with it, the compulsion grew for the Reich to consolidate the budget out of its own resources.)

The 'easy' way out was now blocked by both banks, Reichsbank and Rentenbank, being able and willing to reject the approach of the Finance Minister for easy credits. He was thus obliged and strengthened in his own attempts to balance the budget by paying attention to expenditure and revenue flows and having to approximate the amounts of each within the financial year.

It is interesting to note the central concern with the exchange rate and the need to establish a sustainable fixed rate of exchange. The exchange rate consideration comes first and the corresponding internal note issue is derived from it by the appropriate divisor. The thinking is pure gold standard! External equilibrium comes first and the aggregate note issue for internal stability is derived from it. Nowadays, one might proceed by reducing the rate of growth of some definition of the money supply, of which, in financially developed countries, the note issue would only be an insignificantly small percentage. One might then decide to let the exchange rate then adjust to the slower growth rate in the money supply. Schacht's solution is therefore set in a world of assumptions about the structure of the international payments system different from our own and, in which, the note issue and the money supply are virtually interchangeable terms. Schacht was also quick to point out the advantages in calculating the relationship between the various monies in circulation from such a simple numerical equivalence as 1 'new Mark' = 10^{12} 'old Marks'.

> *ist das runde Umtauschverhältnis von eins zu einer Billion ein wesentliches Erleichterungsmoment gewesen für die Einführung der Goldmark beziehungsweise der Rentenmark.*[5]

(the rounded off rate of exchange of one to one billion was an important factor in facilitating the introduction of the Goldmark or the Rentenmark.)

Having turned off the 'tap' that was pouring fresh supplies of Papermarks into the economy, the next step was to return control over the note issue to the Reichsbank. This meant in effect abolishing the use of Emergency Money that by late 1923 had literally become for thousands of institutions throughout the Reich a print your own notes as you will practice. By this time, it had ceased to be a way of remedying an urgent need for small change or for bank notes that were not supplied by the Reichsbank. It had become a method of obtaining real resources for zero cost in the case of purely nominal value Emergency Money. Often, the notes would carry the advice that they would be redeemed in '*anderem gesetzlichen Zahlungsmittel*', that is, in another form of legal tender. A few weeks or even days from issue, the real value would be close to zero. The decision that such issues would no longer be accepted by the Reichsbank made on 17 November 1923 began the process of removing such private initiative monies from circulation. Having recovered control over the note issue and the ability to resist demands from the government to allow it to increase simply to meet the financing needs of Finance Ministers, the question arose of what to do with the existing monetary situation. Schacht himself was committed to a policy of reducing the note issue in an absolute sense, not merely in establishing control over its rate of growth from its present level.

Reducing the size of the note issue

Before the outbreak of the First World War, the exchange rate fixed parity had been 4.2 Marks = 1 dollar. Stabilization of the financial situation was based on pegging a rate of 4.2×10^{12} Marks = 1 dollar. As this rate held on the Berlin Exchange, it suggested a conversion rate of 1 Rentenmark = 10^{12} Reichsbank Marks. This is referred to by Schacht as the 'dollar divisor'. The use of this term should be obvious; it is the divisor that, when applied to the rate of 4.2×10^{12} Marks = 1 dollar, will re-establish the pre-First World War exchange rate of 4.2 Marks = 1 dollar. These figures make the stabilization policy look numerically very neat and tidy! Using an exchange rate of 10^{12} Papermarks = 1 Rentenmark, we return in November 1923 back to the exchange rate prevailing before the inflationary spiral began. Observation of this suggests a particular interpretation of the motivation that lay behind the choice of divisor. It suggests that the choice was made to secure a return, in terms of exchange rate values, to pre-war 'normality'. Schacht himself this new form of payment, offering by its very nature the highest level of security, will be accepted in circulation with total trust.

The German Rentenbank will be established by representatives of agriculture, industry, trade and the banks. The members of the Board of Directors have already been chosen from prominent circles of the entire Germany economy....

At the same time as Rentenmarks are issued, the Reichsbank will cease discounting the securities of the Reich government. This will close off the source of the depreciation of the Papermark and will enable the Reichsbank to re-establish itself as a true central bank with note-issuing responsibilities....

In order to bring into circulation as soon as possible a significant quantity of a depreciation-free form of payment, the Reich government has decided moreover to issue 1, 2 and 5 dollar units of the Goldloan amounting to 200 million Goldmarks. So that too many different types of money do not remain in circulation for too long, the government is ready in January of next year [i.e. 1924] to exchange these units into Rentenmarks at the option of the holders....

The measures decided today by the Reich government are an intermediate step towards the final solution of the currency question that can only be achieved by the return to the Gold Standard.)

Whether or not a medium of payment is defined to be legal tender does not necessarily determine its acceptability. That the former now virtually worthless Papermark remained legal tender whereas the Rentenmark was not did not prevent the public expressing a strong preference for the latter over the former. Since the Rentenmark was backed by a land charge, a number of other names were possible. As the *Hildesheimer Allgemeine Zeitung* explained to its readers on 16 October 1923,

Die neue Währung

Da es sich dabei um die Leistung einer Bodenrente handelt, so hat man für die Bank den Namen Rentenbank und für die neue Währung den Namen Rentenmark gewählt, während sie zunächst Bodenmark, dann Neumark heissen sollte.

The New Currency

Since it has to do with the payment of a land charge, the name Rentenbank [Land Charge Bank] was chosen for the bank and Rentenmark [Land Charge Mark] was chosen for the new currency, whereas the original intention was to call it Landmark or Newmark.)

The extract above announcing the creation of the Rentenmark and the establishment of the Rentenbank was printed without editorial com-

---

denied that this was the prime reason for choosing the exchange rate to stabilize at this value and restore the old value by an appropriate divisor. The divisor would of course also reduce the value of the note issue in circulation and the actual choice of its precise numerical value would consist of a figure that would simultaneously produce an enduring fixed exchange rate and an acceptable internal contraction of the note issue. On 15 November, the exchange rate of 2.52 billion Marks = 1 dollar was passed and had reached 4.2×10^{12} on 20 November. It was a coincidence that this rate prevailed shortly after Schacht assumed office. The first Rentenmarks issued had been converted at 2.52×10^{12} providing the lucky holders with a windfall gain as the rate rose towards 4.2×10^{12} five days later. Schacht summarized the situation he faced as follows:

bei welchem Kurse dies zu geschehen hatte, das heisst bei welchem Kurse die Aufrechterhaltung, also die Stabilisierung möglich sein würde, das war das grosse Rätsel, vor dem man stand. Irgendeine mathematische Formel hierfür gab es nicht, es kam auf das Gefühl an.[6]

(the big puzzle was at what rate of exchange to achieve and sustain the stabilization. At what rate would this be possible. The choice depended upon feeling for the problem, no sort of mathematical formula existed.)

Notes

1. Hjalmar Schacht, *The Stabilisation of the Mark*, ch. 4, 'The Stabilisation'.
2. Hjalmar Schacht, *The Stabilisation of the Mark*, p. 84.
3. Ibid., p. 85.
4. Ibid., p. 87.
5. Ibid., p. 89.
6. Ibid., p. 73.

CHAPTER NINE

The Stabilization of the Currency

Wer hat die Rentenmark gemacht?
Natürlich unser Hjalmar Schacht![1]

(Who created the Rentenmark?
Our Hjalmar Schacht of course!)

Perhaps excusable as electoral propaganda, this claim was untrue. Schacht did not create the Rentenmark. He was, however, instrumental in carrying through the stabilization programme based on this land charge secured unit.[2]

The economics of what was to be achieved are simple enough to state. The task consisted of replacing one type of note with another. Price stabilization then consisted of ensuring that the Rentenmark notes and credits did not expand at too fast a rate. There was, however, a considerable political battle to be waged to ensure that the policy was successfully carried out.

Schacht was doubtless a forceful individual. He had to be to push through the stabilization policy against the vested interests of those groups standing to lose from the necessary deflationary strategies that would have to be adopted. As J.K. Galbraith pointed out later,

> Schacht was, in fact, like so much else in economics, an accident of timing. If, after 1923, the previous claims on the German budget had continued – the reparations claims and the cost of passive resistance – nothing would have saved the Mark or his reputation. Relieved of these costs and given the desire of people who had experienced inflation for a currency they could trust – and their willingness to abide myth if it sustained this trust – everything was possible.[3]

The Rentenmark was regarded by Schacht as an emergency bridge leading ultimately to the introduction of a definitive gold standard. The Rentenmark was intended to facilitate internal stabilization. Not being readily exchangeable into gold, it was not thought to be suitable for the finance of international trade. How was the introduction of the Rentenmark announced by the press in one town in Germany?

THE STABILIZATION OF THE CURRENCY

Zwischenlösung in der Währungsfrage

Berlin, 15. Okt. Auf Grund des Ermächtigungsgesetzes ha
Reichsregierung die Errichtung einer Deutschen Rentenbank
lossen.

Die Papiermark bleibt das gesetzliche Zahlungsmittel. Nebe
Papiermark ist in der von der Deutschen Rentenbank auszug
den Rentenmark ein wertbeständiges Umlaufsmittel geschaffe
von allen öffentlichen Kassen in Zahlung genommen werden

Die Rentenmark ist gesichert durch auf Goldmark lautend
stellige Grundschulden auf den gesamten deutschen Grund
und erstrangige Goldobligationen der Industrie, des Hande
der Banken. Sie ist jederzeit einlösbar gegen verzinsliche Go
tenbriefe. Es darf mit Zuversicht erwartet werden, dass diese
Zahlungsmittel, das nach seiner Eigenart das Höchstmass ar
erheit bietet, im Verkehr mit uneingeschränktem Vertrauen a
ommen wird.

Die Deutsche Rentenbank wird von Vertretern der Landu
aft, der Industrie, des Gewerbes, des Handels und der l
errichtet werden. Die Mitglieder des Verwaltungsrates si
führenden Kreisen der gesamten deutschen Wirtschaft
gewählt....

Gleichzeitig mit der Ausgabe der Rentenmark wird die
bank die Diskontierung von Schatzanweisungen des Reich
tellen. Dadurch wird die Inflationsquelle der Papiermark ges
und für die Reichsbank der Weg zur Wiedergewinnung ihrer
schaft als einer wahren Goldnotenbank freigemacht....

Um baldmöglichst viel wertbeständige Zahlungsmittel in d
kehr zu bringen, hat die Reichsregierung ausserdem die
von kleinen Stücken der Goldanleihe von 1, 2 und 5 Dollar
Betrage von 200 Millionen Goldmark beschlossen. Damit n
die Dauer zuviel verschiedenartige Zahlungsmittel im Verke
ben, ist das Reich bereit, im Laufe des Januar des nächstei
die kleinen Goldanleihescheine auf Wunsch in Ren
umzutauschen....

Diese von der Reichsregierung heute beschlossenen Mass
sind eine Zwischenstufe zur endgültigen Lösung der Währur
die nur in der Rückkehr zur Goldwährung bestehen kann.

(Interim Solution to the Currency Question

Berlin, 15 October. Following enabling legislation, th
government has decided to establish a German Rentenban

The Papermark remains the legal tender. Alongside the Pa
will be the Rentenmark to be issued by the German Ren
This will be inflation protected and accepted in paymer
public bodies.

The Rentenmark is secured by a Goldmark first charg
totality of German land and first-class gold-based debts of
trade and the banks. It may at any time be exchanged for
bearing annuity bonds. It may be expected with confid

ment. As it stood, it could certainly have been misleading. The reader is invited to think that the backing of the issue by a land charge is what guarantees the real value of the notes over time. Quite how a future holder of devalued notes would get hold of his bit of the asset backing is not considered. It would of course have been impossible. The true future security lay in controlling the total quantity of notes issued and the rate at which the issue was allowed to grow over time. Not allowing Rentenmark notes to be printed to order principally to finance the Reich government's deficit was just as important to their future value as failure to do this had been in causing the depreciation of the Papermark. Editorial comment made this point clear in a leading article on the following day:

Die neue Währung

Das Schicksal der Papiermark bleibt also auch in Zukunft auf sich selbst gestellt. Die Stabilisierung der Papierwährung ist aber trotzdem auch dann gegeben, wenn die Notenpresse ihre Tätigkeit einstellt und nicht wieder in Anspruch genommen wird. Dies soll mit der Einführung der Rentenmark ja geschehen. Von diesem Augenblick an wird die Reichsbank Reichsschatzwechsel nicht mehr diskontieren, d. h. keine neuen Banknoten mehr ausgeben, da die Rentenbank von diesem Augenblick an die Kreditbedürfnisse des Reiches deckt. Das Papiergeld wird sich dann also auf der Wertbasis halten, die es in diesem Augenblick besitzt. Damit soll dem deutschen Währungsverfall Einhalt getan werden, auch wenn die Papiermark und die neue Rentenmark nicht im festen Wertverhältnis stehen. Selbstverständlich kann das aber nur dann so bleiben, wenn die Notenpresse auch tatsächlich als Mittel der Goldbeschaffung ein für allemal ausscheidet.[5]

(The New Currency

The fate of the Papermark thus depends on itself in future. The stabilization of the paper currency is, however, assured even if the note printing press ceases operation and is not called upon again. This is indeed the intention with the introduction of the Rentenmark. From this moment on the Reichsbank will no longer discount government securities, i.e. will no longer issue new banknotes, since from this point onwards the Rentenbank will meet the credit needs of the Reich. Paper money will therefore retain the value which it has at present. In this way a brake will be put on the decline of the German currency, even if the Papermark and the new Rentenmark are not in a fixed relationship. Of course that can only remain the case if the note printing press does in fact cease being a means of acquiring gold once and for all.)

The view presented by the *Hildesheimer Allgemeine Zeitung* is thus that the immediate cause of the inflation had been an excessive printing of paper money and that stability in the future required that this should cease. This had not always been the editorial position of the newspaper. Previously it had argued that excessive expansion of the money supply had not been the cause of rising prices but that the abnormally high rate of price increases had been responsible for a money supply shortage that in its turn had led to rapid expansion; that is, cause and effect were reversed! There were views at the time that quite explicitly excluded an excessive rate of growth of the money supply as being related in any causal way to the rapid erosion of the value of the Mark during this period. An example of this type of argument is to be found one year earlier in the *Hildesheimer Allgemeine Zeitung* of 25 August 1922.

For the author of the *Hildesheimer Allgemeine Zeitung* article, cause and effect are the opposite way round to the conventional explanation of hyperinflation being caused by an excessively high rate of monetary expansion. It is Reparations payments draining the domestic economy of goods in the absence of a level of productivity that allows both the Reparations to be met and the domestic economy to be supplied at the same time. The rise in prices that this process causes on domestic markets means that an increase in paper notes is necessary, not the reduction called for by the Entente. Because of the rise in prices so engendered, the real value of the note issue has fallen. We therefore need more paper money, not less.

> *Die Inlandspreise stiegen infolge der Ueberlastung unserer Wirtschaft durch Zahlungen und Lieferungen an das Ausland rapide weiter, und es machte sich daher bald ein empfindlicher Mangel an papiernen Zahlungsmitteln geltend.*
> *... die Preise sind im Durchschnitt um das Hundertfünfzigfache gestiegen. Die Kaufkraft der mehr als 200 Milliarden Papiermark, die sich im Umlauf befinden, entspricht also nur der von etwa $1\frac{1}{4}$ bis $1\frac{1}{2}$ Milliarden in normalen Zeiten....*
> *Die Wahrheit ist also, dass wir heute nicht zu viel, sondern zu wenig Zahlungsmittel haben, und die Folge davon ist eine Geldnot und Kreditnot, die unser gesamtes Wirtschaftsleben in erheblicher Weise ungünstig beeinflusst.*[6]

(Prices internally are rising as a consequence of the burden on our economy of the payments and deliveries made abroad and that soon gave rise to a shortage of paper money.
... prices have risen on average by around 150 fold. The purchasing power of the more than 200 thousand million Papermarks that are circulating in the form of notes thus corresponds to only around approximately $1\frac{1}{4}$ to $1\frac{1}{2}$ thousand million in normal times....
The truth is therefore that we do not have today too great an amount of forms of payment but too small an amount and the

consequence of this is a lack of money and a shortage of credit that has an unfavourable influence on our whole economy.)

The widespread belief in some quarters that the hyperinflation was not caused by excessive expansion of the note issue was expressed in a number of ways. The belief expressed in editorial comment in the *Hildesheimer Allgemeine Zeitung* already discussed argued that common experience was proof of a monetary shortage in 1923; that is, consumers could not obtain enough money to maintain their previous levels of real purchases. This argument failed to recognize the essential role of a rapidly rising velocity of circulation in hyperinflation as did the following contribution to the debate.

> *Am 31. Januar konnte die Reichsbank ein Jubiläum begehen: Der Notenumlauf hatte sich an diesem Tage, verglichen mit dem Durchschnitt des letzten Friedensjahres, gerade vertausendfacht – statt auf 1,9 Milliarden belief er sich auf 1,9 Billionen Mark. Aber am selben Tage hatte sich die Mark nicht etwa ebenfalls auf ein Tausendstel ihres Friedenskurses, sondern auf das Zehnfache davon, auf ein Zehntausendstel entwertet.*[7]

(On 31 January the Reichsbank celebrated an anniversary. On that date the number of notes in circulation, compared to the average for the last year of peace, had increased 1000 fold, from 1.9 thousand million to 1.9 thousand thousand million. But on the same day the Mark had not fallen to something like one-thousandth of its value in peacetime, but by ten times as much, to one ten-thousandth of its previous value.)

So, comparing 1923 with 1914, the money supply had increased 1000-fold compared to a fall in the value of the Mark to 1/10,000 of its previous value. The author is looking for causal relationships between variables. The necessary and probably sufficient condition for such a relationship is that the changes in the associated variables should be equi-proportional.

> *Der hier oft genug geführte Beweis, dass nicht der Notenumlauf Ursache der heutigen Markentwertung sein kann, dass also von ihm aus keine Heilung möglich ist, wird an diesem Jubiläumstag zahlenmässig besonders drastisch ... es beweist auch, dass wir eine Inflation im eigentlichen Sinne überhaupt nicht haben, dass unsere Inflation nur ein Anhängsel der (vorweigend politisch-psychologisch und zahlenbilanzmässig zu begründenden) Devisenbewegung ist, nicht etwa die Devisenbewegung ein Anhängsel der sogennanten Inflation.*[8]

(The proof often enough cited that the size of the note circulation cannot be the cause of the present depreciation of the Mark has been emphatically illustrated on this anniversary day as well as the fact that no solution is to be found in the money supply. It also offers proof that we do not have inflation in the real sense at all, that our inflation is linked to foreign exchange fluctuations and not vice versa. The causes of the foreign exchange fluctuations are predominantly of a political, psychological and balance of payments nature.)

Having dismissed the idea that an excessively high rate of note printing was causally related to the depreciation of the Mark on foreign exchange markets because equi-proportional changes in these variables had not been observed, editorial comment in *Das Tage-Buch* turned to a consideration of the relationship between the note issue and the depreciation of the Mark with yet another analysis. The required condition for the author to accept a causal relationship between the variables suggests that he had a particular version of the Quantity Theory of Money in mind.[9] The quotation below illustrates the same preoccupation with equi-proportional changes as necessary concomitants of a functional relationship between variables.

> ... mit der Legende, dass der deutsche Markverfall in irgendwelchem Zusammenhang mit dem Notendruck stehe. Schon aus deutschen Ziffern kann man das leicht deduzieren. Ende 1913 betrug der Notenumlauf in Deutschland 2,59 Milliarden, die Golddeckung belief sich auf 1,17 Milliarden. Diese Deckung ist kaum kleiner geworden. Wenn also die Entwertung, die jetzt ungefähr mit dem Divisor 10–12,000 indiziert werden kann, wirklich vom Notenumlauf herrührte, musste auch er aufs 10–12,000 fache gestiegen sein, also auf etwa 25–30 Billionen. Tatsächlich beträgt er nur 1,7 Billionen.[10]

> (... with the myth that the fall in the value of the German Mark is linked in some way to the printing of bank notes. That can certainly be easily deduced from German statistics. At the end of 1913, the note circulation in Germany amounted to 2.59 thousand million Marks with a gold backing of 1.17 thousand million. This backing has hardly fallen. If the depreciation of the Mark to between 1/10,000 and 1/12,000 of its previous value has been caused by the note circulation, then this must have increased by between 10,000 and 12,000 fold to around 25 to 30 million million Marks. In actual fact, it stands only at some 1.7 million million Marks.)

However approximately true an equi-proportional relationship between money supply increase and price changes may be for a particular data set, one situation in which such a relationship will break down is during a period of hyperinflation. As the flight from money into goods gathers speed, people will hold ever-smaller amounts of money for ever shorter periods of time. The velocity of circulation rises in this situation causing the price level to rise more than proportionally in relationship to monetary growth. The figures given also grossly underestimate monetary growth during this period. One major omission was the rapidly increasing Emergency Money issues of the period. Figures given earlier for Notgeld growth show that they dominated official Reichsbank note issue, especially throughout 1923.

There was explicit recognition of the 'veil of money', the problems that arise from not fully recognizing the extent to which the purchasing power of the currency has declined and operating in economic decision making as if the real value of the currency unit were higher than it has actually become.

> Während der letzten Jahre vollzog sich ein guter Teil aller wirtschaftlichen Geschehnisse in Deutschland unter der Decke eines trügerischen Schleiers – eines Schleiers, der den Namen Geldentwertung trug.[11]

(A significant proportion of all transactions in recent years in Germany were completed under the cover of a misleading veil that went by the name of devaluation.)

This author well describes the situation when every poor man was a Mark millionaire with the attendant nightmares of attempting to carry out transactions in money with a currency that was continuously losing value at an ever-increasing rate.

> Milliarden, Billionen – Zahlenspuk! Wer kennt sich noch aus in den Zahlenbegriffen, wer vermag sich unter Ziffern noch Realitäten vorzustellen? Ein Freund erzählt mir dieser Tage mit Befriedigung, er habe sein Vermögen durch glückliche Börsenspekulationen allmählich doch auf $5^{1}/_{2}$ Millionen Mark gesteigert. Daran habe er allerdings monatelang gearbeitet, und jeden Tag, müsse er langwierige Berechnungen in seinem Notizbuch aufstellen. Was sind $5^{1}/_{2}$ Millionen? 500 Friedensmark! Heute noch 500 – morgen vielleicht schon nur noch 400. Ob irgendwer vor zehn Jahren solche Beträge als ‹Vermögen› angesprochen hätte? Zahlenspuk, Zifferntarantalla – bald ist jeder Trambahnschaffner Millionär und freut sich darüber so (und versucht, sich auch so zu benehmen), als ob eine Million wirklich noch eine Million wäre.[12]

(Thousands of millions, millions of millions – haunted by numbers! Who understands all these numerical notions, who can attach any reality to figures? A friend told me recently with satisfaction that he had gradually increased his fortune to $5^{1}/_{2}$ million Marks by fortunate speculation on the stock exchange. Mind you, he had worked at it for months, and every day he had to do lengthy calculations in his notebook. What are 5½ million? 500 peacetime Marks! 500 today, perhaps even tomorrow only 400. Would anybody ten years ago have referred to such sums as a 'fortune'? Haunted by numbers, a wild dance of figures – soon every tram conductor will be a millionaire and as pleased about it (and will probably attempt to behave accordingly), as if a million really were still a million.)

Hyperinflation – a shortage of money?

That a shortage of money may be perceived during a period of hyperinflation was noticed at the time by John Maynard Keynes.[13]

> In the last stages of inflation, the prodigious increase in the velocity of circulation may have more effect in raising prices and depreciating the exchanges than the increase in the volume of notes and the note-issuing authorities cry out against what they regard as the unfair phenomenon of the value of notes falling more than in proportion to their increased volume.

As an illustration of this effect, consider Table 9.1.

Table 9.1 Papermarks and Goldmarks

Date	Number of Papermarks	Number of Marks to buy 1 Goldmark
December 1920	81×10^9	17
June 1922	178×10^9	90

If the money supply is deflated by the price of one Goldmark, then the money supply actually falls from $(81 \times 10^9)/17$ to $(178 \times 10^9)/90$, that is, from 4.8×10^9 to 1.9×10^9. It is possible to show this effect with other given fixed standards of value. Consider the exercise using the exchange rate with the United States dollar (Table 9.2).

Again, a real note issue may be calculated by reference to an external

Table 9.2 Papermarks and dollar values[14]

Date	Number of Papermarks	Number of Marks to buy 1 US$
December 1920	81×10^9	75
June 1922	178×10^9	349

standard of value, this time the United States dollar. The real value of the Papermark note issue falls from $(81 \times 10^9)/75$ in December 1920 to $(178 \times 10^9)/349$ in June 1922, a fall from 1.08×10^9 to 0.51×10^9 or a drop of some 52.78 per cent.

This is the reason for the money shortages noted by Friedrich C.A. Lange, Mayor of Berlin, in his diary.[15] On 17 October 1922, he records that,

> Der Minister für Handel und Gewerbe hat den Gemeinden die Ausgabe kurzfristigen Notgeldes unter Sicherstellung des Betrages anheimgestellt, um dem Mangel an Scheinen abzuhelfen.

> (The Minister for Trade and Commerce has given the municipal authorities the option of issuing short-term Emergency Money, on deposit of the sums involved, as a means of relieving the shortage of notes.)

On 7 February 1923, he further comments: '*Die Geldknappheit wird immer drückender*' ('The shortage of money is becoming ever more oppressive').

Until virtually the introduction of the stabilization policy for the Mark in late 1923, a policy that placed major emphasis on securing control over the money supply, newspapers continued to report a shortage of money in circulation rather than an excess. The struggle apparent to the population was esentially how to finance a given level of real transactions in a situation where the general level of prices was rising more rapidly than the money supply. They were not concerned with monetary theory or with explanations of why prices could rise more rapidly than the money supply, but with how they might maintain their businesses in such a situation. This would have been their major concern even if the solution offered very short-term relief indeed. Employers would have had particular difficulty in financing index-linked wage and salary payments from a payments medium growing at a lower rate than the index of price changes to which their payment commitments were linked. Permission to literally print their own money must have been seen by many entrepreneurs as an unmitigated blessing.

> *Die Zahlungsmittelknappheit*
> *in wenigen Tagen vorbei*

> *Nachdem die Arbeit in der Reichsdruckerei heute nachmittag wieder aufgenommen ist, wird die aussergewöhnliche Stockung in der Belieferung mit Zahlungsmitteln behoben sein. Die am Sonnabend sich ergebenden Fehlbeträge werden voraussichtlich bereits am Sonntag und Montag nachgeliefert werden. Sobald auch die Privatdruckere-*

ien die Arbeit wieder aufgenommen haben, wird in wenigen Tagen eine regelmässige und ausreichende Zahlungsmittelversorgung gesichert sein.

Zur weiteren Behebung der augenblicklichen Schwierigkeiten haben sich Banken und Industrie zu folgenden Massnahmen entschlossen: Die Banken ziehen gegenseitig Schecks aufeinander. Die industriellen Werke werden mit kurzer Frist Notgeld und Gutscheine ausgeben.

Angesichts der schwierigen Lage, in welche die gesamte Bevölkerung durch die Knappheit der Umlaufsmittel geraten ist, darf besonders vom gesamten Einzelhandel erwartet werden, dass er dieses voll gesicherte Ersatzgeld ohne Anstände in Zahlung nimmt.

Die gallopierende Teuerung ist verbunden mit einem verhängnisvollen Mangel an Zahlungsmitteln, unter dem die Lohn- und Gehaltszahlungen leiden. Kein Wunder, dass eine bedrohliche Stimmung in weiten Kreisen der Lohnempfänger sich ausbreitet, die in Lohnstreitigkeiten und Streiks zutage tritt.[16]

(The Shortage of Money
Over in a few Days

Following the resumption of work this afternoon in the Reich press, the exceptional blockage in deliveries of money will be removed. The sums missing on Saturday are expected to be delivered on Sunday and Monday. Once the private presses have also resumed work, a regular and sufficient supply of money will be assured in a matter of days.

In order to further remedy the present difficulties, banks and industrial concerns have decided on the following measures: the banks will offset cheques against one another. Industrialists will issue short-term Emergency Money and notes.

Given the difficult situation for the entire population due to the shortage of money in circulation, it is expected that the entire retail trade will accept the fully guaranteed substitute money without demur.

The galloping inflation is linked with a disastrous lack of money. As a consequence, payments of wages and salaries suffer. It is no wonder that an ominous mood is spreading among workers that expresses itself in disputes and strikes.)

It would not perhaps have helped in the situation described in this report to inform the anxious readers that the sharply rising velocity of circulation was the explanation for a rate of price increase in excess of the rate of increase of the note issue. With strikes and agitation from organized labour, immediate solutions were needed even if they were the cause of more trouble later. A few days' breathing space at this stage of the hyperinflationary process would have been greeted with relief.

In this sort of situation, suggestions that perhaps the rate of growth of the money supply should be curtailed in the interests of achieving price stability would have hardly found receptive ears.

Discussion of monetary theory is, however, to be found in the newspapers of the period. Consider the following example,

Die Lehre vom Gelde
Eine Theorie auf Grund des heutigen Geldwesens
Von Seipio

Hier genügt es zu wissen, dass die Geldschöpfung in einem Staate sich nach der Warenvermehrung zu richten hat, keinesfalls aber den Bedürfnissen des Etates allein folgen darf ... nicht etwa Golddeckung gibt der Banknote ihren Geldwert, sondern einzig die Tatsache, dass der Banknote auf der Warenseite eine entsprechende kaufreife Gütermenge gegenübersteht.[17]

(Monetary Lessons
A theory based on the present monetary system
Von Seipio

It is enough to know that the amount of money created in a country should be related to the increase in output and not solely to the needs of budgetary finance.... Gold backing does not give value to banknotes but solely the purchasing power of the notes in relationship to the quantity of goods available for sale.)

Von Seipio's contribution to the debate is more interesting in the light of future monetary developments. It offers price stability through a policy of controlling the rate of growth of the money supply without the need for a gold backing, essentially the basis of monetary systems after the Second World War.

The alert reader of the *Deutsche Allemeine Zeitung* in 1923 would have found other suggestions that excessive monetary growth was responsible for the depreciation in the purchasing power of the Mark. The example quoted here is from Rudolf Havenstein, President of the Reichsbank.

Die Politik der Reichsbank
Havenstein verteidigt sich

Die Grundursache der Inflation sei das hemmungslose Wachsen der schwebenden Schuld und deren Umsetzung in Zahlungsmittel und Giroguthaben durch Diskontierung der Reichsschatzanweisungen bei der Reichsbank.[18]

(The Policy of the Reichsbank
Havenstein defends himself

> The basic cause of the inflation, he said, is the unrestricted growth in the floating debt and its conversion into forms of payment as a result of the discounting of Reich Treasury bills by the Reichsbank.)

The amounts involved had risen from 22 billion Marks on 30 July 1923 to 194 billion two weeks later. The Treasury bills had been discounted at the Reichsbank essentially to finance the budget deficit. The view expressed is therefore in agreement with the views of Von Seipio discussed above.

This view was presented to the readers as a theory of interest but not with editorial confidence that it offered immediate enlightenment as to the then present collapse of the Mark. Four days later, a leading article occupying half the front page reasserted traditional belief that a return to a gold-backed currency was the essential prerequisite for price stability.

> *Die Beseitigung der Geldinflation*
> *von Friedrich Pilot (Decknamen)*
>
> *Die Papiergeldwirtschaft muss und kann sofort aufgehoben und die Goldwahrung wieder eingeführt werden.*[19]
>
> (The Defeat of Inflation
> by Friedrich Pilot (nom de plume)
>
> The paper money can and must be immediately withdrawn and gold-backed currency reintroduced.)

It is interesting that the author felt it necessary to make this contribution to the debate under a *nom de plume*. There is no worked-out theory presented as to how precisely such a policy would bring about price stability. The view seems to be that the years before 1914 saw both relative price stability and the gold standard. The two will again automatically go together! There is no recognition that the world of 1923 was not the world of 1914 and how the new national boundaries and redistribution of gold stocks as a result of the war might influence the possibility of reintroducing the gold standard.

Before the outbreak of war in August 1914, the exchange rate between the German Mark and the United States dollar was 4.2 Marks equal to one dollar. As Schacht's discussion of the carrying out of the plan to stabilize the currency makes clear, the precise exchange rate at which stabilization was to be attempted was not entirely obvious. It certainly helped the relevant calculations that the chosen rate of 4.2×10^{12} Marks to the dollar meant that the new rate was an exact multiple of the 1914 rate of exchange. It was convenient arithmetic that one Rentenmark of the stabilization currency would just equal one billion (10^{12}) of the virtually worthless old Marks. At the conversion rate adopted in November 1923, the one billion Mark note of the Reichsbahn (German Railways) is just equal in value to the one Rentenmark note. The two notes of equal value are illustrated in Figures 9.1 and 9.2.

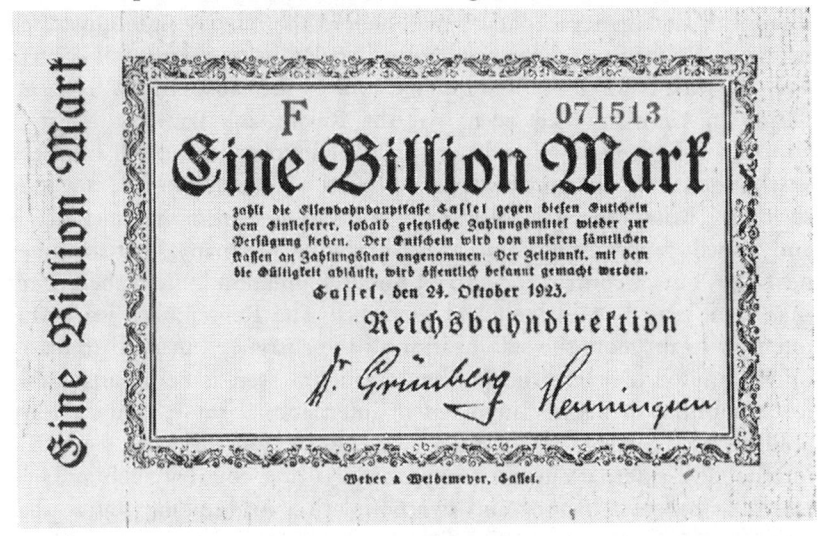

Figure 9.1 One-billion Mark Emergency Money issue of German railways

Figure 9.2 One Rentenmark issued by the Rentenbank. The bank was established in 1923 to issue the Rentenmarks as a key element in the stabilization strategy

The relationship between these notes, *'Eine Billion = Eine Rentenmark'*, illustrates the numbers involved in the stabilization of the German currency in 1923 – one billion (10^{12}) of the previous notes equated to one new Rentenmark. These particular types of notes were both supposed to disappear. Emergency Money issues such as the railway note illustrated in Figure 9.1 had to be removed from circulation to restore full control over the note issue to the Reichsbank. One of the causes of the hyperinflation in Germany had been that the Reichsbank had lost effective control of the note issue and a major contributory factor had been the vast amount of Emergency Money printed to overcome the 'currency shortage'. Britain too had collected in coins minted from precious metals and issued paper Emergency Money. Unlike Germany, British issues never got out of control and fear of possible inflation limited such notes that were issued to insignificant amounts. The Rentenmark issue was intended to promote the stabilization of the currency but itself to enjoy only a limited life. Its principal limitation was seen as being unsuitable for a country so heavily involved in international trade. Only a fully gold-backed currency was seen as being suitable to meet both the internal and external currency requirements of a country such as Germany, whose past history and overpopulation made it imperative that its pre–1914 role in international trade should be restored as quickly as possible. Rentenmark notes and credits, being backed by a land charge, met only the interim internal needs of the economy before the introduction of a full gold standard. This was how the situation was envisaged in Germany in 1923. Return to the gold standard was seen as a return to the international monetary system that existed prior to 1914, a return to the normalities destroyed by the Great War. But at what rate of exchange should the stabilization policy be carried out? There is no detailed discussion in Schacht's work of the problems involved in choosing to stabilize the currency at a particular rate. As he pointed out, he had no time for theoretical discussions. He appears to have sensed a rate at which stabilization would be successful from the signals received from the various foreign exchange markets on which the Mark was traded.

Reducing the money supply depended, of course, on the conversion rate of the old Papermarks into Rentenmarks. The higher the price of the Rentenmark, the greater the reduction in the Papermark circulation that could be achieved by a given Rentenmark issue. Consider some of the prices or divisors considered in the chapter. A price of 4.2×10^{12} would reduce the Papermark issue compared to a price of 630×10^9 by a multiple of $4.2/0.63 = 6.67$.

A price of 4.2×10^{12} would also reduce the nominal value of the outstanding Papermarks to a real value consistent with the restoration of the 1914 Mark/dollar exchange rate, a return to the gold parities.

Conversion would only apply to official Papermarks. The vast quantities of Emergency Money notes of around 1000 trillion (10^{18}) would simply no longer be accepted in exchange for goods and services. The sums involved serve as a quantitative reminder of just how powerful the feedback forces had been during the hyperinflation arising from the increasing velocity of circulation giving the impression of a money shortage.

The money supply was therefore to be brought into line with the requirements of establishing the old parities. Market forces were essentially to be relied upon to bring about the related lining up of prices and wages.

Schacht's views on the cause of this inflation are presented in summary in this chapter. It was overwhelmingly due to the use of the printing press to cover Reich government deficits. On the single day of 15 November 1923, there was a request for the printing of 190×10^{18} (trillion) Marks. Here in a nutshell, cause is stated and cure implied.

Some arithmetic of the conversion

These notes explain the basis of some of the calculations used by Schacht. Consider a dollar rate on the official Berlin exchange quoted as 2.52×10^{12} Marks = \$1. Relate this back to the 1914 exchange rate of 4.2 Marks = \$1, that is, 4.2 gold standard Marks = \$1. There is therefore a relationship between the November 1923 and 1914 Marks of $(2.52 \times 10^{12})/4.2 = 600 \times 10^9$. As both values were at different times equal to the price of a dollar, the quotient may be thought of as the 'Goldmark'.

Goldmark value of the money supply

What is the gold value, that is, the 1914 value of the November 1923 Papermark money supply? On the date in question, there was a Papermark circulation of some 60×10^{18}, that is, 60 trillion Marks. The Goldmark price was 150×10^9 Marks, that is, 150 milliard. The Goldmark value of the note circulation was thus the quotient $(60 \times 10^{18})/(150 \times 10^9) = 400 \times 10^6$, that is, 400 million Goldmarks.

Profiteering from the Rentenmark conversion

Figure 9.3 should make clear the arguments about profiteering presented in this chapter.

Official Berlin rate
2.52×10^{12}
= $1. 17.11.1923

Conversion → 4.2 Rentenmarks = $1

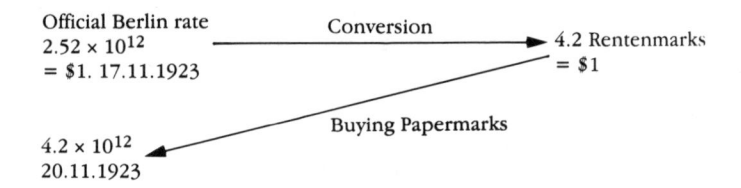

Buying Papermarks

4.2×10^{12}
20.11.1923

Figure 9.3 Profiteering

The profit available is clearly the difference between the two rates, that is, 1.68×10^{12} Papermarks per dollar. This makes clear the pressure described by Schacht to respond to this situation by closing the gap, by adopting a policy of increasing the Papermark price of the Rentenmark.

*Wo sich mit Gewalt nichts machen lässt,
ist Vorsicht und Klugheit die Basis.*

(Where force can achieve nothing,
Be guided by prudence and sense.)

Figure 9.4 A 25 pfennig note

Cuxhaven's own Emergency Money did not significantly contribute to inflation. It did not issue the large nominal value notes of other cities but rather only the notes intended to overcome the shortage of small change.

The inscription on Figure 9.4 in Plattdeutsch is an exhortation to overcome German military impotence after 1918 by skilful policies and diplomacy!

In describing the currency reform to its readers, the *Cuxhavener Zeitung* was quite happy to use the term 'Bodenmark' instead of the official 'Rentenmark'.

Die neue Währungsbank

> ... Die Bank ist selbstständig in Verwaltung und Geschäftsführung.... Die Währungsbank stellt auf Grund ihres Kapitals auf Goldmark lautende Rentenbriefe aus, die als Deckung für die von der Währungsbank auszugebenden Bodenmark dienen. Die Bodenmark ist in 100 Bodenpfennige eingeteilt.... Eine Bodenmark entspricht dem Wert von 0. 358 Gramm Feingold.[20]

(The New Currency Bank

> ... the Bank is independent in adminstration and in the conduct of business. The Currency Bank, based on its capital, issues Goldmark denominated annuity bonds. These serve as backing for the Groundmark notes to be issued. The 'Groundmark' is divided into 100 'Groundpfennigs'.... A Groundmark corresponds in value to the value of 0.358 grammes of fine gold.)

This article contains much that must have reassured the reader of the *Cuxhavener Zeitung* in September 1923. Its independence in administration and conduct of business must have contrasted with the total dependence of the Reichsbank that had made the latter the note-printing department of the Reich government. What would they have made of the idea of a backing for the new notes based on a land charge? It seems unlikely that any of the readers actually thought in terms of ever having to acquire the land that served in theory as the backing for the new notes. Some reassurance might have been found in the gold value of the new notes. There was no realistic hope of ever acquiring 0.358 grammes of fine gold for each Mark. Any Goldmark backing would have meant at the most the current Papermark equivalent of that amount of gold.

But what would determine the success of the Rentenmark issue in November 1923? According to the *Cuxhavener Zeitung*, a number of factors would be involved.

Vertrauen zur Rentenmark

... Dieses Zahlungsmittel müsse aber vom Vertrauen des ganzen Volkes getragen sein und dies Vertrauen könne nur geschaffen werden durch die unbedingte Zuversicht, dass die Reichsregierung und alle nachgeordneten Stellen mit grösstem Nachdruck die Tatsachen bekämpfen würden, die bisher eine Gesundung der Währung verhindert hätten. Dazu sei vor allen Dingen eine auswärtige Politik notwendig, die der stark herabgeminderten deutschen Wirtschaftskraft entspreche, ferner die Ausbalancierung des Reichshaushalts, wobei unter Hintansetzung aller Parteirücksichten auf eine unbedingte Sparsamkeit gedrungen werden müsse. Notwendig sei ferner der Abbau des Beamtenapparats, die Beseitigung aller produktionshindernden Steuern und statt dessen die Einführung weniger, verständlicher und einträglicher Steuern, die Verselbständigung der Finanzen der Länder und Gemeinden unter Oberaufsicht des Reiches, aber unter deren eigener Verantwortung sowie Loslösung der Reichsbetriebe aus dem allgemeinen Etat.

Die Voraussetzung für die Wertbeständigkeit des neuen Zahlungsmittel sei im übrigen die Aktivierung der Zahlungsbilanz, die nur durch Förderung der Ausfuhr erreicht werden könne. Deshalb müsse die deutsche Produktion wieder wettbewerbsfähig gemacht werden. In diesem Zusammenhange sei die Aenderung des Arbeitszeitgesetzes und die Befreiung von den Tarifverträgen zu fördern. Eine vollständige Umstellung der Erwerbslosenfürsorge werde sowohl der Wirtschaft als auch der Entlastung des Reichshaushalts zugute kommen....

Nur unter der Voraussetzung, dass diese Forderungen erfüllt werden, würde nach Ansicht des Verwaltungsrats der Rentenbank die Rentenmark Vertrauen im Volke gewinnen und erhalten können.[21]

(Confidence in the Rentenmark

... This form of payment must have the confidence of the entire nation and this can only be achieved by the absolute certainty that the Reich government and lower levels of government will vigorously deal with the problems that have until now prevented the establishment of a healthy currency. The principal necessity is for a foreign policy that meets the needs of the seriously reduced German economy. Furthermore, the balancing of the Reich budget must be achieved by extreme economy regardless of all party political interests. A reduction is required in the size of the Civil Service, the removal of all taxes that adversely affect production and the introduction of fewer and understandable and bearable taxes, the establishment of independent finances for the provinces and municipalities under the supervision of the Reich government but with their own financial responsibility. Financial responsibility for businesses conducted by the Reich government should be removed from the general budget.

The condition for the maintenance of the real value of the new form of payment rests finally on the improvement of the balance of payments which can only be achieved by the promotion of exports. Therefore, German output must be made competitive again. In this connection, the laws relating to the hours of work and wage agreements must be changed. A complete overhaul of unemployment benefit will both assist the economy and reduce the burden on the Reich budget.

Only on condition that these demands are met will, according to the Administrative Council of the Rentenbank, the Rentenmark gain and maintain the confidence of the people.)

The list of prerequisites for the success of the Rentenmark issue could form the basis of a party-political manifesto as well as listing ideas that have interested economists over the years. The labour market is to be made competitive with legislation on wages and the length of the working day to be abolished. The willingness of labour to work is to be encouraged by changes in unemployment pay. Although it does not actually say so, the intention would be to reduce the level of financial support for the unemployed.

The desire to increase German exports is understandable enough. It would increase the possibility of the Reichsbank obtaining reserves of gold and foreign exchange and help to restore the gold standard at least partly in the form of the proposed Gold Discount Bank. The generation of a trade surplus would tend to slow the depreciation of the Mark and allow food imports to be obtained more cheaply from abroad. It is arguably the case that an increase in German exports was much more dependent in 1923 on the level of demand in those countries with whom Germany had successfully traded before 1914, and a willingness in Britain and France to 'buy German', than on changes in Germany's own domestic labour market. Faith in the Rentenmark would then presumably be strengthened by the population simply observing the correlation between the issue of the new currency and the benefits flowing from an improved trade balance. A true causal relationship might be difficult to find given that the Rentenmark was explicitly issued to assist in internal stabilization of the Mark and not as a means of stable value payment for foreign trade purposes. There is a major problem of interpretation of an article of this type. It is strong on assertions but non-existent in terms of spelling out linkages and mechanisms.

The comments on achieving an elimination of the domestic budget deficit concentrate more on how this might be achieved than on the desirability of so doing. Civil servants are to be reduced in numbers and general thrift required of all departments. Similar demands are reported in Hildesheim. It seems in part to be a ritual scapegoating of civil servants. The reduction in the level of taxes demanded reflects a view that there is a negative relationship between the tax rate and the yield from the particular tax. The reduction in tax rates is therefore presumably intended to increase the tax yield, raise government revenues and thereby contribute to reducing the overall deficit.

At the time this article was published, the deficits of the posts and railways contributed to the overall budget deficit of the Reich. Making them responsible for their own budgets after privatization would therefore reduce the Reich deficit. Making the various levels of regional and local government responsible for their own finances would also have a similar effect on the Reich deficit.

There is a mixture of policies advocated in this article. In summary, they are intended either to curb the demand side or to promote and stimulate the supply side of the economy.

Perhaps the keypoint of all is not made. Balancing the budget was important in Germany in 1923 because the deficit was covered by note printing. There was a direct relationship between the deficit and the money supply. The success of the measures advocated would result in greater price stability by enabling the money supply to grow at a much slower rate than hitherto. One is left wondering! Is the omission to make this point explicit because it is so obvious or because it is not clearly recognized?

While many reports published in the newspapers did not explicitly state that the excessive printing of paper money was the immediate cause of the inflation, many most certainly did take this line. Many were merely reports in the local press of communications issued in Berlin by the Reich government and were not particularly the considered editorial views of the local newspaper proprietors. Particularly, however, in the second half of 1923, the citizen was certainly informed that the government believed the inflation to be due to excessive printing of Papermarks. Consider the following extract from the *Cuxhavener Zeitung*.

Die Währungsreform

Vom Reichsfinanzministerium wird mitgeteilt, dass die Arbeiten für die Schaffung eines wertbeständigen Geldes so weit gefördert sind, dass der Entwurf vorliegt. Die Reichsbank wird von den Reichsfinanzen völlig losgelöst und dadurch in den Stand gesetzt, die Funktion einer Goldnotenbank für das Wirtschaftsleben im vollen Umfange zu erfüllen. Reichsschatzscheine werden bei der Reichsbank nicht mehr diskontiert, sodass eine ausgedehnte Vermehrung des Papierumlaufes nicht mehr stattfindet....

Gleichzeitig wird nach einem bereits vorliegenden Finanzplan die stärkste Einschränkung der Ausgaben des öffentlichen Haushaltes erfolgen. Bei der Wertbeständigkeit der Einnahmen wird eine grössere Ergiebigkeit der Steuerquellen und damit eine fortschreitende Deckung der Ausgaben erzielt werden....

[Es] wird nur möglich sein, eine wertbeständige Währung zu schaffen, wenn das Defizit im Reichsahushalt beseitigt wird oder in absehbarer Zeit beseitigt werden kann. Während im Frieden der Geldumlauf rund 5 Milliarden betrug, stellt sich der heutige Papiergeldumlauf in Gold umgerechnet auf etwa 100 bis 150 Millionen Mark. Dass die deutsche Wirtschaft mit diesem minimalen Betrag heute auskommt, ist darauf zurückzuführen, dass der Umlauf im schnellen Tempo vollzieht....

Da das Reich seine Schatzwechsel nicht mehr bei der Reichsbank diskontiert, kann sich die Menge an Papiergeld nicht mehr vermehren und die Entwertung muss aufhören.[22]

(The Currency Reform

It has been announced by the Ministry of Finance of the Reich government that work for the creation of an inflation-protected currency is so far advanced that the draft proposal is complete. The Reichsbank will be completely separated from the finances of the Reich government and thus placed in a position to fully carry out the functions of a Gold Note Bank for the economy. Government securities will no longer be discounted by the Reichsbank so that widespread increases in the circulation of money will no longer take place....

At the same time, according to the already prepared finance plan, the largest possible reduction in budgetary expenditure will take place. Given the inflation-linked receipts, taxation sources will produce very much more revenue and a progressively greater coverage of outgoings....

It will only be possible to create an inflation-proof currency if the Reich budget deficit is removed either immediately or in a foreseeable period of time. Whereas in peace time the money in circulation amounted to about five thousand million Marks, paper money today in circulation amounts to 100 to 150 million Goldmarks. That the German economy manages today with this small amount is explained by the speed of the circulation of money....

Since the Reich government can no longer discount its securities at the Reichsbank, the money supply can no longer increase and the depreciation of the currency is bound to cease.)

The German press was able to point out to its readers that the velocity of circulation rose enabling the price level to rise at a faster rate than the money supply. A quantitative estimate is provided by the *Economist* magazine for 7 July 1923. From 1914 to 25 June 1923, there was a 2000-fold increase in the money supply in Germany but a 24,618-fold increase in the general level of prices. The explanation offered by the *Economist* was that 'this increase in speed is an outcome of the rapid depreciation, which causes salaries and wages, where possible, to be drawn at short intervals and immediately converted into goods.'

There can perhaps be no clearer Quantity Theory explanation of German inflation in 1923 than the one in this extract from the *Cuxhavener Zeitung*. The conditions for stable-value money are clearly stated. The printing press must not be used to finance the Reich budget deficit! Only by increasing revenue and decreasing expenditure can this be achieved. The extract actually claims that the money supply was smaller in 1923 than in 1914. That the smaller amount of money has financed a much larger aggregate of transactions by value in nominal terms is attributed to an increase in the velocity of circulation. Such a comparison of money supplies needs to be interpreted with extreme caution. The nominal money supply for the later date has been deflated by the depreciation of the Mark as measured by exchange rate changes. As discussed elsewhere, the exchange rate is not necessarily the most appropriate deflator to use to convert nominal to real values. A better picture of inflationary pressures would have been conveyed if the article had given the money supply data in nominal terms. Thus, 100 million Goldmarks would convert to 10^{20} Papermarks when multiplied by the conversion rate to be used in the November stabilization of the Mark. This would give a more dramatic impression of the flow of paper to finance the Reich deficits. A certain sophistication would be required of the non-specialist reader to understand that an increase in the velocity of circulation is required if the price level rises by a higher percentage than the supply of money. The average citizen might still be left wondering how the money supply could shrink in real terms and still be the cause of hyperinflation.

But what about the actions of the private sector? Could not the financing strategies of this sector also contribute to hyperinflation? The finances of the public sector are stressed because initially only the government had the power to compel the Reichsbank to print the notes necessary to cover its deficit. Inflationary impulses could also originate in the private sector.

The private sector contributed to inflation by printing its own large nominal value Emergency Money notes. This can be viewed as a response to an apparent shortage of money as a rapidly increasing velocity of circulation caused prices to rise at a faster rate than the money supply. It could also speculate on future price rises and borrow larger sums from the Reichsbank in anticipation of the repayment obligation being reduced or even wiped out in real terms by further increases in inflation. Schacht himself was to curb the private sector in 1924 by a credit stop, simply denying further credit advances. He was to reject the use of discount rate policy because the required rates would be so high that damage would be done to 'deserving' sectors of the economy. However, in September 1923, the *Cuxhavener Zeitung* obviously considered the times normal enough to permit the use of discount rate policy to curb the financing demands of the private sector.

Die Goldwährung

Beseitigung der privaten Inflation durch scharfe Diskontpolitik hat nebenher zu erfolgen.[23]

(The Gold-based Currency

The elimination of private inflation must proceed in parallel through a harsh discount rate policy.)

There were attempts in 1923 to create islands of monetary stability. One of these attempts was in Danzig. The essentials of the scheme are outlined in the following extract from the *Cuxhavener Zeitung*.

Neue Währung in Danzig

Danzig, 19. Juli. Wie bereits bekannt ist, legte der Finanzsenator von Danzig, Dr. Volkmann, dem Finanzkomitee des Völkerbundes eine Denkschrift über die Währungsreform für Danzig vor. Als bleibendes künftiges Geld wird Gulden und Heller vorgesehen. Der Heller soll ein Hundertstel des Gulden sein. Guldermünzen sollen als Metallgeld von der Freien Stadt Danzig ausgeprägt werden; 100 Gulden-Stücke so, dass sie das gleiche Roh-und Feingewicht haben, wie die englischen 1 Pfund-Stücke, also fast genau so, wie die alten 20 Markstücke. Die Denkschrift stellt fest, dass diese Geldmünzen vorläufig nicht in grösseren Beträgen hergestellt werden können, wohl aber wird die Ausprägung von Silbergeld sowie von Nickel- oder Kupfermünzen ins Auge gefasst. Die Silbermünzen sollen ein Rohgewicht von 1 Gramm für je 5 Gulden haben. Der Umlauf von Silber-, Nickel- oder Kupfermünzen darf 100 Gulden auf den Kopf der Bevölkerung nicht übersteigen. Dieser Gulden wird durch bestimmte währungstechnische Massnahmen in feste Beziehung zum englischen Pfund gestellt und zwar so, dass 100 Gulden gleich 1 Pfund sind. Ein Gulden würde also den Wert von etwa 20 Goldpfennigen oder nach dem heutigen Kursstand von etwa 10000 Papiermark darstellen. Es ist die Gründung einer Danziger Notenbank vorgesehen. Vom Tage des Inkrafttretens der neuen Währung würde die Reichsmark wie ausländische Valuta behandelt werden.[24]

(New Currency in Danzig

Danzig, 19 July. As is already known, Dr Volkmann, the Senator for Finance of Danzig, has put a formal proposal to the Finance Committee of the League of Nations for the reform of the currency in Danzig. Future money will consist of the guilder and the heller. The heller will be one-hundredth part of the guilder. Guilder coins will be minted by the Free State of Danzig. 100 guilder coins will have the same weight as the English pound and almost the same as the old 20 Mark coins. The proposal states that these coins can not for the time being be produced in large amounts, but minting in silver, nickel or copper is certainly being considered. The silver coins will contain 1 gramme of the metal for every 5 guilders. The circulation of silver, nickel or copper coins may not exceed 100 guilders per head of the population. Technical measures will be adopted to maintain these guilders in a fixed relationship to the English pound with a relationship of 100 guilders to the pound. A guilder would thus have the same value as around 20 Goldpfennigs or about 10,000 Papermarks at today's exchange rate. The creation of a Danzig Central Bank is envisaged. From the date of the introduction of the new currency, the Reichsmark would be treated as a foreign currency.)

The idea of establishing an area of monetary stability would be readily received by the population in July 1923. The principle of restricting monetary growth as a precondition of price stability is evident in the article envisaging a money supply of no more than 100 guilders per head of population. The aim to fix the relationship of the new currency to the pound sterling, presumably by foreign exchange market operations, is interesting in view of the major preoccupation of the German press with the value of the United States dollar.

Not stressed or even mentioned are some of the consequences of establishing a Danzig currency zone. It represents the disintegration of the monetary system of the Reich. Normally, as countries became more unitary states than collections of separate regions, the monetary systems became integrated into one national system with one currency and one central bank. Even the proposed names of the new units, gulden and heller, are a throwback to nineteenth-century names before the Mark became the currency of the united Reich. With the Mark now to be treated as a foreign currency, a market would be necessary to trade Marks against gulden. There would thus be a foreign exchange risk in transactions between Danzig and other parts of the Reich. A new currency boundary would cut across trading areas imposing extra trading costs. As these points are not dealt with in the article, it is not clear to what extent they would have been appreciated at the time by the readers of the *Cuxhavener Zeitung*.

Notes

1. Democratic Party slogan for the Reichstag elections, 4 May 1923.
2. The actual origins of the Rentenmark are uncertain. The nature of the scheme shows the possible influences of many contributors. For a detailed discussion on this point, see H. Pentzlin, *Hjalmar Schacht. Leben und Wirken einer umstrittenen Persönlichkeit* (Ullstein Books 1980), especially ch. 3, 'Die Väter der Rentenmark'.
   See also K.R. Bopp, 'Hjalmar Schacht: Central Banker', the University of Missouri Studies, vol. XIV, no. 1, January 1939.
3. J.K. Galbraith, *Money: Whence it Came, Where it Went* (London: Pelican Books 1976), p. 171.
4. *Hildesheimer Allgemeine Zeitung*, Tuesday, 16 October 1923.
5. *Hildesheimer Allgemeine Zeitung*, Wednesday, 17 October 1923.
6. *Hildesheimer Allgemeine Zeitung*, Friday, 25 August 1922. *Der Dollar an 2300!*: The Dollar near 2300!
7. S. Grossman, *Das Tage-Buch* (Berlin: Athenäum Verlag 1923), Heft 37, Jahrg. 4, p. 191.
8. Ibid.
9. The form of the Quantity Theory of Money assumed is M = kPY where k = 1/V. For a discussion of this particular version of the theory, see G. Ackley, *Macroeconomic Theory* (MacMillan 1961), especially p. 118.
10. S. Grossman, *Das Tage-Buch* (Berlin: Athenäum Verlag 1923), Heft 37, Jahrg. 4, p. 16.
11. Ibid., p. 495.
12. Ibid.
13. J.M. Keynes, Section V of 'Reconstruction in Europe' in the *Manchester Guardian*; 'Inflation as a Method of Taxation', quoted in the *Economist*, 5 August 1922, pp. 232–3.
14. The choice of values for any one day is uncertain. With the precipitate falls in the value of the Mark daily in terms of other currencies, a difference of a few days or even hours in the dates of the values used can make a major difference to the arithmetic.
15. Friedrich C.A. Lange kept a diary of political, social and economic events in the life of Berlin from 1920 to 1933. See his *Gross-Berliner Tagebuch 1920 – 1933* (Berlin: Westkreuz Verlag 1982).
16. *Deutsche Allgemeine Zeitung*, 12 August 1923.
17. *Deutsche Allgemeine Zeitung*, 19 August 1923.
18. *Deutsche Allgemeine Zeitung*, 27 August 1923.
19. *Deutsche Allgemeine Zeitung*, 23 August 1923.
20. *Cuxhavener Zeitung*, Monday, 24 September 1923.
21. *Cuxhavener Zeitung*, Friday, 16 November 1923.
22. *Cuxhavener Zeitung*, Wednesday, 19 September 1923.
23. *Cuxhavener Zeitung*, Saturday, 8 September 1923.
24. *Cuxhavener Zeitung*, Wednesday, 19 July 1923.

CHAPTER TEN

Relevance of the Events of 1923 for Economic Policy Today

The political violence in Germany that attended the events discussed in this text is acknowledged in the Berlin suburb of Grunewald. The murder of Walther Rathenau, the Foreign Minister, was simply one of the most easily remembered acts of political violence of the years of the Weimar Republic.

Until 1933, Taubertstrasse was called 'Rathenauallee' in memory of the Foreign Minister, Walther Rathenau, killed by right-wing extremists in 1922 and in memory of his father, Emil Rathenau, the founder of AEG.

Figure 10.1 Commemoration of Walther Rathenau, Berlin 1990

The consequences of these events

The *Hildesheimer Allgemeine Zeitung* reported in 1923 a banking development of enormous significance for the future conduct of monetary policy in Germany. It was reported without comment, so the eventual significance of the change does not appear to have been fully realized.

> Sie [die Rentenbank] darf mit dem Erscheinen der Rentenmark keine auf Papier lautende Schatzwechsel des Reiches mehr diskontieren.[1]

(It [the Rentenbank], with the appearance of the Rentenmark, may no longer discount paper securities of the Reich.)

Considering this period in retrospect, the Bundesbank would write that,

> Bei Ausbruch des Ersten Weltkrieges wurde sowohl die Goldeinlösungspflicht als auch die Notensteuer aufgehoben. Die Deckungsvorschriften wurden zwar nicht völlig abgeschafft, aber entscheidend aufgeweicht. Als Bardeckung wurden nämlich auch Darlehenskassenscheine und als bankmässige Deckung auch Reichsschatzwechsel sowie kurzfristige Schatzanweisungen des Reichs zugelassen. Damit war Tür und Tor zur Kriegsfinanzierung mit Hilfe der Notenbank geöffnet und der Weg vorgezeichnet, der zur grossen Inflation führte. Die Reichsbankleitung war in dieser Zeit praktisch nur noch ein ausführendes Organ des Reichsfinanzministeriums.... Das Bankgesetz von 1924 bestimmte ausdrücklich die Unabhängigkeit der Reichsbank von der Reichsregierung. Die Leitung der Bank und die Verantwortung für die Geldpolitik lagen nun allein beim Reichsbankdirektorium.[2]

(At the outbreak of the First World War both the duty to convert gold and the tax on notes were suspended. The regulations for backing (of note issues) were not entirely abolished, but decisively weakened. Loan certificates were accepted as cash backing, and short-term paper securities of the Reich were also allowed as bank backing. With the help of the Notenbank the way was thus opened to war financing, and the path was marked out which led to inflation. The Reichsbank management was at this time in effect only an executive organ of the Reich Ministry of Finance.... The 1924 Banking Law expressly defined the independence of the Reichsbank from the Reich government. Management of the bank and responsibility for monetary policy now lay solely with the Reichsbank directorate.)

The Banking Autonomy Law of 1922 formally ended the dependence of the Reichsbank on the government. It could no longer simply be required to discount whatever amount of securities were presented by the government. Perhaps just as significant was the readiness of the Reichsbank to use these powers in 1923 and to ensure the success of the stabilization policy by denying the government the credits it desired. This principle of the independence of the central bank from the government was incorporated in the Banking Law of 1924 and in the legal framework of the Federal Republic in 1949. The latest statement of the independence of the Bundesbank was made in July 1990 when considering the currency arrangements on the merger of the Federal Republic of Germany with the German Democratic Republic to form one country.

> Since the entry into force of the monetary union on July 1, 1990 the Bundesbank, 'by deploying its instruments on its own responsibility and, pursuant to section 12 of the Bundesbank Act, independent of instructions from the governments of the contracting parties', has regulated 'the circulation of money and the credit supply in the entire currency area with the aim of safeguarding the currency' (Article 10, paragraph 3 of the State Treaty). To enable the Bundesbank to discharge the mandate laid down in the State Treaty effectively in the territory of the GDR as well – i.e. to enable it to exercise monetary policy control over the money and credit creation process – specific regulatory prerequisites also have to be met in that part of the extended currency area, so as to ensure that the Bundesbank's traditional interest rate and liquidity policy measures will work there too.[3]

The events of 1922 and 1923 still play a significant role in party politics in Germany today. Figures 10.2 to 10.4 are perhaps rather amusing examples of this reality. It also ensures that a strong case will still be put in many circles for the maintenance of the policy-making independence in monetary policy matters of the Bundesbank (formerly the Reichsbank) against any sharing of that responsibility with the Bundesregierung (formerly the Reichsregierung). Seventy years after they took place, the experiences of those years still affect the election campaigns in Germany.

Although these illustrations represent Christian Democrat electoral propaganda against the Social Democrats, they must have touched deep worries about the likely repetition of the monetary history of the 1920s to have been worth producing. It is worries of this nature that probably ensure a fairly broad consensus across the political parties to ensure that the independence of the central bank in monetary matters from the federal government is preserved. The accompanying ditty (Figure 10.4) contains some of the key words from the 1920s: *Schulden* (debts), *Loch* (deficit), *Entwertung* (depreciation, loss of value of the currency), *Schutz für Sparer* (protection for savers), *dein Erspartes baden geht* (your savings come a cropper), *Inflation* (inflation).

Figure 10.2 The unmodified note – the 100,000 Mark note of 1923

Figure 10.3 The modified note for 1980s party-political propaganda – an attack by the Christian Democrats on the Social Democrats led by Helmut Schmidt, implying that the alleged financial impropriety of the latter would lead to serious inflation

Alles steiget in die Höh',
Drum ein »Hoch« der EsPeDe
Bald die Mieten, bald die Preise
Ach, es ist schon eine Schlimme Sache
Die Verwahrlosung der Jugend
Steigt viel mehr als ihre Tugend.
Raub, Erpressung, Geiselmord
Schaffen Recht und Ordnung fort.
Riesig gehn die Schulden hoch,
Apels Kasse hat ein Loch.
Zahl der Arbeitslosen steigt
ständig höher — Kanzler schweigt.
Schnaps wird teurer vor der Hand,
Ach, wie schad für Willy Brandt.
Alles steigt, wohin ich seh'.
Drum: »Sieg Heil« der SPD!
Für 100 kaufst Du heute ein,
bald werden's 100.000 sein!
Das nennt Schmidt: Lebensqualität,
wenn Dein Erspartes baden geht.
Entwertung frißt den Wohlstand auf,
die Linksmarxisten warten drauf!
Mit Wirtschaftswachstum ist es aus,
Brandt bracht uns Inflation ins Haus,
auch Schmidt und Apel reden nur,
von Schutz für Sparer — keine Spur.
Die Preise setzen sich in Marsch,
der Wohlstand ist jetzt bald am ... Ende!
Hoch zu Roß auf gelbem Wagen,
mit Schmidt und Genscher geh'n wir baden!

Figure 10.4 Party-political ditty on the theme of inflation, 1980s

The propaganda poem was an attack on the Social Democrats by the Christian Democrats. The concern and fear about inflation that the attack plays on harks back to 1923.

> Everything is going up!
> Shout 'Hurrah' for the SPD.

Soon rents and prices will be going up,
It's already pretty bad.

There are ever more problems with youth!
Robbery, extortion and the murder of hostages
destroy law and order.
Deficits cause debts to accumulate and the
number of those unemployed continuously increases.
The Chancellor says nothing.
Booze gets more expensive as you buy it!
Oh! how bad for Willy Brandt.
Everywhere I look, everything is going up!
Shout 'Long live the SPD.'
You can buy today for 100 what will soon cost 100,000.
Schmidt calls that quality of life if your savings are ruined.
Depreciation of the currency destroys welfare,
just what the left-wing marxists are waiting for!
It's all over with economic growth,
Brandt has brought inflation into our house and
Schmidt and Apel say absolutely nothing about protection
for savers.
Prices have started to move.
Prosperity has practically disappeared.
Sat high up in the saddle, on the yellow cart,[4]
We'll really come a cropper with Schmidt and Genscher.

The litany of criticisms of the government in the Christian Democrat attack would have been instantly recognizable to the average citizen in 1923. The shape of party-political propaganda in the 1980s was still being moulded by a view of the events of 1923.

Notes

1. *Hildesheimer Allgemeine Zeitung*, Friday, 2 November 1923. *Unser tägliches Geld*: Our daily Money.
2. *Die deutsche Bundesbank, Geldpolitische Aufgaben und Instrumente*. Sonderdrucke der Deutschen Bundesbank, Nr. 7, April 1985, pp. 2–3.
3. 'Monthly Report of the Deutsche Bundesbank', vol. 42, no. 7, July 1990, p. 16. The monetary union with the German Democratic Republic.
4. '*Hoch zu Ross auf gelbem Wagen*' translated here as 'Sat high up in the saddle, on the yellow cart' is a line from a very popular German folk song and is a reference to pompous, self-opinionated and incompetent luminaries 'sat up on high', occupying positions they really are not capable of holding. I am indebted to John Sinden for this point.

CHAPTER ELEVEN

Postscript

The poem below summed up the sentiments of many Germans in 1923. The first verse resents the abyss into which the national currency has plunged and its loss of purchasing power against the United States dollar. The second verse resents the occupation of German territory by the French and, in particular, by French colonial troops. A landscape created by German inspiration and strength is under the control of the enemy. The third verse stresses the impotence of the League of Nations to help Germany free itself from the murderous French occupation.

The language is powerful and emotional. The cartoons emphasize the brutality of living under the heel of the French and the suspicion that French territorial ambitions go much further east than the limits of the occupation of 1923. The last two lines have enormous historical significance. 'You poor German Fatherland, where is your Saviour?' The accession to power in 1933 of Adolf Hitler, in 1923 already a minor political activist, would lead Germany into a far deeper abyss than that experienced in 1923.

The sentiments of the day were captured in cartoons as well as in the lines of more dramatic poetry. The two cartoons illustrated in Figure 11.1 are typical of many that appeared in the German press of the day. The French are seen as blocking trade by road and river. The French soldier stands astride the road between Bochum and Essen. The advice in the cartoon to its German readers is to stop buying French and Belgian goods while the rape of Germany continues. Raymond Poincaré, the French Prime Minister, is shown as the new Napoleon, seeking ever more territorial gains at the expense of Germany and able to interfere with shipping on the Rhine. Is the ultimate destination of French imperialism to be Moscow as it had been for the first Napoleon? Although economic technicalities were admitted and are to be found discussed in press reports, the causes of Germany's economic difficulties were widely assumed to be political in nature.

The *Nordwestdeutsche Zeitung* wrote of these matters in words that were echoed in other German newspapers when it stated that,

> *Der Expansionsdruck der französischen Aussenpolitik.... An Ruhr und Rhein ist die Bevölkerung auf Generationen hinaus über französisches Wesen aufgeklärt, über diese Mischung von Affe und Tiger.*[1]

Figure 11.1 Cartoons expressing some of the sentiments discussed in the text

(The expansionism of French foreign policy ... the people of the Rhine and Ruhr have now seen the light about the French character, about this mixture of ape and tiger, for generations to come.)

A few days later, it informed its readers that financial reform in Germany depended upon a resolution of essentially political problems.

Es wird jedoch in englischen Kreisen als feststehend erachtet, dass eine ... Finanzreform nur dann wirksam werden kann, wenn die Reparationsverpflichtungen endgültig festgestellt werden und das Ruhrgebiet wieder an Deutschland zurückgegeben sein wird. Diese beiden Voraussetzungen werden als die grundlegenden Faktoren für eine deutsche Wiedergefundung betrachtet.[2]

(It is, however, considered in English circles as established fact that financial reform can only be effective when the reparations obligations have been finally determined and the Ruhr returned to Germany. These two conditions are regarded as basic to a German recovery.)

Mignons Lied

Kennst du das Land, wo die Devisen blühn,
in dunkler Nacht die Nepplokale glühn?
Ein eis' ger Wind vom nahen Abgrund weht –
wo tief die Mark und hoch der Dollar steht.
Kennst du es wohl?
Dahin – dahin mit frohem Sinn
Valutastarke ziehn.

Kennst du den Berg, den Wald, den Strom, das Tal,
von deutscher Art ein flammendes Fanal?
Was Wille wollt' und deutscher Geist ersann
schafft dort mit starkem Arm der deutsche Mann –
Kennst du es wohl?
Dahin – dahin mit frohem Sinn
Spahis und Turkos ziehn.

Kennst du den Bund auf schwachem Wolkensteg,
den Völkerbund? Zu dem gibt's keinen Weg.
An Rhein und Ruhr haust ekle Drachenbrut,
speit feigen Mord und wüsten Hasses Glut
wild um sich her.

Du armes deutsches Vaterland –
wo kommt der Retter her.[3]

Mignon's Song

Do you know the land where the currencies bloom,
In dark night the clip joints shine?
An icy wind blows from the nearby chasm –
Where the Mark stands low and the dollar high.
Do you know it perhaps?
Thence – thence with joyful spirit
Strong currencies journey.

Do you know the mountain, the forest, the river, the dale,
A flaming beacon of the German character?
What the will wished and the German mind devised
Is created there by the German man –
Thence – thence with joyful spirit
French native troops journey.

Do you know the league on flimsy bridge in the clouds,
The League of Nations? There is no path to it.
On the Rhine and the Ruhr lives a foul breed of dragons,
Spitting craven murder and the fire of vicious hate
Wildly all around.

You poor German Fatherland –
where will the saviour come from?

Notes

1. *Nordwestdeutsche Zeitung*, 28 July 1923.
2. *Nordwestdeutsche Zeitung*, 2 August 1923.
3. *Nordwestdeutsche Zeitung*, 5 July 1923. This is a parody of a song sung by the character Mignon in Goethe's novel *Wilhelm Meisters Lehrjahre*. See for example Stefan Zweig, *Johann Wolfgang Goethe Gedichte* (Stuttgart: Philipp Reclam Jun., 1990), p. 88 for the original.

Index

agriculture 4, 11–23, 21–2
Agriculture Committee 22
Aisne, River 30
Alsace-Lorraine 26, 36
Antwerp 31
arbitrage 48
Argonne 31
Armistice 7, 15, 24, 35, 51
army
  British 41–2
  German 7, 24–36, 39–41
atrocity stories
  in British press 26–34
  in German press 36–40
Austria 133, Fig 7.8
Autonomy Law (1922) see Banking Autonomy Law
Aventoft 133, Fig 7.7

balance of payments surpluses 4, 9, 42, 51–2
Bank of England 132
Banking Autonomy Law (1922) 143–4, 175–6
banknotes see notes
banks 75–7
Barlieux 29
barter 17
Belgium 30, 31, 52–3
  army 3
Berlin 1, 7, 11, 15, 24, 26, 108
  civic budget 121–2
  foreign exchange market 44–7, 53, 64–5, 68, Fig 4.7
  Grunewald, Rathenau memorial 174, Fig 10.1
  occupation of 12
  Tramway Operating Company 121–2
Bielefeld 137, Fig 7.10
Bismarck, Otto von 24
blockade 4, 18
Bochum 37–8, 180
Bodenmarks see Rentenmarks

boundaries 18–19, 25, 133, Fig 2.1
Bouvines 29
Bradbury, John 131
Bradburys 131, Fig 7.6
Brandt, Willy 179, Fig 10.4
bread prices 41, 63, 66
Bremen 80–1
Britain 98, 167
  army 41–2
  emergency money 131–2, 162, Fig 7.6
  and Germany 35–6, 41–3
  see also pound
British High Command 42–3
Brückmann, Peter, & Co. 128
budget deficits 2–4, 18, 20, 49, 93–7, 100, 108–9, 111, 115–16, 132, 163
  and Reichsbank 144, 160, 169
  see also council expenditure and income
budget, Reich, balancing of 166–8
Bundesbank 87, 175, 176
bureaucracy 99–100
burial of dead 89–91
Buzancy 31

Calwaert, Mme de 30
cartoons 180, Fig 11.1
Cassell, Gustav 50–1
causes (of hyperinflation) 2–4, 115–21, 152, 168–72, 180–2
Central Bank 2
Christian Democrats 176, 178–9, Fig 10.3
'cipher stroke' ('zero stroke') 77
City Money (*Stadtgeld*) 119, 131
civil service, overstaffing of 100, 166, 167
coal market 4–6, 15, Fig 1.1
coins
  hoarding of 119
  minting of 119, 128, 162
  replacement by notes 131–2
collectors (of *Notgeld*) 127–8, 135

INDEX

Cologne 37–8, 44, 68
Confederation of the Rhine 9
consumer groups 66
Convent of the Virgin, Fschenstochowa 27
cost of living indices *see* price indices
cost-effectiveness, in public sector 110
council expenditure and income 108–14, 121–2, 128
    indexing of 112
council housing 111
courts-martial 40, 43
Craven, Yorkshire 35–6
Craven Herald 35
credit squeeze 14–15
cremation 90–1
Crossland, John 43
crowding out 99
crowns, Swedish 50–1
currency reform 168–70
Cuxhaven
    average citizen in (1923) 72–7
    banks in 75–7
    emergency money 165
Cuxhavener Zeitung 47, 48–9, 75, 77, 120, 165–7, 168–70, 171–2

Daily Express 1, 7, 15, 26–34, 48
Danzig 47, 171–2
Darlehenskasse 106–7, 131, 175
Dawes Committee 52
demobilization 115, 116
Denmark 133
Deutsche Allgemeine Zeitung 126, 159
Deutsche Bank 132
discounting of bills 2, 61–2, 115, 133, 160, 169, 175
dog tax 92
dollar/Mark exchange rate 1, 3–4, 44–8, 50, 53–7, 63, 68, 79, 81, 82, 93, 96, 101, 120, 128–9, 136, 144–7, 156–7, 160, 163, 170, 172, 180, Table 4.1
'Dollarkurs' *see* dollar/Mark exchange rate
dollars
    demand and supply 44–7
    and German cost of living index Fig 4.2
Dortmund 38, 39
Douai 31

Dresden 12, 82
Dresdner Bank 133
Duisburg 39–40

Eberswalde 67
Ebert, Fritz 15
Economist 169–70
Ehrenbreitstein 37–8
emergency money *see* Notgeld
emigration 21
Emilie-Rudolf-Mosse Foundation, Berlin 121
England *see* Britain
Erhardt Naval Brigade 12
Ersatz foods 17
Ersatzgeld 131
Essen 180
exchange rates *see* dollars, dollar/Mark exchange rate
exports
    prohibitions on 51
    promotion of 167

Festmarkbank, Bremen 80–1, Fig 5.1
Festmarks 80–1, Fig 5.1
Fieberbrunn 133, Fig 7.8
First World War (Great War) 7, 18, 131
'flight from money' 3, 116–17, 154–5
food
    Ersatz 17
    shortages 11, 15–18, 38–9, 63
foreign currencies, appreciation of 124
foreign exchange markets 44–53, 68, 142
foreigners, contempt for Germany 124–7
Fourteen Points 35–6
France 180–1
    army 3
    German withdrawal from 24
    imports from Germany 167
    see also Occupation
Franco-German hatred 24–40
Frankfurt 37–8
Frankfurter General-Anzeiger 124
Fresnoy 29
Fschenstochowa 27

Galbraith, J.K. 148
Gelsenkirchen 38

Genscher, Hans-Dietrich 179, Fig 10.4
Germania 99
Germany
 army 7, 24–36, 39–41
 and Britain 35–6, 41–3
 merger of Federal Republic with Democratic Republic 176
 navy 12
 see also Franco-German hatred
Glasenapp, Vice-President von 84
Goeb, Dr 14
gold, replacement of, in currency 131–2, 165
Gold Discount Bank 167
gold standard 2, 62, 79, 82, 148, 150, 160
Goldloan 64–5, 77–8, 84, 150
 coins 102
 see also guaranteed real value loan
Goldmarks 53–5, 79–86, 96, 128, 135, 140, 141, 146, 149–50, 156, 163, 172, Table 9.1
Goldnotes 80
Goldpfennig note 82, Fig 5.2
grain prices 41
Greenwall, H. J. (Harry) 1, 7, 15–18, 24, 26–34
guaranteed real value loan (*Wertbeständige Anleihe*; indexed/ inflation-protected loan; Goldloan) (1923) 101–6, Figs 6.3, 6.4
Gui d'Ossus 29
guilders 171–2

The Hague, American legation 34–5
Hamburg 77
Hanover 31
Havenstein, Rudolf 115, 116, 159–60
Heichen, A. 60
Heilbronn 41, 128
Helfferich, Karl 11, 97
hellers 171–2
Herbert, Felix 33
Herne 38
Hildesheim 81, 167
 1923 budget 108–14, 121
 shopping in 83–6
Hildesheimer Allgemeine Zeitung 4, 6, 9, 13, 20, 36–41, 52–3, 54, 65, 87, 96–7, 99, 103–4, 113, 150–3, 175

advertisements in 81, 83, Figs 5.3, 5.4
Hitler, Adolf 180
hoarding
 of currency 51, 68–70, 119
 of supplies 17, 68–70
Holtfrerich, Carl-Ludwig 115
Honnef railway station 37–8
housing 111
Hugo Stinnes Linien 128–31
hunger 14, 15, 51, 67
Hythe 48

importation of goods 60–1
index-linking 61–2, 101–6, 112, 113, 135, Figs 6.3, 6.4
 see also discounting of bills; price indices
industrialists 1, 128–33
inflation-protected loan *see* guaranteed real value loan
inflation-protected payment medium 79, 80–1, 83, 84, 135, 168–9
inheritance tax 98
interest rates 74, 98–9
internal colonization 13

Jobst, Heinrich 128

Kapp, Wolfgang 11
Kapp Putsch 11–13
Kastrop 38
Keynes, John Maynard 42, 156
Kluck, Alexander von 30

labour market, and currency reform 167
land charge tax 14
Lange, Friedrich 1, 18, 44, 54, 63, 68, 90–1, 119, 121, 157, Table 4.1
Langedreer 38
League of Nations (*Völkerbund*) 171–2, 180, 182, 183
Liebknecht, Karl 16
Liège 30
Lisogne 28
living-space (*Lebensraum*) 21
Lloyd George, David 131
loan, compulsory (1922) (*Zwangsanleihe*) 93–9
 and interest rate 98–9

loan notes (*Anleihstücke*) 103, 176
loans
　interest-free 127, 129
　and public sector finance 93–114
　repaying in devalued currency 87–9
local authorities *see* council
　expenditure and income
Lock, Josef Michael 128
Long-la-Ville 29
Longwy 29
looting 67
Louis XIV, King of France 9
Lünen 38
Luther, Dr 68
Luxemburg, Rosa 16

Mainz 39–40
Mark
　illicit trading in 48
　stabilization of 62–70
　value of, *see also* dollars, dollar/
　　mark exchange rate
　see also Festmarks; Goldmarks;
　　Papermarks; purchasing power
　　of Mark, decline in; Rentenmarks
Marne, River 27
Marseilles 33
Le Matin 28
Meuse valley 28
migration into cities 21
monetary disintegration 119
Mont Saint Martin 29
morality, public, and inflation 87–91

Napoleon I, Emperor 9
nationalism 25–6, 133
navy, German 12
Néry 33–4
New York 47
Nordwestdeutsche Zeitung 180–2
North Schleswig 133
notes
　alternative uses for 123
　export of 51
　high-denomination 118, 122–7,
　　128–9, 136, Figs 7.2, 7.3, 7.5, 7.9,
　　7.10, 9.1, 10.2, 10.3
　lack of control over issue 143–4
　low-denomination 118, 133–4, 165,
　　Figs 7.1, 7.7, 7.8, 9.2, 9.4
　political messages on 134, Figs 7.7,
　　7.8, 10.3
　reducing size of issue 146–7
Notgeld (emergency money) 1, 2, 19,
　104, 113–14, 115–38, 139–43, Fig 2.3
　and collectors 127, Fig 7.4
　increase in issues 155
　indexed 135
　as interest-free loan 127, 129
　origins 119–20
　redemption 134–6

Occupation (by Allies) 3, 7–9, 68, 126,
　180, Fig 1.2
Occupied Zone 44
Old Comrades Association, 231st
　Regiment 40–1

Palatinate 2
Papermarks 54, 63–5, 77, 79, 81–3, 87,
　93, 96, 102, 128, 135, 149, 151–2,
　156
　contraction of 139, 140
　conversion to Rentenmarks 162–4
　and dollar values 156–7, Table 9.2
　and Goldmarks 163, 170, Table 9.1
　and guilder 172
　see also Notgeld
Paris 1, 7, 26
party-political propaganda 178–9, Fig
　10.4
Pennewang 134
pensions 99
Pentzlin, Heinz 107
'Pilot, Friedrich' 160
plebiscite (on self-determination of
　citizenship) 133
Plötzensee Prison 87, Figs 5.5, 5.6
Poincaré, Raymond 117, 180, Fig 11.1
Poland 27
population growth 4, 21
Post-War Credits (UK) 98
postal service, deficit in 168
pound 57, 172
poverty 18, 63, 83, 110, 121
Pram-Oesterreich ob der Enns 127,
　128, Fig 7.4
press 2, 25
　and apparent money shortage 157–8
　English 26–34
　German 26, 36–41

see also *Craven Herald*;
Cuxhavener Zeitung; *Daily Express*; *Deutsche Allgemeine Zeitung*; *Economist*; *Frankfurter General-Anzeiger*; *Hildesheimer Allgemeine Zeitung*; *Nordwestdeutsche Zeitung*; *Vorwärts*
price indices 3–4, 53, 54–62, 120, 135, 157, Tables 4.2, 4.3
  cost of living index 72–4, 109
  deficiencies in use of 59
  official wholesale index 61
prices
  determination of 68–70, Fig 4.3
  requirement to display 66–8
printing of banknotes 3, 49, 140, 141, 158, 163, 168, 169
private sector, curbing 170–1
privatization 168
production, collapse of 26
profiteering 66, 164, Fig 9.3
Public Records Office (UK) 43
public sector, expansion of 100
purchasing power of Mark, decline in 1, 44, 50, 77, 106–7, 180
Purchasing Power Parity Theory 50–1

quantity theory of money 154, 170
Queen's Bays regiment 33–4

racialism 25–6
railways, German
  currency issue 161, 162, Fig 9.1
  deficit 168
  railway station attacks 37–8
Rathenau, Emil 174
Rathenau, Walther 15, 115, 174, Fig 10.1
Rathenau Memorial Fig 2.2
rationing of food 11, 15, 63
Reichsbahn (German Railways), currency issue 161, Fig 9.1
Reichsbank 1, 2, 3, 14, 25, 42, 44, 46–7, 51, 61, 87, 93, 107, 115, 117, 119, 175
  asserts independence 143–6, 169, 176
  and budget deficit 144
  and Hugo Stinnes 131
  and printing of notes 140, 141, 142

Remarque, Erich Maria 1
  Der schwarze Obelisk 53–4, 123
Rennes 31
rent, calculation of 72–7
Rentenbank 145, 149–50, 161, 167, 175
Rentenmarks (Bodenmarks) 14, 55, 70, 77, 83–4, 103–4, 146–7, 148–51, 160–2, 165, 175, Fig 9.2
  factors for success of 165–6
reparations payments 3, 4, 9, 24, 26, 42, 51–3, 97, 115–17, 152, 182
reporting, bias in 4–5, 7
  see also Franco-German hatred
resettlement 19–20
Rhine, River 7–9, 25–6, 180–2, 183
Rhineland 2
  Commission 37–8
Rhineland Society (*Verein der Rheinländer*) 83, Figs 5.3, 5.4
Romain 29
Romanovsky 67
Rotterdam 34–5
Roubaix 31, 33
rounding off sums 75–7
Ruhr, occupation of 2, 3, 26, 36–9, 47, 49, 139, 141, 180, 182, 183

Saar- und-Mosel-Bergwerkgesellschaft (mining company) 132–3
St Maurice-sous-les-Côtes 28
Saint Mihiel 28
Schacht, Hjalmar 1, 3, 11, 12, 14–15, 20–1, 34–5, 50, 51–2, 55, 68, 107, 115, 132–3, 139–47, 148, 164
  and exchange rate 160, 162
  and private sector 170–1
  The Stabilisation of the Mark 139
  views on causes of inflation summarised 163
Schlittler, Herr 133
Schmidt, Helmut 179, Figs 10.3, 10.4
schools, closure of 1
Schröter, Secretary of State 5
securities, government (*Reichsschatzanweisungen*) 2
Seipio, von 159, 160
settlers 19–20
shortages
  of coal 4–6, 15
  of food 11, 15–18, 38–9, 63

of money (apparent) 3, 119–21, 152–8, 170
Social Democrats 98, 99, 176, 178–9, Fig 10.3
social security, expenditure 110
social services 116
Sperrgesetz ('Blocking Law') 87
stabilization of currency 1, 3, 13, 14–15, 21, 62–70, 93, 103, 113, 116, 135, 139–47, 148–73
  local areas of stability 171–2
state benefits 14, 18, 167
State Loans Office (*Darlehenskasse*) 106–7
  note 107, Fig 6.5
Statistical Bureau (Reich) 59, 61
Stinnes, Hugo 1, 57, 115, 116, 128–31, 132, 142
Stresemann, Gustav 101–2
strikes 3, 11, 26, 158
  General Strike 11
Stuttgart 12
Sweden, currency 50–1

taxation 14, 25, 37, 49, 51, 92, 93, 97, 98, 100, 101, 115, 121, 166, 167–8
  index-linked 113
territorial losses 11, 12, 13, 15, 18, Fig 2.1
theft 89
Thyssen, August 132–3
Treasury Notes (UK) 131–2, Fig 7.6
Troisdorf 37–8
'Turnip Winter' 11

unification 24
United Kingdom *see* Britain
United States of America 42

'vampire note' 25
'veil of money' 155
velocity of circulation, increasing 3, 119–20, 153, 154–5, 156, 158, 169–70
Versailles, Treaty of 3, 4, 6, 9, 11, 12, 13, 18–20, 24, 26, 35, 52–3, 67, 96, 97, 133, 137
Vincent, Louis 33
Vogelgesang, Karl 31
Vohwinkel 136, Fig 7.9
Volkmann, Dr 171–2
Vorwärts 54–5

War Loan (1915) 93, 102, 103
  certificate Fig 6.1
  interest coupons Fig 6.2
war loans 106–7
War Money (*Kriegsgeld*) 119, 131
Wattenscheid 38
wealth tax 101
Wertbeständige Anleihe see guaranteed real value loan
Wilson, T. Woodrow 35
withdrawal from France 24
Wurm, Dr 17

Zehden, Emmy 1, 87, Figs 5.5, 5.6
'zero stroke' ('cipher stroke') 77
Zollern, Colonel 27
Zwangsanleihe see loan, compulsory (1922)